DEMOCRACY AND PROSPERITY

Democracy and Prosperity

Reinventing Capitalism through a Turbulent Century

Torben Iversen and David Soskice

PRINCETON UNIVERSITY PRESS

PRINCETON AND OXFORD

Copyright © 2019 by Princeton University Press

Published by Princeton University Press
41 William Street, Princeton, New Jersey 08540
6 Oxford Street, Woodstock, Oxfordshire OX20 1TR

press.princeton.edu

Jacket art: Joseph Stella (1877–1946), *Old Brooklyn Bridge*, c. 1941.
Oil on canvas. 193.67 × 173.35 cm. (76 ¼ × 68 ¼ in.) Museum of Fine Arts, Boston.
Gift of Susan Morse Hilles in memory of Paul Hellmuth, 1980.197

All Rights Reserved
Library of Congress Control Number: 2018949305
ISBN 978-0-691-18273-55

British Library Cataloging-in-Publication Data is available

Editorial: Eric Crahan and Pamela Weidman
Production Editorial: Leslie Grundfest
Jacket/Cover Design: Carmina Alvarez
Production: Erin Suydam
Publicity: Tayler Lord
Copyeditor: Emily Shelton

This book has been composed in Adobe Text Pro

Printed on acid-free paper. ∞

Printed in the United States of America

10 9 8 7 6 5 4 3 2 1

CONTENTS

TABLES AND FIGURES

Tables

Figures

This book started from our discussions of a paradox.

Yet despite its importance it has been curiously little discussed in the academic literature.

On the one hand, the last century of advanced capitalism in the developed world has been one of deep and conflictual instability: two world wars (as well as Vietnam and Korea), technological revolutions, massive social and economic transformation, the collapse of the white colonial empires, fascism, the rise and then fall of the communist bloc and the Cold War, and two great financial crises with subsequent extended deep recessions.

On the other hand, this same developed world of advanced capitalism in this same last century has been spectacularly successful in any remote historical comparison in massively raising living standards, in widely diffusing education, and in remaining highly egalitarian in comparison to states elsewhere. Equally it has been a century in which democracy—established in all the then industrialized countries by the early 1920s—has remained in place (leave aside the 1935–45 exceptions).

As we see it, the advanced capitalist democracies, for all their instability and social problems not least at present, have been remarkably resilient and effective over this whole period. What we want to understand in the book is what mechanisms have driven that resilience and effectiveness over this long century.

In seeking to understand this resilience we want to propose a theory of advanced capitalist democracy, covering its many different forms. Of course, we make much use of the large body of work on varieties of capitalism. But the goal of the book is to develop an *overall framework* theory of how advanced capitalism works in the different advanced democracies. With the theory we address the key question of resilience.

This is a central historical question. Moreover, if the mechanisms *are* understood, they may also shed light on the questions that trouble thoughtful observers today: the rise in inequality, the consequences of globalization, the financial crisis, the growth of populism, the meaning of Brexit and Trump, and so on.

Whatever the analysis of current problems, our understanding of the long term has become reasonably clear from our research over the last decade or so. Very broadly, democracy and advanced capitalism have been symbiotic in the advanced nation-states. Democracies positively reinforce advanced capitalism and well-functioning advanced capitalism reinforces democratic support. In our framework theory advanced capitalism is driven by the advanced democratic nation-state: democracy drives advanced capitalism. And in this process the autonomy of the advanced nation-state has increased even as globalization and mutual dependence have risen.

This is very far from any received view.

The great theorists of advanced capitalism—among them Marx, Schumpeter, Hayek, Polanyi, and Poulantzas—all saw its relation to democracy as deeply problematic, although from very different political vantage points.[1] The same is true of major contemporary commentators, notably leading Marxists including Streeck and Piketty, but also Buchanan, Tullock, and other public choice theorists, on the right of the political spectrum. More generally in the political economy and political science literatures, a very widespread assumption is that the interests of capital and labor are opposed. We have come to a different conclusion.

What, then, are the key elements of the symbiotic relationship? We see three:

(i) *The role of government is central:* The state/government has to ensure that companies operate in a broadly competitive environment; it has to ensure that labor is cooperative, allowing management the right to manage; and to provide an effective system of education, training, and research as technology develops. All these in turn mean that the state is powerful enough to carry through these broad strategies. But what is its incentive to do so? Capitalism left to itself will hardly choose to operate in a competitive environment. We argue next that advanced democracies supply the incentive.

(ii) *Parties to be electable have a reputation for managing advanced capitalism effectively:* There is typically a significant proportion of the electorate who would not vote for parties without a reputation for economic competence and concern for the advanced sectors of the economy. A key empirical fact is that advanced capitalism is (relatively) skilled-labor intensive, so that it demands and has demanded a large skilled workforce. Because the cooperation of such a workforce is important, efficiency wages align the interest of skilled labor (and its unions) with the broad success of advanced capitalism. Add to this, aspirational voters concerned that they and/or their children get jobs in these advanced sectors. This does not imply support for a particular party, left or right, but instead that electable parties have a reputation for effective management of advanced economies.

(iii) *Advanced capital is geographically embedded in the advanced nation-state rather than footloose:* The third element of our approach rules out "race to the bottom" welfare states and/or imposition of subsistence wages in the advanced sectors, and more generally it also justifies advanced governments making huge investments in education, training, and research, which footloose companies might otherwise carry abroad perhaps with their skilled workforces. The value added of advanced companies is geographically embedded in their skilled workforces, via skill clusters, social networks, the need for colocation of workforces, and skills cospecific across workers and—given their limited codifiability—the implicit nature of a large proportion of skills. The nature and pattern of industrial organization has changed substantially through the century but the insight of economic geographers that competences are geographically embedded has not. Thus, while advanced companies may be powerful in the marketplace, advanced capitalism has little structural power, and competition makes it politically weak. (As noted above, this is a major difference from the less advanced world, to which Rodrik's analysis of globalization applies.)

These are the three basic ideas—the central role of the state, the concern by a significant part of the electorate for economically competent government, and the geographical embeddedness of advanced capitalism—which have together generated symbiosis between democracy and capitalism in advanced nation-states over the past century despite many ups and downs.

Are capitalism and democracy still symbiotic in the advanced world today?

There may be many problems with advanced capitalism. But electorates turn to populism when they feel let down by established politicians they see as ineffective economic managers. If "good jobs" dry up, then middle-class voters can easily lose faith with politicians whom they see as having failed to deliver. When they do, the audience for anti-establishment populist parties grows. This is the unsurprising consequence of the contemporary prolonged recession (as it was in the 1930s), and of an expansion that creates low-paid employment instead of graduate jobs. The problem is particularly urgent in countries such as the US and the UK with inegalitarian access to quality education, which perpetuates inequality and makes upward mobility harder (a relationship known as the Great Gatsby curve).

We see the division between the new knowledge economy and those low-productivity labor markets as a new socioeconomic cleavage that has crystallized along educational lines and a deepening segregation between successful cities and left-behind communities in small towns and rural areas.

Yet we do not see this cleavage as a fundamental threat to democracy, because it does not undo the basic elements of the symbiotic relationship. Democracy has a built-in mechanism to limit antisystemic sentiments. Parties need to build majority coalitions to govern, and they consequently need to extend opportunities to a majority through education and social policies. The fact that populist values are less pervasive in countries with more equal access to the educational system is a testament to this logic. The capacity of the state to address grievances through the welfare state has also not waned.

Despite the doom and gloom of much contemporary scholarship and commentary, we show how the middle class has been able to retain its share of national income over time, in part because of redistributive tax and transfer systems. When the economy grows, the middle advances. But this does not imply that the bottom benefits. Indeed, the rising educated middle classes may have little interest in redistribution to the poor because they are themselves relatively secure. A general problem in the existing literature is that by talking broadly about redistribution it does not adequately separate the interests of the middle class from the interests of the poor or from those who have lost out in the transition to the knowledge economy. A theme that runs through this book is that when we seek to understand the roots of inequality, we should pay more attention to how democracy works and interacts with economic change.

A related theme is the primacy of politics. The huge transformation from a Fordist to the knowledge economy was set in motion by major policy reforms in the 1980s and 1990s, which were induced by democratic governments responding to an electorate demanding economic results and reasons to believe in the future. Information and communications technology (ICT) enabled the transition, but nothing about the technology itself ensured that it would succeed the way it did. The forces set in motion by these reforms led to the unprecedented expansion of higher education and empowerment of women, which would have been unimaginable in the 1950s and 1960s. Somehow this huge success story has been forgotten in contemporary debates that tend to cast new technology and "neoliberal" reforms as villains in a gloomy story about decline.

Perhaps some of the tension between our own view and those that dominate the current debate is a matter of historical perspective. In this book—which covers a hundred years of history—we deliberately focus on a longer period of time. In contrast to the pessimism that permeates contemporary debates, from this perspective advanced capitalist democracies have generated massive improvements in prosperity. This has been made possible by the repeated democratic reinvention of capitalism through a turbulent century. We believe it is such reinvention that should be the target of our current debates.

ACKNOWLEDGMENTS

We have accumulated many intellectual debts in writing this book. We want to thank most particularly Peter Hall for his continued encouragement and comments over a long period, as well as his huge intellectual contribution to the field; similar debts are due to Kathy Thelen and Cathie Martin. In the same vein, as our close and intellectually supportive colleagues in comparative political economy, we thank Jonas Pontusson, Philip Manow, Philipp Rehm, and John Stephens and Evi Huber.

Equally important, and emphasizing the "electoral turn" in the field, we have benefited greatly from the work of, and exchanges with, first and foremost, Herbert Kitschelt, together with Pablo Beramendi, Silja Häusermann, Hans-Peter Kriesi, and David Rueda. We also had the advantage of extended discussions with Sara Hobolt, Mark Thatcher, and Magnus Feldmann over much of the material. In this context we want to thank Billie Elmqvist Thurén, Frieder Mitsch, Alice Xu, and Delia Zollinger for superb research assistance and beyond that for their intellectual contributions to understanding the different forms of populism.

In a graduate seminar at the LSE that Cathy Boone ran with us, she played a key role in making us clarify our arguments as well as justify our claims. She did this for us at a critical period in our writing. We are deeply grateful to her as well as to the participants in the seminar.

For continuing discussion of macroeconomics, as well as the financial crisis and the extended recession, we thank Wendy Carlin, and also David Hope, very warmly. We are very grateful to Ciaran Driver for advice on innovation and corporate governance, as well as highly pertinent comments on advanced capitalism more generally.

Economic geography plays a major role in the book, and we have been extremely fortunate to have interacted over some time with the exceptional group of economic geographers associated with the LSE, most notably Michael Storper, Simona Iammarino, Neil Lee, and Thomas Kemeny. Mike Savage, who led the Great British Class Survey, also made a major intellectual contribution by making us think seriously about culture and social networks—in turn closely related to economic geography.

Among many other colleagues from whose comments we benefited in the UK and the US, we want particularly to thank Chris Adolph, Jim Alt, Lucio Baccaro, Bob Bates, Jeff Frieden, Simon Hix, Chandran Kukuthas (finishing his own important book on immigration), Paul Lewis (for extended discussion of Hayek and competition), Steve Levitsky, Anne Phillips, Thomas Plümper, Vera Troeger, Gunnar Trumbull, Eric Wibbels, David Woodruff and Anne Wren. Additional influences are: Nick Crafts on the central importance of market competition; Steve Vogel and his latest work, *Marketcraft: How Governments Make Markets Work,* which appeared too late for us to take fully on board; and Orfeo Fioretos's marvelous *Creative Reconstructions,* which examines how governments rethought capitalism in postwar Europe.

We also thank two huge and hugely encouraging intellects, Margaret Levi and Paul Pierson, for their support. Margaret organized a workshop at the University of Washington, Seattle on a very early version of this book, which helped us refocus and sharpen our argument. We also benefited greatly from early book workshops in the Department of Political Science at Duke and at the Center for European Studies at Harvard.

By awarding a Centennial Professorship to Torben, the LSE gave us the opportunity to work together in the same location for a year, which was critical for the completion of the book. This was hosted by the Government Department and the International Inequalities Institute, and we owe very special thanks to John Hills and Mike Savage, the codirectors, and Liza Ryan, the administrator, for having created such a friendly and intellectually stimulating working environment.

Torben is grateful to Charla Rudisill for hosting many small book "meetings" in our home in Brookline, and for her unwavering support and encouragement in writing this book, while reminding us not to lose sight of real politics. Thanks also to Esben and Isabelle for fun and enlightening discussions about AI and how it will transform work and social relations (see concluding chapter), while reminding me what really matters in life.

David owes a huge debt to Niki Lacey for just about everything, for keeping him on the intellectual and human straight and narrow, for marvelous gossip, for reminding him (and Torben) that rational choice has some limits, and for being just about the cleverest person he knows, and certainly the most lovable. To William for long and stimulating discussions on capitalism and macroeconomics; and to Juliet for her intelligence, wit, and delightful company and her two most entertaining and smart children, Gus and Fordie.

And thanks to both Charla and Niki for putting up with transatlantic houseguests so brilliantly and so long—and bringing us back to the project each time we were about to let go!

Princeton University Press has done us proud. We want to acknowledge our most outstanding editor, Eric Crahan, our reason for choosing PUP. Also for constant support from editorial associate Pamela Weidman and a most meticulous and efficient production editor, Leslie Grundfest. Very many thanks indeed to them.

Finally, Andrew Glyn, dearest and most generous of friends and the finest Marxist economist of his generation in the UK. Deeply sadly he died in early 2007, after having finished *Capitalism Unleashed*. We had very divergent views! But he would be smiling were he reading this now.

DEMOCRACY AND PROSPERITY

1

Introduction

Much of the academic and nonacademic literature on advanced capitalist democracies over the past two decades has painted a critical and pessimistic picture of advanced capitalism, and—closely linked—of the future of democracy in advanced societies. In this view, the advanced capitalist democratic state has weakened over time because of globalization and the diffusion of neoliberal ideas. With advanced business seen as major driver and exponent, this has led to liberalization, privatization, deregulation, and intensified global competition. In Esping-Andersen's (1985) striking metaphor, it is "markets against politics" with markets winning out. This explains, inter alia, why there has been a rise in inequality (labor is weakened) and why this rise has not been countered by increased redistribution. If governments attempted such redistribution, the argument goes, it would cause footloose capital to flee. In Piketty's (2014) hugely influential account, the power of capital to accumulate wealth is governed by fundamental economic laws which democratically elected governments can no longer effectively counter. If they try, capital just moves somewhere else. Democratic politics is then reduced to symbolic politics; the real driver of economic outcomes is capitalism (Streeck 2011a, 2016).

1

In this book we argue that the opposite is true. Over time the advanced capitalist democratic state has paradoxically become strengthened through globalization, and we explain why at length. The spread of neoliberal ideas, we argue, reflects the demand of decisive voters from the middle and upper middle classes to fuel economic growth, wealth, and opportunity in the emerging knowledge economy. The "laws" of capitalism driving wealth accumulation are in fact politically and, largely, democratically manufactured. This was true to a large extent at the formation of advanced economies in the late nineteenth and early twentieth centuries, but it is especially true in today's supposedly borderless economy.

Drawing on a wide literature in economic geography, in innovation studies, and in management, we explain how knowledge-based advanced companies, often multinational enterprises (MNEs) or subsidiaries of MNEs, are increasingly *immobile* because they are tied to skill clusters in successful cities, with their value-added embedded in largely immobile, highly educated workforces. A central aspect of our book is the extent to which advanced capitalist companies are tied geographically into national systems. In our perspective, which reflects a large research program of recent decades, knowledge is geographically embedded—in advanced nations, in regions, cities, and towns—typically in clusters of skilled workers, engineers, professionals, and researchers. Also geographically embedded are institutions, public and private. One way of reading our book is therefore to see it as tying together economic geography, national and regional systems of innovation, and political economy.

As is increasingly understood in contemporary economic geography, the topographical distribution of knowledge competences is of hills and peaks rather than of a flat earth. This reflects the combination of the importance of tacit knowledge (even if partly codifiable), and of the need for colocation in the generation of tacit knowledge. Educated workers colocate in skill-clustered networks (which for them is valuable social capital) and therefore cannot be transported abroad, and companies cannot typically find alternative specialized knowledge competences elsewhere; thus, in business school jargon, "Capital chases skills." In the modern literature on knowledge-based MNEs, MNEs are seen as networks of increasingly autonomous companies, which get their value from the colocation with geographically differentiated skill clusters; and the payoff to the MNE derives from the complementarities which may be generated across the network from access to these differentiated knowledge competences.

In turn, skilled employees benefit both from this increased demand from foreign direct investment (FDI) from abroad and also as a result of the knowledge complementarities from the FDI abroad of domestic knowledge-based MNEs. An even more profound benefit from globalization comes from specialization in advanced goods and services in the knowledge economy: the ICT revolution both decentralizes the level and multiplies up the number of groups capable of autonomous projects. This is the basis of specialization manifested in the great expansion of varieties traded across the advanced world. Rising inequality and increased poverty is a consequence of the government-sponsored shift toward the new economy and it is not effectively countered, because the new middle classes are relatively secure and because the old middle classes are opposed to redistribution to the poor. The Meltzer-Richard model fails to predict such opposition since median/decisive voters see themselves as contributors, not recipients. We have put some of the key references and researchers into a long footnote to avoid cluttering the text.[1]

The book can at least partially be read as an attempt to integrate economic geography with political economy. As noted, the national embeddedness of advanced capitalism is not new. We will argue that it goes back a long way and is fundamentally rooted in skilled workforces and a broad range of public and private institutions that promote investment in human capital and in new technology, together resulting in economic growth and prosperity. Central to the creation and continuation of this beneficial interaction between policies, institutions, and investment is democracy itself. When the middle classes are educated and tied into the advanced economy, or have strong expectations that their children will be, they start to favor policies that promote growth, and vote for parties and political leaders with a reputation for doing so. Those with low or obsolete skills may not go along if they cannot see themselves or their children benefiting from advanced capitalism, and here we find a large audience for populist appeals—in the twentieth as well as the twenty-first century. Our goal in this book is to present a new picture of the relationship between advanced capitalism and the democratic nation-state that runs counter to the standard markets-against-politics perspective and explains the remarkable resilience of advanced capitalist democracies, from their beginnings in the early twentieth century and through the arguably most turbulent century of human history.

1.2. The Argument Summarized

This book starts from what appears to us a major puzzle in political economy, though paradoxically one that the literature pays little attention to. This is the exceptional resilience of advanced capitalist democracies (in comparison to any other type of nation state in the last century or so). All the economies which industrialized in the nineteenth and early twentieth centuries were democracies shortly after the end of the First World War; and apart from temporary German and Italian lapses they have remained advanced capitalist democracies ever since.[2] (Czechoslovakia, tenth most industrialized democracy in the early 1920s, is the exception—as a result of external forces.) This resilience is also true of the small number of newly advanced capitalist economies since the end of the Second World War (Japan, Israel, Hong Kong, Singapore, Taiwan, South Korea, Ireland): once they became advanced capitalist democracies they have remained so (with the arguable exception of Hong Kong, again the result of external forces).[3] While the correlation between per-capita income and democracy is well-known (Lipset 1959), and while the near-zero probability of rich democracies reverting to authoritarianism is well documented (Przeworski and Limongi 1997; Svolik 2008), why this is so remains a black box.

What is particularly puzzling about this resilience is that it took place over arguably the most perturbed century in European recorded history (apart perhaps from the fifth century). In any case, a dominant theme in the book is how advanced capitalist democracies have responded to and shaped interactively two great technological regimes. The second industrial revolution (or the scientific regime) started in the last third of the nineteenth century and morphed into an organizational revolution of giant Chandlerian conglomerates, often described as the Fordist regime. And then the Information and Communication Technology (ICT) revolution that followed ushered in so-called "knowledge economies." A fine analysis of changing technological regimes is by Freeman and Louca (2001). In addition to encompassing technological change, the advanced world has seen major wars, the end of empires, the rise and fall of communism, the rise of Asian manufacturing, and exceptional social, occupational, and locational change, including a massive entry of women into the labor market. Most dramatically, two deep financial crises led to prolonged depression and deep recession and slow growth.

The reader will be likely to read this book in the light of the financial crisis. That is partially intentional. But from our perspective it is written in the light of the performance of the advanced capitalist democratic nation-states, both as resilient and as responsible for the huge rise in living standards, decline in poverty, and, relative to other countries, fall in inequality over more than a century, as will be seen in the next section.

Our initial motivation is to understand this striking resilience of advanced capitalist democracies. So one concern of this project has been to develop a broad model of advanced capitalist democracies to explain the resilience. We sketch key elements of this model here. We also see how this may help to solve several other puzzles about advanced capitalist democracies, such as the continued differences in institutions and public policies despite the globalization of production.

In contrast to almost all other approaches, apart partially from Lindblom (1977), we argue that there are powerful *symbiotic* forces explaining why democracy, the advanced nation-state, and advanced capitalism are generally mutually supportive and have been so over this perturbed last century.[4] In common with Hayek (1944, 1966),

Lindblom (1977), Schumpeter (1942), and Poulantzas (1973), we see a strong state as necessary to promote successful innovation-oriented advanced capitalism, notably by enforcing competition on advanced capitalist companies (who would prefer protection and stable profits) and labor market rules to ensure workplace cooperation (against predatory unions). For both Hayek and Schumpeter, and also Poulantzas, capitalism and social democracy are both enemies of such enforcement—capitalism because it eliminates monopoly profits and social democracy because it undermines monopoly wages. But in our model a central component is that the large skilled workforces of the advanced sectors of the economy, and the aspirational voters who seek to join these workforces, have interests aligned with the promotion and success of advanced capitalist sectors, and are generally decisive voters. This contrasts with the general assumption in almost all this literature that democratic capitalism is a clash of interests between labor and capital.[5]

Our approach, building on the alignment of decisive voters with the success of advanced capitalism, assigns a very different role to democratically elected governments, in which they play a central and activist role in an uncertain technological environment promoting change in their advanced capitalist sectors. Democratic governments construct and reconstruct their economies, conditioned by past choices, in response to voter demands for effective economic management and internationally competitive economies and a better life for themselves and their children. This draws heavily on our academic background in the rich comparative political economy of advanced capitalism.[6] A dominating concern in this literature is how democratic governments guarantee the effective organization and reorganization of their advanced capitalist sectors. This literature has also been concerned with understanding heterogeneous socio-economic institutions across different advanced economies which underpin specialization of economic activities: a specialization we also seek to understand in this book. Given the scope for variety, advanced capitalist democracies evolve over time in response to technology and other shocks, but in turn also reshape them; and they are themselves embedded in different electoral and legislative rules. Common for all are the incentives for governments to promote the advanced sectors of the economy and construct and reconstruct institutions in order to further this goal. We see new technologies as political opportunities, and their adoption is politically determined.

The most distinctive element of advanced capitalism in our approach has already been mentioned—the large skilled and educated workforces of the advanced capitalist sectors. Some of our understanding about skills has developed from comparative political economy, and much has developed from the literature on innovation (Dosi (2000), Malerba (2004), Lundvall (1992, 2016), Freeman (2008), Nelson (1993), Casper (2007), Whitley (1999, 2007). The skills of these workforces are tacit and cospecific both with each other and with company technologies; technologies are themselves partially codifiable and perhaps patented, but, as Teece (1986) underlined, protected by the cospecific skills of the workforce even in the absence of patents. Moreover, their tacit skills are generally learned from each other, in an overlapping generation (OLG) logic. This implies colocation in work environments and/or skill clusters over time. This is widely recognized in the economics of agglomeration (Glaeser 2010), despite the role of the internet and global trade and finance; it is also true of the different environment of giant Chandlerian corporations, in an earlier technological regime with Fordist and earlier technologies (Chandler 1967, 1977). Quite generally it has pinned down advanced companies or their subsidiaries to the national environment where education and training takes place; the high value-added activities of an advanced company are thus generally embedded in the national or regional or local environment—advanced capitalism is geographically specific and not footloose (irrespective of where the shares or patents are held). Knowledge-based multinationals (typically but not necessarily with core technologies in a particular national environment) may have many geographically embedded skill-intensive subsidiaries (Cantwell 1989). It is only across the low-skill subsidiaries that multinational companies (MNCs) can easily move between locations at low cost, leaving little rent to the countries they are in.

A second implication of the colocation and cospecificity of skills and capital is geographical specialization. Specialization is deeply embedded in innovation-oriented activities. Again, this follows both from the literatures on comparative and international political economy, and also from the innovation literature including that on national systems of innovation (Lundvall 1992, 2016; Nelson 1993; Cooke 2001). Geographically embedded skills and specialization in turn lead to another symbiosis, namely that each advanced nation in general derives complementarities from trading and capital mobility with other advanced economies. Thus advanced nations gain from globalization with other advanced nations, at least in the advanced sectors. This then is a game of strategic complementarities. In our broad model the greater the specialization, the greater the value the community of advanced governments gain from each individual advanced economy: hence the symbiosis between the advanced nation-state and the extent of advanced globalization. A hegemon may be important in protecting an advanced economy from military threats by nonadvanced economies; but it is not relevant within the community of advanced economies.

The colocation and cospecificity of skilled workers, enabling and enabled by specialization, are in turn what endow the nation-state with power, and in democracies this power is used to improve the lives of a majority by creating the institutional conditions for innovation, skill formation, and growth, and by responding to demands for social insurance and sometimes redistribution. This then suggests a third implication: there exists a strategic complementarity, or symbiosis, between democracy, the advanced nation-state, and advanced capitalism. Democratic parties and politicians that successfully promote the prosperity and welfare of a majority will be rewarded by winning elections, and the majority will be skilled workers who are keen to see the advanced sectors of the economy thrive.

Spelled out in greater detail below, we thus see our broad approach going some way in explaining the resilience puzzle. It also explains, we believe, five related puzzles which we elaborate below: first, the middle-income trap, and why so few countries have developed into advanced capitalist democracies after the Second World

War. Second, it shows why a thoroughly integrated world economy has not undermined the existence of different forms of advanced capitalist democracies, since their institutional differences cause and are caused by distinct patterns of specialization. Third, it illuminates how democracy reinforces advanced capitalism when it is widely thought to cause "decommodification" by majoritarian demands for policies that undermine markets in the name of equality. Fourth, and related, it goes a long way in understanding the distinct paths to democracy of the different advanced economies, and the limitations of generic arguments such as that of Acemoglu and Robinson (2005). Finally, it helps us understand why advanced democracies, despite generating prosperity and greater income equality than most non-advanced countries, have not responded to rising inequality since the late 1970s. Closely related is the question why advanced capitalist democracies have given rise to populist political movements that oppose the very elites that grow out of the knowledge economy as well as open borders and the prosperous cities and the live-and-let-live values that they give rise to. But first we highlight some key conceptual distinctions, causal claims, and empirical hypotheses that make up our basic argument.

1.3. Our ACD Framework Approach

Our broad thesis is that a relatively simple framework model of advanced capitalist democracies (ACD) evolved over a long period of time, at least over the last century—from roughly the end of the First World War, by which point all the early industrialisers had become democracies. In summarizing this framework more closely than above, we attach central importance to the *symbiotic* relationship between five core elements:[7]

1.3.1. THE ROLE OF THE STRONG NATION STATE

We follow many analysts before us (for example, Poulantzas (1973), Hayek (1944, 1966), and Schumpeter (1942), among the major theorists of advanced capitalism from quite different political perspectives) in paying close attention to the central role of the state in putting and maintaining in place key necessary conditions for the operation of advanced innovation-oriented capitalism. The state, to be successful, can be thought of having four sets of tasks:

(i) Imposing on business the requirement that product markets are competitive; this is a key requirement, for there is considerable evidence that competition (so long as not too intense) is a precondition for innovation. It requires a strong state to impose competition because businesses prefer protected markets with low-risk and high-profits which they can share with politicians. The first country to emerge as a modern capitalist economy, Britain, did not take off until the rampant rent-seeking and corruption that characterized the political system up until the end of the eighteenth century was eliminated (Popa 2015).

(ii) Imposing on labor the requirement that businesses are allowed the right to manage and to cooperate with management. If labor is too powerful, it may prefer to control production and to limit innovation and skill replacement, or with cospecific skills in a technology to "hold up" management once the technology is installed. Thus a strong enough state is needed to organize labor market rules to prevent this.

(iii) In addition to these rules of the game, the third role of the state is to invest in a range of public goods, especially in the areas of education, training, and research. Here the problem for the nation-state is that if advanced capitalist companies are mobile, they will take the benefits of these investments and locate elsewhere. Thus the benefits of knowledge generated in the nation-state need very broadly to remain there.

(iv) Finally the state needs to negotiate out through the political system and interest groups how advanced capitalism and the state can reset rules and reinvest in response to shocks. Fioretos 2011 shows this with insight over the whole postwar period in relation to France, Germany, and the UK). More generally, in periods of deep uncertainty—as in the early 1980s—it needs to debate the direction to be taken to promote advanced capitalism. In an important recent book, *Marketcraft: How Governments Make Markets Work*, Vogel discusses this process at length, in particular in relation to the United States and Japan since the 1980s.

1.3.2. ALIGNED INTERESTS OF DECISIVE VOTERS WITH ADVANCED CAPITALISM

Why should a strong enough state behave in these market-enhancing ways? If capitalism is politically strong it will be tempted to demand protection from the state, and politicians will be tempted to make bargains with it. Advanced capitalists will exchange profits with the state for protection and the quiet life. Poulantzas (1973) saw this as a fundamental problem facing capitalism. Arguably one of the most brilliant Marxist theorists from the 1960s to the 1980s, his "regional" theory simply posited that the state had the "function" of maintaining a competitive environment; this both geared business to innovation and prevented businesses from collective action such as investment strikes because of the collective action problem they faced when competing against each other. This approach may appear slightly mystical, but it showed how Poulantzas was aware of the problem.[8] Hayek (1944, 1966) was equally aware of the need to impose competition requirements on businesses if they were to innovate. His concern was with democracy: he believed that voters as workers would vote for protection to guarantee their jobs. And Schumpeter (1942) was equally aware of the problem and thought that advanced capitalism would lead to corporatism and an end to a competitive environment, or that voters would choose socialism.

We take a quite different position. Along with Lindblom (1977), but without his emphasis on the structural power of capital, we argue that governments pursue policies supporting advanced capitalism in the nation-state because the electorate, or at least decisive voters, punish governments which don't.[9] We argue that they do so because a large number of voters see themselves as benefiting from advanced capitalism, whether directly as employees or as aspirational voters: thus we take the opposite position to the standard view of political economy, that the interests of workers are opposed to those of capitalists.

Within advanced capitalist democracies, political parties and their leaders need to build up reputations among decisive voters as effective economic managers to be electable: that is to say, they need to build up a reputation for maintaining and, where necessary, changing the product and labor market rules (mainly, product market competition and labor market cooperation) and the public infrastructural investments (education, skills, research, universities) necessary for innovation-oriented capitalism. We can think of these as electable parties. An important question is what ensures a majority, or decisive vote, for these policies and parties. Who are these voters?

First, there is a large vote from employees in advanced capitalist companies. Advanced capitalism has required since the second (or scientific) industrial revolution from the last third of the ninteenth century, a large skilled and educated labor force, cospecific and collocated with the technology of the company in question (Thelen 2004; Goldin and Katz 1998). It is often wrongly thought that the knowledge of the company is a technology which can be codified and patented; but technology is almost always cospecific with the tacit skills of the workforce (Teece, 1986). The level of skills and education is relative to the prevailing technology, but management in the advanced sectors has always had to secure the cooperation or motivation of the labor force, because of the significant costs of hiring and firing. This is as true of semiskilled workers under Fordism as of contemporary software engineers: they could easily stop the line, and replacing them involved both strikes and significant retraining costs, especially if training new workers required the tacit cooperation of existing semiskilled workers. Thus we can think of this skilled workforce as gaining rent from advanced capitalism above the competitive market value of their skills. In one form or another this aligns the interests of the skilled worker with advanced capitalism. Because advanced capitalism is skill-intensive, this electorate is very large.

Second, the aspirational vote has a particular relevance in relation to advanced capitalism. By contrast to status-ordered societies, *growth* in the demand for skilled and educated labor is core to the idea of advanced capitalism as a result of technological change (Goldin and Katz 2009). Hence, while aspirational individuals, parents, and families have always existed to some extent, it is particularly associated with advanced capitalism. Even if parents may not themselves be skilled they can aspire to their children becoming skilled, which is equivalent to upward intergenerational mobility. Thus the aspirational voter has interests aligned with the success of advanced capitalism. Our analytic approach thus explains why advanced capitalism must grow, since growth is needed to provide the new jobs for aspirational voters and/or their children.

By this token, when some families are blocked from experiencing upward mobility they tend to react politically against the system, which we see as the root cause of populism. For reasons we will spell out below (and in detail in chapters 3–5), the transition to the knowledge economy has produced blockages, and this raises the question of whether populism is a threat to advanced democracy.[10] We think not. The reasons are discussed in detail in chapter 5, but the most fundamental in our view is that those benefiting from the knowledge economy have an obvious incentive to make sure that a solid majority will continue to feel included in, and benefit from, the knowledge economy in the future. That said, we do not want to minimize the challenges of potentially creating a large left-behind minority who feel alienated from society and democratic institutions. Even if populist parties will never attain majority status, populist appeals could prove a destabilizing force in democracy (as they arguably have in the United States and in Britain), and we do not want to underestimate the social costs of large minorities losing hope in the future and turning to drugs or crime as a consequence. This is a serious problem *for* democracy, even if it is not a serious threat *to* democracy (or advanced capitalism, or the nation-state). As we spell in out in chapters 3 and 5, this problem has been addressed much more effectively in some democracies than in others (in particular through the training and educational system).

1.3.3. SPECIALIZATION AND LOCATION COSPECIFICITY

This is perhaps the most novel element of the argument, and it underpins the symbiosis discussed above, between decisive voters and governments promoting the framework rules and infrastructural investments needed for advanced innovation-oriented to function effectively.

A critical and major empirical assumption we make about advanced capitalism is that (at least since the scientific revolution) it has been skill-intensive. That is an empirical assumption, and Braverman (1998) argued to the contrary that the microprocessor would result in a fall in skill-intensity. That has not happened so far in the advanced sectors; it has, arguably, as in Asian manufacturing, turned what had been advanced sectors in the Fordist era into less skilled sectors today. We will discuss in the conclusion different future scenarios depending on the nature and trajectory of technological developments. In the contemporary world, however, advanced capitalism is built on a large skilled labor force. More than forty-two percent of twenty-five-to-thirty-five-year-olds today have tertiary degree in the OECD (compared to twenty-six percent among fifty-five-to-sixty-four-year-olds), and more than half of the current university-age cohort will acquire a tertiary education, with the great majority of those who do not acquiring a higher secondary degree. Many of the latter will expect their own children to go to university. Almost eighty percent of the working-age population in contemporary OECD countries have at least a higher secondary degree (OECD 2016, 41). In a middle-income country like Turkey, the number is thirty-seven percent.

Not only is labor skill-intensive in the advanced sectors, those skills are tacit (i.e., difficult to codify) and cospecific with other skilled workers, and they are also cospecific with the relevant technology, even in cases where the technology is itself is codifiable and thus (generally) patentable. This in turn implies that the skilled workforces of advanced companies are colocated and have to work physically together. The great Chandlerian companies of the Fordist era typically had huge plants or connected sets of plants—the advanced sector of their era—which housed the skilled workforce, often from sophisticated manufacturing through to research and development. Many find it surprising that colocation has increased in the knowledge economy, despite the internet. This is often today in the form of skill clusters, so that knowledge is geographically confined, and both workers with the relevant skills and knowledge-based companies wanting to tap into the relevant knowledge cluster have strong incentives to locate there.

This is then a picture of the value-added of companies being constituted by their skilled workforces. Because whole workforces are extraordinarily difficult to relocate (especially to another country), and because of the costs of training relevantly skilled workforces abroad, advanced companies (or their subsidiaries) are relatively immobile.

This is consequential for how we understand modern capitalism. First, the common view of footloose capitalism makes little sense in relation to advanced companies, or at least their knowledge-based part. This is different from the behavior of MNEs in nonadvanced countries. It is different to financial assets, including the ownership of companies. And it is different to the ownership of patents. But even if the technology or discovery is codifiable, it is typically cospecific with skilled workforces. (Not always, as in the case of patents for therapeutic drugs.) In the substantive sense of the value-added of their knowledge, advanced companies are relatively immobile. Equity capital is liquid and can be owned in many different national markets, but its value is still tied to firms that are nationally embedded, hence also to the skilled workforces on which they depend. Short-term financial assets, such as foreign currency holdings or short-term bonds, impose constraints on macro-economic policies—notably, the capacity of governments to build up large debts or to use currency devaluations—but these are self-imposed constraints, as we will see in chapter 4. Besides, they have no effects on the capacity of governments to use balanced budgets to redistribute, or to use countercyclical fiscal or monetary policies in times of high unemployment.

Second, collocated and relatively immobile workforces are generated both by economies of scale and scope. In the scientific revolution and, increasingly, under Fordism, this required colocation in vast plants covering multiple interlinked activities gaining great economies of scale and also frequently of scope. It also took the form of smaller skilled companies carrying out interrelated activities. And it typically included many high value-added service sector activities, as skill clusters do now. Both in the past and now it has required differences, major and minor, across advanced nation states in knowledge competences.

Our argument about the immobility of capital in ACDs runs counter to common claims to the contrary. Among the more prominent examples in the academic literature are Streeck (2010), Piketty (2014), and Rodrik (1997, 2017), who all argue that capital mobility undermines the capacity of governments to tax and finance the welfare state. For Piketty this is the basis for his prediction that $r > g$, which will produce ever-greater concentration of wealth. Yet Piketty's own data show that after taking account of destruction of capital and capital taxation, in fact $r < g$ for the entire period from 1913 to 2012—that is, basically during the period of democracy (see figures 10.10 and 10.11). The dire prediction for the future relies on the key assumption "that fiscal competition will gradually lead to total disappearance of taxes on capital in the twenty-first century" (2014, 355), coupled with a sharp drop in growth rates.[11]

A look at actual capital taxation rates instead reveals remarkable stability. While top statutory capital tax rates have come down in most countries since the 1980s, Swank and Steinmo (2002) show that such cuts were accompanied by a broadening of the tax base that left effective tax rates virtually unchanged from 1981 to 1995. The most ambitious attempt to estimate capital tax revenues as a share of the capital base (called the implicit tax rate) by Eurostat shows no tendency for decline in European ACDs between 1995 and 2015 (see table 1.1). If anything, the opposite is true. The United States is an exception because corporate tax rates were cut in the Republic tax

TABLE 1.1. The implicit tax rates on capital, Western European countries, 1995–2015

	1995	2000	2005	2010	2015	Diff 2015–1995
Belgium	24.7	28.8	31.1	27.4	38	13.3
Denmark	27.9	31.6	45.3	38.7	34.4	6.5
Germany	20.8	26.4	20.4	19.2	24.2	3.4
Ireland	.	17.2	22.3	16	14.5	−2.4
Spain	.	27.9	35.9	26.2	30.3	2.2
France	36	42.3	44.1	43.5	52.7	16.2
Italy	24	24	24.7	28.6	34.3	10
Netherlands	19.6	18.6	13.5	10.9	12.1	−7.5
Austria	25.9	26.8	24.3	23.4	29.9	4
Portugal	19	28.4	24.4	25.4	26.5	7.4
Finland	31.5	40.6	28.6	29.2	31.4	−0.1
Sweden	18.8	39.2	31.5	27.5	32.7	14
UK	24.4	34	33.4	32.6	31.6	7.2
Norway	38.7	42.5	41	42.7	30.3	−8.5

Source: Eurostat–European Commission. 2017. *Taxation trends in the European Union. Data for the EU member states, Iceland and Norway*. Luxembourg: Publications Office of the European Union.

reform, but only to about the average rate of other OECD countries, which is twenty-one percent (the United States had exceptionally high rates before the reform). Of course, there is no reason that governments should rely on capital taxation to fund the welfare state, and such taxation rarely exceeds twenty-five percent of revenues (with income and consumption taxes making up the bulk of the rest).[12] The composition of taxation is a political choice, not a matter of the structural power of capital to exit.

1.3.4. STRATEGIC COMPLEMENTARITIES AND INSTITUTIONAL HETEROGENEITY

Because of nationally rooted specialization in an integrated world economy, the advanced capitalist democracies are engaged in a game of strategic complementarities. Globalization between them increases the payoffs from the game, as opposed to constraining domestic political choice or suborning democracy of the advanced economies.

In Chandlerian companies in a Fordist regime, free trade and freedom of foreign direct investment movement are both important, as they are in knowledge economies. In knowledge economies, as knowledge competences become more decentralized, so knowledge-based MNEs become more like networks of autonomous subsidiaries with complementary knowledge competences. In both cases there is a political incentive to promote globalization across the advanced economies; but it is arguably more important in the contemporary world. There are several implications of this insight:

A. *The political power of advanced capitalism is unlikely to be strong.* Advanced capitalist companies need to operate in an international competitive environment in the advanced democracies. That makes it difficult to solve the collective action problems (such as mutual punishment) needed for carrying out, for example, an investment strike, as well as sharply reducing the temptation to doing so. Even in coordinated systems, business action against a government is both costly and limited to areas like training, technology transfer, and wage restraint, where advanced companies are unlikely to want to follow disruptive activities.

Equally, as we have seen, since companies are relatively immobile geographically, it limits both actual exit and the credibility of exit threats. The critics of capitalism are right that footloose capital constrains what states can do; it is just that advanced capitalism is not footloose.[13] Thus we find the idea thoroughly unpersuasive that advanced capitalism has suborned the autonomy of democracy through globalization, and is responsible for austerity, poverty, and cutbacks in redistribution and the welfare state. One can of course find examples of governments giving tax concessions to companies that promise to retain jobs instead of moving them to low-wage countries. Such pressures and temptations arise naturally as part of Vernon's (1966) product life-cycle as production becomes more routinized and can be performed by robots or low-skilled workers abroad. But we think it is far more remarkable that governments in ACDs routinely shun such temptations. At the height of deindustrialization in the 1980s governments across ACDs engaged in policies that accelerated the decline of sunset industries by cutting back subsidies, privatizing unproductive public enterprises, and removing barriers to competition from low-wage countries while betting on new high value-added industries moving in to take advantage of an abundance of high-skilled labor (and the associated institutional supports). Nor are such "tough" industrial policies catering to the collective interests of "capital"—even in the broadest Poulantzas(1973) or Lindblom (1977) interpretation. The Rehn-Meidner model informing the economic strategy of the Swedish LO, the major union confederation, and of the Social Democratic Party was deliberately designed to force low-productivity firms to die or to innovate. A right-wing version of this modernization strategy was pursued in the UK and it was vehemently opposed by business. Sometimes the siren song of jobs from declining companies are too hard to resist, but more often than not these companies are shown the door.

B. *Redistribution and the welfare state is democratically decided, for better and (often) for worse.* In understanding inequality before and after redistribution and the policies toward the welfare state in advanced societies, there is consequently little mileage to be gained from focusing on the political power of advanced capitalism; in ACDs (though not elsewhere) capital is politically weak. Instead, for understanding "bad" outcomes, the focus should be on three aspects of advanced democratic systems: first, that the winners from advanced economies are typically the decisive voters—they choose policies to re- and in some measure also predistribute; they may or may not make those choices to compensate the losers; and in particular they may choose not to compensate the poor. (Moreover, if we think of populists as losers of advanced capitalism, they are if anything more hostile to compensating the poor.) Second, that "rules of the democratic game" differ as one moves from consensus PR-based systems to majoritarian "winner-takes-all" Westminster systems (Iversen and Soskice 2006); and further still to the porous American system in which primary elections and semidisciplined parties enable money to influence outcomes (Hacker and Pierson 2010). Third, the level of political information among the electorate exacerbates bad outcomes (Iversen and Soskice 2015). In understanding the problematic of inequality and poverty in the advanced world, it is at these aspects of democracy that we will look, and it is on these aspects that critics of contemporary politics in advanced democracies should focus. We are, needless to say, strong proponents of democracy, but the failure of adequate redistribution in advanced economies lies in the workings of democratic systems rather than in the political power of capital.

C. *A key underlying condition for a democratic system to support heavy investments in education and research infrastructure is their geographical immobility.* Geographic immobility relates to the rents of skilled workers and the alignment of their interests with advanced capitalism. Critically it also explains the logic behind the heavy infrastructural investments needed to support advanced capitalism in the first place. For if it could be taken abroad (as companies could do in the absence of the tacit skills of the domestic workforce and their cospecificity with company technology), then incentives for governments and voters to invest would collapse.

1.3.5. THE FUNDAMENTAL EQUALITY OF DEMOCRACY

We have established above that advanced capital in ACDs is immobile and that the state for that reason is powerful. We have also argued that democracy and capitalism are in a symbiotic relationship in the sense that decisive voters—skilled or aspirational or both—vote for parties and policies that promote the advanced sectors, which raise the demand for skills, and so on. In this section we suggest that the essence of democracy is not redistribution or equality, as so commonly assumed, but the advancement of middle class interests, and we capture this idea as the "fundamental equality of democracy" (to distinguish it clearly from Piketty's (2014) "fundamental inequality of capitalism").

The interests of the middle classes are aligned with advanced capitalism via two key mechanisms. The first is direct inclusion into the wealth stream created by the continuous progression of the advanced sectors. By far the most important path to such inclusion is education, since the advanced sectors are skill intensive. Even when the skills of middle-aged workers fall behind the needs of the advanced sectors, these workers can benefit indirectly if their children acquire the skills needed to move up in the economy. Such intergenerational mobility creates aspirational voters who will also support policies that push forward the advanced sectors—notably through investment in education and research and development (R&D), coupled with strong competition rules.

The second mechanism is the welfare state, broadly construed to include cash transfers, social insurance, and public services. Accounting for more than one-third of GDP on average, wide-ranging tax-financed middle-class programs ensure that those with high and rising incomes share some of their wealth with the rest of society. This is especially important in the transition to the knowledge economy because gains of new technology have been concentrated at the upper tail of the income distribution. The tax-and-transfer system ensures that these gains are shared with the middle classes.

Exactly who benefits and how much from the knowledge economy is a matter of democratic politics, which varies with the institutional framework of each country. In this book we pay particular attention to electoral and party systems, but for now we can capture the role of electoral politics with the simplified notion of a "decisive voter." Given that democratic governments ordinarily depend on support from a majority and given that politics is broadly organized around class and economic interests, this decisive voter will be someone from the middle of the income distribution (although not necessarily the median). With a right-skewed distribution of income, a majority has income below the mean and the decisive voter will therefore also typically be someone with income below the mean.

Contrary to standard notions, the overriding concern of the decisive voter is neither equality nor redistribution, but rather his or her own income and welfare, with due attention to efficiency costs of taxation. Although the literature tends to equate political equality with economic equality, there is no reason that the decisive voter should care about those at the bottom of the distribution, except insofar as he or she fears falling into the ranks of the poor (or fears that his or her offspring will)—an insurance motive we discuss in subsequent chapters. Nor is there any reason for decisive voters to oppose rising incomes for those above them, as long as such windfalls are shared. There are clearly efficiency limits to taxing the rich but whatever the optimal level of taxation from the perspective of the decisive voter, we should expect democracy to ensure that the net income of the decisive voter keeps up with the capacity of the economy to generate income. This capacity is reflected in per-capita income, or average income, and we can therefore represent the political logic of ACDs as a simple identity: $Y_D / \bar{Y} = k$, where Y_D is the disposable income of the decisive voter, $\bar{Y}$ is average disposable income, and k is a nationally specific constant (defined over some suitable length of time to smooth out short-term fluctuations).[14] Needless to say, this assumes that the decisive voter does not change over time because of, say, declining voter turnout or reforms in the electoral system.

Much of the contemporary literature on advanced capitalism implies, however, that any such equality of democracy has ended—if it ever existed. Globalization critics like Rodrik imply that footloose capital has undermined the capacity of labor—which presumably includes our decisive voter—to maintain its share of national income. In Piketty, what he calls the "fundamental inequality of capitalism" ($r > g$) guarantees that national wealth and income will increasingly accrue to those at the top of the distribution. In the more political interpretations of Streeck (2016), Bartels (2008), Gilens (2012), and Hacker and Pierson (2011), the will of the majority is subverted by the outsized political resources of business and the rich, again causing a concentration of income at the top while the middle and lower classes lose out.

At first blush these pessimistic conjectures seem to be borne out by the data. No matter what measure is used, inequality has risen significantly since the 1980s across all ACDs. For example, Piketty shows that the top decile share of US national income rose from about thirty-five percent in 1980 to about forty-seven percent in 2010 (Piketty 2014, 24). Goldin and Katz (2007) show a similar rise in US wage inequality. Across twenty-two ACDs the Gini coefficient of market household income has risen an average of eleven percent from 1985 to 2014, according to data from Solt (2016), and the disposable income Gini (after taxes and transfers) increased a more modest seven percent. (The pattern is illustrated in figure 1.1, panel a.)

Yet there has been no corresponding decline in the $Y_D/\overline{Y}$ ratio if we proxy Y_D by median disposable income and $\overline{Y}$ by mean disposable income. This is shown in figure 1.1 (panel b) for a sample of ACDs for which we have comparable data starting in 1985 and ending in 2010. The $Y_D/\overline{Y}$ ratio in 2010 is more or less the same as it was in 1985 for most countries (the observations lie close to the 45-degree line), and the average difference in the ratio between the two years, Δr, is indistinguishable from zero: $\Delta r = [-0.043; 0,047]$. So it appears that the median income group has been exceptionally successful in keeping up with the overall growth of income. We think this is also bound to be true for more accurate measures of decisive voter income since decisive voters tend to be closer to the means as voter nonturnout is concentrated among the poor.

New Zealand is something of an outlier with a drop in the $Y_D/\overline{Y}$ ratio from .92 to .87 between 1985 and 2010, or about six percent. Even in this case, however, it is notable that average real incomes rose by thirty-five percent in the same period, so the middle class was much better off in 2010 than in 1985. The Gini of disposable household income in this period rose by twenty percent, according to data from Solt (2016). This highlights the general fact that while income inequality has been rising fast, the relative position of the median has been fairly stable, even in an "outlier" like New Zealand. This is also true in the case of the other negative "outlier": Germany. Here the relative income of the median declined from .93 to .90, or about four percent from 1985 to 2010 (undoubtedly in large part because of unification); yet the mean income rose by more than fifty percent. Even in cases where relative income of the median has slightly slipped, the middle group of income earners is thus clearly enjoying rising incomes despite increasing inequality.

The stability of $Y_D/\overline{Y}$ is particularly remarkable considering that the data cover a period with the most dramatic increase in inequality since the emergence of democracy. The middle class is a critical constituency for democratic governments, yet it has no interest

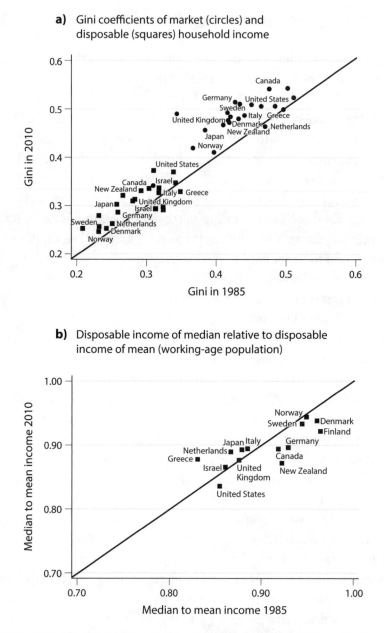

a) Gini coefficients of market (circles) and disposable (squares) household income

b) Disposable income of median relative to disposable income of mean (working-age population)

FIGURE 1.1. Measures of distribution of income, 2010 vs. 1985. (a) Gini coefficients of market (circles) and disposable (squares) household income; (b) Disposable income of median relative to disposable income of mean (working-age population). Labeled observations are the countries for which data are available in panel (a). The first observation for the United States refers to 1995, not 1985. *Sources*: (a) OECD Income Distribution Database (IDD): Gini, poverty, income. Data extracted on December 31, 2017, 13:11 UTC (GMT) from OECD.Stat. (b) Solt, Frederick. 2016. "The Standardized World Income Inequality Database." *Social Science Quarterly* 97. SWIID Version 6.2, March 2018.

in inequality per se; only in seeing its own fortunes rise with the economy as a whole. Even when the gains are concentrated at the top, the middle benefits. As we discuss below, in the United States about seventy percent of federal tax revenues comes from the top ten percent of earners, and about forty percent from the top one percent. Indeed, we argue in this book that the reforms that enabled the knowledge economy to take off created huge inequalities, yet were supported by a majority of voters. Those left out of the new economy are generally also weak in the political system. Indeed, a recurrent theme of this book is that democracy, not capitalism, is to blame for the rise of low-end inequality. Phrased positively, greater equality is a democratic choice, which is little constrained by capital.

Our argument may seem to run counter to the evidence in Gilens (2005, 2012), Bartels (2008), Peters and Ensink (2015), and others that the rich are much more politically influential than the middle class. But as we will discuss in detail in chapter 4, this evidence does not in fact say much about whether the economic interests of the middle class are attended to in government policies. The reason is that these analyses compares preferences for policy change with actual policy change, and many policy changes are at the margin and do not much affect how well the broader interests of different classes are represented. If it was truly the case that the rich almost monopolized political power, it would be very hard to understand the emergence and persistence of large-scale middle-class programs such as Medicare and Social Security, let along why the top one percent of earners pay almost half of the bill for these programs. Moving outside the United States, the notion that middle-class interests are ignored in public policies is even less plausible. Those with high education and income may simply understand the constraints on government policies better than others—the obvious example here is the need for countercyclical fiscal policies—and this will show up as congruence between preferences for change and actual change (see Elkjær and Iversen 2018 for evidence). But this is not synonymous with deciding whose class interests are favored by government policies; the fundamental equality of democracy is an expression of middle-class power.

In the following we develop our argument further by applying it to the five puzzles we identified above in addition to the resilience of ACDs: the middle-income trap; the strengthening of advanced capitalism by democracy; the rise of democracy; persistent varieties of capitalism in an age of globalization; and the lack of response to rising inequality.

1.4. The Middle-Income Trap Puzzle

A remarkable fact is that the group of advanced democracies has only been slightly expanded since their rise in the nineteenth and early twentieth centuries. The distribution of world income has become marginally more equal since the 1980s, but this is virtually all due to the rise of a few populous poor countries to the ranks of middle-income economies, notably China and India, and not the rise of middle-income countries into the high-income group. For more than a century, entry into the advanced group has only occurred in the instances of Singapore, South Korea, Taiwan, Israel, Ireland, and Hong Kong.

We can illustrate this using patent data because the number of patents per capita is a measure of the size of the advanced sector (as opposed to GDP per capita, which is affected by oil and other natural wealth). If we focus on OECD and major middle-income countries with at least five million citizens, figure 2.1 shows the number of patents per one million working-age adults in 1976 compared to 2015. The data are from the US Patent and Trademark Office, where nearly every major patent is taken out by individuals, labs, and firms from around the globe.[15]

It is apparent that the ACDs are clustered in the top right corner and that only South Korea, Taiwan, and Singapore have made the transition into this group from 1976 to 2015. This ties into our argument, since in each of these cases powerful governments were deeply committed to becoming advanced capitalist countries. Taiwan, South Korea, and Singapore were semi-authoritarian and in each case, governments were powerful enough to impose competition (in different ways, but always involving trade) and shift massive resources into the educational system. Taiwan and South Korea have since become democracies with powerful electoral

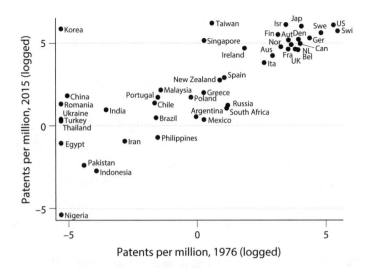

FIGURE 1.2. Number of patents per one million people (logged) in the working-age population, 2015 vs. 1976. The data are from the US Patent and Trademark Office and show the total number of patents granted as a share of working-age population in millions, by the country of residence of the inventor. Countries all the way to the left received zero patents in 1976 and have been assigned an arbitrarily low value (since numbers are logged). *Source*: OECD.Stat. Data extracted on March 3, 2018, 02:19 GMT.

lobbies for advanced capitalism. Singapore has only slowly moved in a fully democratic direction, but its commitment to education and open trade has been unwavering; it is in fact the only advanced country that is (still) not fully democratic.

The difficulty of breaking into the rich ACD club is known in the economic literature as the "middle-income trap" (e.g., Kharas and Kohli 2011). Eichengreen et al. (2012) have persuasively argued that the key barrier is the creation of large knowledge-intensive sectors sustained by internally driven innovation. It is precisely the existence of such dynamic, skill-intensive sectors that define advanced capitalism as we use it in this book. This is as true today as it was at the turn of the previous century.

In fact, if one considers the distribution of the *world population*, the share who lives in rich democratic countries has *declined* since the Second World War, and the total number of people living in these countries has barely risen. Paradoxically, in the face of this evidence most of the recent work on globalization has focused on the concern that rich countries might fail in global competition with "low-wage" countries and decline into the middle income group. But no country has suffered this fate, and the gap to middle-income countries is stable. Simply put, there is no convergence, whether viewed from above or from below.

Our framework explains the middle-income trap at least in part:

1. The advanced capitalist democracy requires (ab initio) a strongly organized government with both the ability and the incentive to impose the relevant labor and product market rules as well as to build the requisite education and research infrastructure. The incentives for nonadvanced governments to do so are not likely to be fulfilled since they will have strong incentives to do protectionist deals with companies; or a wish to control the companies in the first place; or with natural resources to exploit. Post–1945 exceptions were initially strongly organized states with effective bureaucracies, an absence of natural resources, and a need for the revenues to maintain a powerful military—Singapore, South Korea, and Taiwan. Israel is a related case in point, where the electorate understood the military need. But absent that special case, and absent initially large skilled and educated workforces supportive of advanced sectors, there is no democratic incentive for governments to behave in this way (Doner and Schneider 2016).

2. The professional social networks and skill clusters do not generally exist to create the capacities and requisite knowledge to build innovative companies with the necessary marketing and financial linkages with other companies and the relevant markets (themselves nearly always in advanced capitalist democracies). Israel and Taiwan were able to benefit from social networks and skill clusters composed of returnees and also between networks strung between them and Silicon Valley (Saxenian 2007); Singapore and South Korea from MNEs; and in all cases from rapid build-up of skills and research. These now constitute skilled and educated electorates supportive of government promotion

of advanced capitalism. But it is only the rare cases where governments had the relevant incentives, connections, and capacities (Breznitz 2007).

3. The democratic institutions necessary to support advanced capitalism are mostly absent. First, there has to be government support for broad-based public investment in education (and a range of supporting institutions that we discuss later), and this in turn requires disciplined political parties that are preeminently concerned about their reputation in a political system where governments must continually appeal to electoral majorities. Reputation-based political parties are also necessary for the government to be sufficiently independent of local strongmen and business interests to ensure that they will not allocate resources or restrict competition for short-term political support. Such reputation-based democratic institutions failed to emerge in most countries. Instead, the middle-income countries tend to be characterized by an economic system where firms seek rents from the political system by offering bribes in exchange for protection against market competition, while politicians accept bribes for personal gain and in order to wage personalized electoral campaigns or party-internal contests. Consistent with this logic, Svolik (2013) shows that voters in in such a setting will rationally conclude that all politicians are bad, giving even honest politicians reasons to act like them. While Latin America has many candidates for moving out of the middle-income trap, this logic captures the Latin American dynamic of weak product market competition legislation ensuring the market dominance of large, typically family-owned conglomerates, *Grupos*, with close links to the political systems (Schneider 2009).

From this we can begin to understand why it is so difficult for middle-income countries to join the rich camp. Unlike the neo-classical notion that technology is available to every country, it is in fact embedded in immovable national workforces. Advanced technologies therefore have to be built from within, and for middle income countries to acquire this capacity requires two simultaneous revolutions: one economic and another political. The economic revolution is that firms have to abandon their current product market strategies and make major investments in new technology, at the same time as the supply of highly skilled workers expands dramatically. The latter requires a political revolution, since politicians have to free themselves from both educated elites who have no interest in such a major supply shock, and from clientilistic networks of existing producers and their dependent workers who want to remain protected. Competition is a requisite for technological progress, but it can be the death knell for many middle-range producers that have to confront global competition. Moreover, because mid-range technologies rely on easily replaceable skills, any attempt by governments to impose costs or demands on business can be met by exit. So, unlike advanced capitalism, the nation-state in middle-income countries is generally weak and short-sighted, while capital is strong.

1.5. The Puzzle of Democratic Politics Strengthening Capitalism

It is natural to think that democracy and capitalism are on a collision course. One is based on a principle of equality ("one person, one vote") while the other is based on a principle of market power ("one dollar, one vote"). Esping-Andersen captured this tension succinctly in the title of his 1985 book *Politics Against Markets*, and it underpins the entire power resources approach to capitalist democracies.[16] Streeck (2013) interprets every major institutional change, economic crisis, and distributive outcome in the post–WWII period in terms of the struggle between (egalitarian) democracy and (inegalitarian) capital, with capital gradually winning out as its mobility rises.[17] Piketty (2014) concurs but does not even perceive a need to analyze democratic politics because mobile capital inevitably undermines the capacity of democratic governments to either arrest the growth of capital or accelerate the growth of the economy. So how can we claim that democracy prevents markets being undermined, leading to divestment and capital flight?

The first reason is that a majority of voters want to see advanced capitalism succeed. They derive their prosperity from the success of the advanced sectors, and they therefore have an incentive to support parties that promote the advanced sectors using a variety of policies, including exposing business to competition as a means to spur innovation and growth. These policies are market-enhancing, and therefore entirely compatible with the success of capitalism as an economic system, though not of individual companies, and they typically garner broad cross-class support. In advanced countries with large skilled workforces, advanced democracy promotes geographically embedded advanced capitalism.

When the threshold into a modern economy is passed, the mutually beneficial, and reinforcing, relationship between advanced capitalism and government takes the following form:

> Governments provide and/or underwrite an *institutional framework* which enables advanced sector companies to develop and carry forward their comparative advantages—we see the provision of the conditions in which advanced capitalism can flourish as a central function of advanced governments. This institutional framework covers a wide range of areas, which notably include education, vocational training and higher education, technology transfer and innovation systems, regulation of skilled labor markets and industrial relations, corporate governance and markets for corporate control, those aspects of the welfare state relevant to advanced capitalism (its insurance but not redistributive functions), trade, competition and intellectual property policy, and the macroeconomic regime.

Politically, what sustains the equilibrium is a large electoral constituency of educated workers attaching importance to the competence of government parties in managing the institutions promoting successful advanced capitalism. This constituency is supplemented in multiple ways by those who are not direct beneficiaries of advanced capitalism: there is a wide aspirational community of families concerned that their children can access these advanced sectors. And there is a wider set of "sheltered" service sectors whose prosperity depends on the success of the advanced capitalist system; these include both high-skilled sectors such as culture, the media, entertainment, much of the health and fitness system, the education system at all levels, and large parts of retail, law and finance, but also some lower-paid workers employed in successful cities in transport care and so on. Specifically:

> The electability of parties requires that they are credibly seen by this broad electorate as having the competence to manage and promote advanced capitalism. As voters choose politicians for their reputation for good performance, bad types are crowded out (Svolik 2013). In our perspective, the possession of this reputational competence is a valence issue across parties, although the particular form that advanced capitalism is promoted—the "growth model"—involves distributive conflict. Thus we will argue that there is a symbiosis between democracy and advanced capitalism in advanced societies. So long as the constituency of actual or aspirational direct or indirect beneficiaries of advanced capitalism is large enough that it includes enough decisive voters, then there will be pressure on governments to promote the conditions for the success of advanced capitalism.

Our key assumption is that that constituency is big enough in the advanced economies. And that if governments are seen as successfully promoting these conditions, then that constituency is reinforced. Under these conditions there is a symbiotic relation between democracy and advanced capitalism.[18]

One element of institutional frameworks that needs highlighting is the one governing industrial relations and the power of unions. This gets to the core of the relationship between capitalism and politics. First, as with all other aspects of the institutional framework, governments (and the political system more generally) can only impose legislatively feasible frameworks; in the UK neither the early-twentieth-century Liberal government nor the 1950s Conservative government could have legislated against unions had they wished to, because decisive voters were, respectively, craft workers and then, in the 1950s, semiskilled workers, who would have suffered from "right to manage" legislation. Crafts (forthcoming) argues the failure of UK governments to introduce serious competition legislation through this long period explains its weak economic performance; and it is plausible to argue that serious competition would have required the "right to manage." But Thatcher did introduce effective competition requirements in the 1980s and Blair accepted her legislation because they did not face this electoral constraint, and because they saw this as benefiting the innovative capacity of advanced capitalist sectors. Second, disciplined industry unions and employee representation within the company have been integral to competitiveness in skill-intensive export-oriented manufacturing industries in coordinated capitalism and hence part of the relevant institutional frameworks. This was not always the case, and it only holds when companies see cooperative unionization as a better alternative in managing highly skilled employees with autonomous responsibility than individual wage/career structures and/or company-based social protection. This highlights another point:

> The development, maintenance, and modification of institutional frameworks is neither simple nor transparent nor typically consensual. There is nearly always conflict when major changes occur since the interests of some particular groups will be damaged. In coordinated economies organized interests have greater negotiating rights and therefore play a greater role in the process of change in institutional frameworks, while in liberal and majoritarian countries governments may simply impose decisions against the will of business (as Thatcher did in eliminating collusive agreements in finance or ending protection against hostile takeovers) let alone against unions. Our contention is that governments of advanced nations—often after long processes of consultation, argument and sometimes open conflict—generate institutional frameworks which effectively promote comparative institutional advantages, given the preexisting patterns of know-how and coordination.

In exchange, the economic success of advanced capitalist sectors cashes out in many ways for governments, from electoral success to military resources; governments of all political colors are therefore concerned to build appropriate institutional frameworks, sometimes conflictually—so long as they remain electorally and politically successful. To a far greater extent than is recognized in the literature, governments and mainstream political parties are concerned with their medium and long-term viability, and voters reward parties for sustained good economic performance. Political parties represent distinct interests, especially in multiparty PR systems, but they also serve as bridges between the present and the future which enable voters and companies to thrive over long periods of time.[19] This does not mean that parties have no incentives to pursue short-sighted policies, but rather that such policies come at a cost in terms of lost reputation. When the economic gains from far-sighted policies are sufficiently large—in the context of an advanced economy—the costs of reputation from short-sighted policies are correspondingly large.

The exchange between business and governments has many benefits for advanced capitalism, but it is far from maximizing the interests of capitalist companies. Their basic strategic interest at any given moment is in protected markets in which they can make secure profits with minimal- and low-risk investment. That, however, is against the interests of governments who are concerned inter alia with tax receipts, value added and productivity, competitiveness and exports, skills and innovation, and the provision of sustainable high value-added employment. Again, it is possible that some politicians are unconcerned with these issues but instead with personal enrichment, but we argue that it was an element of the coevolution of the political systems of our countries (i.e., those with advanced capitalist sectors) that this incentive was minimized. Thus:

> A critical element of the institutional frameworks which governments with advanced capitalist sectors (and thus sectors capable of innovation) provide is some requirement on companies that they compete in domestic and/or export markets in order to incentivize them to innovate.

By contrast to Marxist arguments, as well as Lindblom's (1977), we do not see political systems setting the frameworks which capitalists would have chosen. On the contrary, the institutional frameworks of the advanced countries forced capitalists to compete and take risks rather than guaranteeing them safe and high returns on their capital. These national frameworks (in different forms) both supplied the public goods necessary for innovation, and imposed the competitive incentives to generate innovation. The political basis for these policies were educated workers and aspirational constituencies.

But within these broad efficiency mandates, governments have considerable discretion to tax and redistribute as they see fit since they are not constrained by capital mobility. Indeed, advanced democracies tend to be more redistributive compared to both non-democracies (where governments have little incentive to redistribute) and to nonadvanced democracies (where governments have little discretion to redistribute). This is very clearly illustrated in figure 1.3. Lower inequality is especially evident for net income, after taxes and transfers, reflecting higher levels of redistribution in advanced countries compared to other countries. Greater redistribution is partly a reflection of the role of middle classes in demanding a share of income through the democratic system, partly a result of democratic coalitions that include representatives of lower classes, and partly a reflection of the role of social insurance as a complement to skill-intensive production, as we discuss in greater detail in subsequent chapters. But it also reflects the strength of the state to redistribute, which is largely missing in low- and middle-income countries (democratic or not). These differences are very stable over time.

1.6. The Puzzle of the Rise of Democracy and Advanced Capitalism

The historical parallel to the question of how democracy and advanced capitalism can coexist and indeed reinforce each other is how democracy emerged in the first place. Contemporary dominant theories of democratization by Boix (2003) and Acemoglu and Robinson (2005) assume that the establishment of democracy provides a commitment to each side (as it were, to rich and poor) that from then on redistribution would be based solely on democratic processes. But it is not clear why that commitment is credible; and in many nonadvanced economies democracy has been overturned or subverted or put at risk.

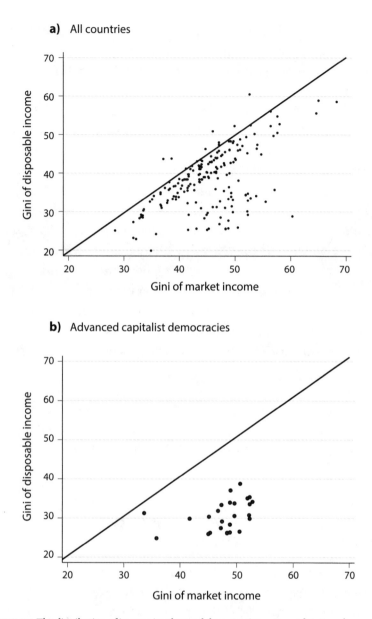

a) All countries

b) Advanced capitalist democracies

FIGURE 1.3. The distribution of income in advanced democracies compared to nonadvanced countries. *Notes*: (a) displays the pre- and post-fisc Ginis for 192 countries. The years are the latest available, where 85% are from 2008 or later and only 5 observations are from before 2002. (b) includes Australia, Austria, Belgium, Canada, the Czech Republic, Denmark, Finland, France, Germany, Greece, Iceland, Ireland, Israel, Italy, Japan, Korea, Luxembourg, Netherlands, New Zealand, Norway, Portugal, Spain, Sweden, Switzerland, the UK, and the United States. *Source*: Solt, Frederick. 2016. "The Standardized World Income Inequality Database." *Social Science Quarterly* 97. SWIID Version 6.2, March 2018.

Next, neither theory gives a role to advanced industrialization in democratization. This contrasts with the most plausible reading of Lipset (1960; see also Wucherpfennig and Deutsch 2009). Lipset's measures of what might be thought of as a proxy for advanced capitalism (industrialization, urbanization, wealth and education) is not only strongly correlated with democracy but also with the stability of democracy. We have outlined why advanced capitalism is associated with stable democracy, and the question is then how this shapes our understanding of the origins of democracy.

There are clearly predemocratic forces pushing forward advanced capitalism. This is true for the advanced countries that emerged before the Second World War, and it is true for those that emerged after the war. They were all characterized by an authoritarian regime strong enough to impose a set of rules and invest in research and education infrastructure and to have a (nondemocratic) incentive to promote advanced capitalism. Under those conditions, skilled and educated workforces are built up, generally in Chandlerian corporations in the case of the early industrializers (Thelen 2004). These workforces, with skills cospecific with each other and with the company's technologies, are central to the value-added of the company.

Once the transition to democracy has occurred, the sustainability of the system depends on these skilled workforces because a) they want the system of advanced capitalism to continue, since their market income depends on its market success, and b) they have the organizational capacity to block or render a return to authoritarianism very costly. By contrast to Boix's (2003) condition that capital be mobile to prevent expropriation, the "functionally equivalent" condition is that these skilled workforces support the system of advanced capitalism. By contrast to Acemoglu and Robinson (2005), the nonreversibility of democracy does not lie in the institutions themselves ("credible commitment to redistribution") but in the organizational capacity and economic importance of skilled workers.

This then explains the conditions for democratization in advanced capitalist systems: the skilled workforces with their cospecific skills will eventually be well-entrenched enough to have the bargaining power to impose democracy on governments. And nondemocratic governments—promoting advanced capitalism—will eventually accept democracy, since these skilled workforces also wish to promote it. As advanced capitalism promotes the number and bargaining strength of skilled workers, democracy becomes highly stable.

As we explain in detail in chapter 2, advanced capitalist democracies did in fact not all develop from worker pressure in nondemocratic advanced capitalist states. In the United States and the UK, as well as Australia, New Zealand, and Canada, democracy was elite-imposed (Collier 1999). In our interpretation, this happened because a modernizing elite—though in very different ways in the United States on the one hand and in the UK and its settler colonies on the other—wanted to minimize the influence of conservative landowning or plantation-owning classes who were opposed to the education and modernization needed to build an advanced capitalist system. In the UK and the settler colonies, it was designed to bring skilled workers into the class of decisive voters, diminishing the role of landowners in the House of Lords and other upper houses, as well as in local governments. In the United States, the Republican ascendency of the late nineteenth century in effect permitted the conservative plantation-owning Southern states, hostile to industrialization, to opt out of the development of advanced capitalism in the North.

1.7. The Puzzle of Varieties of Advanced Capitalism in an Age of Globalization

A large literature, mainly in economics, has been devoted to the idea that there is a single optimal way—a best practice—of organizing economies to pursue growth or maximize GDP. At various stages, especially in the 1980s and 1990s, the OECD, the World Bank, and the IMF propagated these beliefs, sometimes referred to as the Washington Consensus.[20] It might have been expected that advanced capitalist democracies would have seen convergence, especially in corporate governance, labor market rules, as well as institutions playing roles in training and in technology transfer. Moreover, advanced companies face broadly similar conditions in international product and financial markets, and with respect to overseas direct investment.

But that has not generally been the case, despite major relaxation of government rules in the last quarter-century and despite the fact that companies are free to move (Hall and Soskice 2001). In fact, although corporations are now organized with greater flexibility and are more decentralized, each advanced capitalist democracy has remained different from each other: some advanced capitalist democracies are closer to each in broad variety of advanced capitalism terms, but there are many institutional differences between even Denmark and Sweden (Ibsen and Thelen 2017). As already noted, redistribution and welfare states, while they have changed over time, remain different across advanced capitalist democracies. These institutional differences are for the most part at the national level. In particular, there are great differences in knowledge competences and patterns of specialization across, but also within, countries.

Our approach is quite consistent with these differentiated patterns, even in a global world in which financial markets are competitive and capital movements are unconstrained. These results are of course widely known (Garrett 1998; Swank 2002), but our approach provides a clear analytic framework for understanding them as "equilibrium" phenomena.

1. The first key point is again the limited mobility of skilled knowledge-based workforces in the advanced economies. Nor can companies usually replicate the skills of the workforce elsewhere because training in tacit skills depends largely on new employees working with existing ones who can impart the tacit knowledge. Nearly always companies or skilled educated employees depend on other companies or other facilities (including research) in the area. This is strongly reinforced by and reinforces geographical specialization.

2. Not only can the advanced company not move, but it cannot seldom threaten credibly to do so. Capital does not have structural power in this sense. Moreover, advanced companies generally lack collective action capacity since the state imposes competitive product market rules. As Poulantzas (1973) puts it only slightly differently, the

nature of capitalism is competition, especially if legally reinforced, so we should not expect advanced capitalism to act collectively as a class for itself. Hence advanced capitalist companies (even if they should want to do so) cannot force the state to lower corporation taxes or limit redistribution or cut back welfare states. Nor by the same token can they force states to change rules governing varieties of capitalism.[21]

3. A key implication is that advanced capitalist democracies will have an incentive to support globalization, at least relative to the sectors in which the economies specialize. Each advanced country benefits more from globalization the more specialized advanced countries are drawn to the table. In this sense, it is a classical strategic complementarities (or network externalities) game.

4. Finally, note that this is reinforced in a world of knowledge-based MNEs. Together with the geographical immobility of these sophisticated innovation-oriented research, development and production clusters, the impetus for nation-states to encourage the globalization of FDI by knowledge-based MNEs is clear. Pushed by the immobility of knowledge and the benefits of accessing via FDI complementary knowledge based in other advanced countries, the autonomy of the advanced state is enhanced (Cantwell and Mudambi 2005).

All this enhances the power of the individual advanced capitalist democracy, for the specialization of each advanced state is desired by the others. This permits institutional, political, and policy differentiation.

1.8. The Puzzle of Rising Inequality without Redistribution

Unlike those who see the rise of inequality as the result of a subordination of democracy to capital, we see rising income and wealth inequality instead as a function mainly of technological change and choices made by politicians trying to satisfy the demands from middle- and upper-middle-class constituencies.[22] Skill-biased technological change (SBTC) is a well-established driver of income inequality, with a clearly articulated economic logic. Because ICT technology substitutes for semiskilled, routine tasks while it complements high-skilled, nonroutine tasks, demand drives up relative wages of the high-skilled (Autor, Levy, and Murnane 2003; Autor, Katz, and Kearney 2008). Yet, even here politics is essential because the SBTC thesis only speaks to the demand side, and the supply of skilled labor is heavily influenced by government policies, in particular spending on higher education (Goldin and Katz 2007).

Democratic politics is even more important in explaining wealth accumulation. If we assume—very loosely—that the middle and upper middle classes are key constituencies for governments, following the logic above, then we must ask what these groups want from the government. Clearly, they want to become wealthier, and a large portion of the wealth that Piketty (2014) assigns to capital is in fact in the form of housing and pension funds, which are also owned in large numbers by middle and upper middle classes. It is hardly a surprise that they see an interest in policies that help increase the value of these assets, and politicians of all stripes obliged from the 1990s onwards by making it easier to own real estate and to build up pension funds (Popa 2016). Indeed, as we show in detail in this book (especially in chapter 4), the entire reconfiguration of financial, educational, and regulatory institutions in the 1990s and 2000s was induced by politicians eager to satisfy the demands from those who stood the best chance to benefit from the emerging knowledge economy. Especially those in the rising cities were richly rewarded by higher housing prices, better education, and ballooning private pension funds (associated with rising bond and equity markets). In fact, as is now well-known, most of the great increase in wealth in the advanced economies which Piketty associated with business capital stemmed from the increase in house prices in urban agglomerations resulting from the rise of knowledge economies in the past three decades (Bonnet, Bono, Chapelle, Wasmer 2014).

But if the democratic state is powerful and advanced capital weak, why was rising inequality from the 1980s not accompanied by increased redistribution? As we suggested above, this puzzle is rooted in what we see as a misunderstanding of the politics of ACDs. There are two parts to this puzzle; one is about the top half and the other is about the bottom half. At the top end there is no doubt that financialization of the economy, coupled with the extraordinary fortunes made by top professionals and entrepreneurs in the new high-tech sectors, has stretched the income and wealth distribution, as documented by Piketty (2014) and others. But it is a mistake to think about this as a zero-sum game. In the most extreme case of rising top-end inequality, data in the United States from the Internal Revenue Service show that the share of federal income tax revenues paid by the top one percent has risen from about twenty percent in the early 1980s to nearly forty percent in the 2000s. The latest figures released by the IRS are for the year 2014 and show that 39.5 percent of federal income tax revenues were paid by the top one percent of earners, while 19.9 percent came from the top .1 percent.[23] The bulk of total federal income tax revenues, seventy-one percent, were accounted for by the top ten percent of earners. The average tax rate paid by the top one or ten percent has not changed much from the 1980s to 2014—there was a slight drop in the 2000s that was reversed under Obama—so this dramatic increase in top-end shares is driven by rises in top incomes.[24] Still, high incomes are the main funders of the major middle-class programs such Medicare, Social Security, and public higher education. If rising inequality is driven by the transition to the knowledge economy, the middle and upper middle classes have benefited, either directly through the market or indirectly through the tax-financed welfare state. Across ACDs, while marginal tax rates have fallen, after accounting for deductions, the overall burden of financing the welfare state has not shifted from the top to the middle.

Moving to the lower half of the distribution, across most advanced democracies there has been no or little effort to address rising inequality. We argue that the reason for this lack of government responsiveness is declining political support in the middle and upper middle classes for expanding redistributive social programs—and the unwillingness of even the lower middle classes to redistribute to the poor. This unwillingness is reflected in terms such as the "undeserving poor" in contemporary populist discourse. Underpinning this shift is a breakup in an alliance between skilled and semiskilled workers, which had characterized the postwar industrial economy, and the rise of new middle and upper middle classes of highly educated and relatively secure workers. Only where there are strong political-institutional incentives to include representatives of low income groups in government coalitions have policies been responsive to rising inequality and insecurity at the bottom. Indeed, it is not only the poor being left behind; in some advanced economies it is also the old middle classes who had their heydays under the Fordist economy.

More work is needed in this area to understand the demand of current and former industrial workers. It is clear that they are concerned to maintain access to "their" welfare state but also to close that access to immigrants; also that they want to block redistributive transfers to the "undeserving poor," especially in the form of "benefits"; thus it may be that in some advanced economies there is a yet wider group of decisive voters against relief of poverty.

As we set out in more detail in chapter 3, a major underlying cause of the challenge to the postwar consensus over the welfare state was the decline of Fordist mass production since the 1970s, and the concomitant shift toward knowledge-intensive production. These changes have severed previously strong complementarities in production between skilled and semiskilled workers. Deindustrialization contributed to this process by gradually segregating many low- and intermediary-skilled workers into insecure, often part-time or temporary, service jobs (Wren 2013). The combined effect of new technology and deindustrialization has been a divergence in employment security and income between core and peripheral workers (Kalleberg 2003), with the college-educated in much more secure positions.

A key question for our entire understanding of the role of democratic politics in redistribution is the extent to which governments have stepped in to compensate and assist workers who have been adversely affected by deindustrialization and technological change.[25]

In past work, we have argued that in multiparty PR systems where each class is represented by its own party, there is an incentive for the middle-income party to ally with the low-income party because the size of the pie to be divided rises with the wealth of those excluded from the coalition. Majoritarian systems with a center-left and a center-right party are different because with incomplete pre-election commitment, the middle might end up with fewer benefits and higher taxes under a center-left government dominated by the left, whereas lower benefits are likely to be partially offset by lower taxes if the right dominates in a center-right government.

The qualification to this logic is for PR systems with strong Christian democratic parties. Following Manow (2009) and Manow and Van Kersbergen (2009), if parties under PR represent more than one class it opens up the possibility for governing coalitions that exclude both the left and right. The historical example is Christian democracy, because these parties represent multiple groups, including skilled workers, technicians, and upper-middle-class professionals and managers. These parties do not need to win elections by appealing to the "median voter," as in majoritarian systems, but because they allow group differences to be bargained out inside the party, they end up closer to the center, where they can often govern with "pure" center parties, shunning compromises with the left.

In addition to these coalitional dynamics, however, the transition to the knowledge economy has reconfigured political divisions and the party system. Semiskilled workers—and sometimes their children—have largely lost their foothold in the dynamic sectors of the economy and are increasingly segmented into precarious low-end jobs in service sectors, including social care and personal services, delinked from their erstwhile peers in industry. Some continue to be employed in industry, but industrial employment has been declining rapidly in most advanced economies. Instead, a new web of interdependencies has emerged in the urban centers of the new knowledge economy, organized around those with higher education. Workers with high school degrees and lower-level secondary vocational training in the old manufacturing cores are left out of this new economy, and they increasingly live in small towns and rural areas, which have for the most part lost their importance as suppliers for the urban economy.

Politically, many among these left-behind groups have abandoned traditional center-left parties, which are increasingly chasing the emerging urban, educated voters with liberal, cosmopolitan views. Instead, many have thrown their support behind populist parties, which promise to restore the status of the old industrial (mostly male) skilled workforce while retaining core elements of the old welfare state. Immigrants, who are seen as a threat to the white working class, are deliberately left out of this scheme. This new divide is not synonymous with the "insider-outsider" conflict identified by Rueda and others, because many of the "insiders" in that story are in fact the losers in the new knowledge economy, even as "outsiders" (many of whom are immigrants) fare worse. It is better approximated by the rise of a new "cultural" (or "libertarian-authoritarian") dimension in politics, which has been convincingly documented by Kitschelt (1995), Häusermann (2010), Oesch (2012), Kriesi and Pappas (2015), Häusermann and Kriesi (2015), and others, but it has deep material roots. Attitudes about this new dimension are closely related to education, occupation, and location. In chapter 5 we interpret the new political divide from the political economy framework developed in this book, with a strong emphasis on the role of education and educational institutions.

What ultimately makes advanced democratic capitalism resilient in the face of technological change and the rise of the populist challenge is the continued expansion of education combined with opportunity in the advanced sectors. Only in an extreme crisis like the Great Depression is there a serious risk that populism may grow so widespread that the foundations of both advanced capitalism and democracy will come under attack. Nonetheless the cleavage in PR systems between traditional mainstream parties and sometimes green parties, especially on the center-left, and rising populist parties is the most salient political division in the knowledge economy, just as in majoritarian systems the most salient political divisions may be within the mainstream parties themselves. It is also an economic, social, and cultural division, for it undermines the quality of democracy, even if it does not upend it.

1.9. Conclusion: Coevolving Systems

In political economy there is a long tradition for analyzing the interplay of markets and politics, but while it offers a nuanced view of politics, it substitutes a detailed understanding of the organization of firms, production, and labor for broad notions of "markets." The modern literature on voting behavior in the advanced democracies, political parties, electoral systems, or the operation of legislatures, or even economic policy-making and the welfare state, talks little of the world of advanced capitalism or organized business or multinational companies. By contrast, firms and their organization are often at the center of analysis in business schools, industrial economics, and business history, but this literature rarely considers the role of political institutions: governments, political parties, electoral systems, and voters. The Marxist tradition, and some of the work inspired by it, considers structural constraints on democratic politics, and this is what leads it to erroneously conclude that the nation-state is weak and capital strong. Precisely the opposite, we argue, is the case.

We attempt in this book to move beyond the above approaches, and in this concluding section we briefly summarize the main elements of our theory and its implications for the study of politics and capitalism.

1. *The primacy of the democratic state.* The central idea in our basic theory of the relationship between politics and capitalism is that advanced capitalism is driven and maintained by national governments who are concerned about the long-term competitiveness and strength of their national economy. Governments are comprised of leading politicians, typically with careers within a political party, whose concern for economic strength largely derives from the long-term economic concerns of party supporters, determining whether they vote or abstain or even switch party adherence—hence feeding back into their future careers directly and via the support from

lower-level party politicians. Economic strength in turn increases the capacity of government in a wide range of areas, and from this leading politicians also benefit. Thus we see the framework of advanced capitalism being conditionally promoted within the political framework of relatively long-lived parties with overlapping generations of politicians and supporters as well as—critically—potential voters with equally long-term and often loose party identification to whom a well-functioning economy is of great importance. Political promotion of the framework of advanced capitalism is conditional on its being consistent with winning elections.

A central element of the institutional framework is the requirement that advanced sectors are exposed to competitive export and/or domestic markets in effect to force companies to innovate. This goes against the interests of capitalists, who want to create monopolies and to reduce risk, but business has limited ability to pressure governments to adopt its preferred policies for two basic reasons: (i) Advanced companies are domestically anchored, so they cannot threaten exit. (ii) Companies are set up as independent to compete and make profits, so that their collective voice is limited. We have underscored the role of coordination across companies in coordinated market economies or of their buying into the political and regulatory system in the United States, but these fundamental institutional weaknesses of capitalism remain. (iii) With a high stock of location cospecific investment and long-term oriented politicians, the gains from, and opportunities for, rent-seeking are limited.

This political weakness of advanced capitalism extends into all areas outside the institutional framework. In particular, advanced capitalism has no impact on decisions over redistribution and poverty, or the protection of the low-skilled, including their unionization and the operation of low-skilled labor markets. These issues are determined by majorities or coalitions in legislatures. Whereas political positions on institutional frameworks are nonpartisan, positions in these other areas are likely to be partisan. It is true, of course, that business opposes redistribution, but it has no credible way to threaten exit or disinvestment because it depends and thrives on the infrastructure of locational cospecific assets that is embedded in advanced sectors of the economy. Massive redistribution where such threats would become credible are not in the interest of politicians who largely cater to the winners of the transition to the knowledge economy, who have no interest in such redistribution.

2. *Political economies are spatially anchored.* Our argument explains how institutions (especially overlapping generations of knowledge bearing companies and workers) remain within the same *space* over long periods of time; indeed it explains how knowledge—which should in principle be almost costless to move—remains in particular locations. Unlike most work in the comparative political economy literature but in line with that of business history, the knowledge-bearing company of advanced capitalism is seen as the carrier of technical, market and organizational "know-how" across time but within a national or more narrowly defined space. We model such companies as complex webs of locational cospecific assets embedded in overlapping generations of employees.

Knowledge-bearing companies range from great long-lived multinationals to short-lived high-tech start-ups in agglomerations of such companies. High-skilled workers share know-how embedded in locational cospecific assets with other workers in companies, but they also share social locational cospecific assets with families and friends and colleagues, frequently in high-skill agglomerations in the major cities. Networks of highly skilled employees of any size cannot be moved geographically by companies without great cost. High-skill agglomerations are nearly always defined within the advanced nation-state and generally within a narrow area. If companies want to access the know-how of an agglomeration they have to set up subsidiaries located in the agglomeration; this is a major motivation for the spread of MNC subsidiaries across the developed world in pursuit of complementary technologies. In addition, companies and their employees operate within institutional frameworks covering technology transfer, universities and research institutes, training systems, industrial relations, and corporate governance. We argue that these forces reinforce agglomerations and generate centripetal pressures at local, regional, and national levels. In these senses we describe advanced capitalist sectors as domestically anchored. Thus methodologically we see our work—microfounded in complex spatially defined webs of cospecific assets—as tied to the economics of geography and specifically the economics of agglomerations and social networks.

If advanced companies are the spatially defined "people-carriers" of know-how over time, political parties are the spatially defined "people-carriers" of their interests. Precisely because interests are locally embedded, political parties representing these interests have to be as well. This is why the communist dream of an international labor movement has largely remained unfulfilled.

3. *The system of representation underwrites the economic system.* The institutional patterns of both advanced capitalism and of (usually) democratic politics have varied across the advanced nations but with stability over time. In particular, coordinated capitalism has been associated with negotiated political systems and liberal capitalism with competitive political systems. There have been relatively stable differences within these broad varieties, as between the centralized British and decentralized American political system, and associated differences in their institutions of capitalism. Other notable relatively stable differences are between Sweden, Germany, and Japan.

In our model the stability of these institutional patterns reflects the nature of investments which advanced companies have made given the degree of protection afforded by the political system, and the concern of governments to maintain a political system supportive of the comparative advantages of companies. The clustering of coordinated market economies with consensus political systems, and liberal market economies with majoritarian political systems, follows directly from our logic of the set of rules and understandings governing the production and maintenance of skills and their insurance. Yet we want to underscore commonalities. Whatever the set of rules and understandings, its framework is underwritten by the democratic political system. This is what sets advanced capitalism apart from nonadvanced countries, whether democratic or not.

4. *Wage coordination and welfare states secure cospecific assets.* Union centralization and/or coordinated wage bargaining plays a

major role in determining the equality of the earnings distribution. For us this derives from the different nature of skills in different varieties of capitalism. Groups of workers are strong when they can credibly threaten to hold up employers. This is a consequence not of employment or skills per se—employers can in principle replace workers with general skills at low cost—but of skills that are costly to replace and whose withdrawal is costly to the employer in lost production. Thus *cospecific* skills cause particular problems for employers; and for employers to invest in them, they need the assurance that wages will be set at least partially *outside* the company, whether across the industry or more widely. Otherwise they risk holdup by their skilled workers. Hence, employers support disciplined unions and industry or economy-wide bargaining, just as they also support strong rules governing co-determination within companies.

Workers with cospecific assets also have an insurance need for strong unions and coordinated wage bargaining. The reason is that they face a similar holdup problem by employers since it is difficult for them to employ their skills elsewhere, and they also face the risk that their skills could be made obsolete by technological change. So, just like employers, they need to know that the return on their investment in cospecific assets is safeguarded. Hence we see coordinated wage bargaining and social protection as stemming in part from an insurance need for cospecific asset investment by both employers and workers in coordinated economies. Equally, employees need the guarantee of codetermination within the company to ensure retraining and employment security if they are to be supportive of technological change by the company.

5. *Globalization strengthens the state.* In our analysis globalization is not capitalism unleashed but the choice of advanced national governments in response to the collapse of Fordism as a competitive organizational technology and the onset of the information technology revolution. Eliminating barriers to trade and capital mobility is seen to promote the interests of their advanced sectors—both to enable domestic multinationals to access complementary foreign technologies and markets requiring customization, and to enable foreign multinationals to access their national technologies and markets.

They are not, we argue, threatened by footloose multinationals, still less by political coordination of foreign multinationals. Indeed, protectionism in the 1930s came on the heels of the hitherto most globalized economy, and it happened because of domestic pressure for social protection in the face of mass unemployment, and against the interest of big capital.

The welfare state has since assumed the role that trade protectionism once disastrously filled, what Ruggie calls embedded liberalism, and globalization has come in response to the endless search of advanced country governments for greater prosperity. Trade facilitates specialization in lines of production in which companies have a comparative advantage because of the institutional framework. Trade therefore also entrenches and facilitates cross-national differences in institutions, and this is reinforced by foreign direct investment. We see more tendencies toward convergence in nontraded, low-wage service sectors where flexibilization of labor contracts is a common trend in the past two decades. Still, most evidence confirms that there have not been races to the bottom in redistribution or corporate tax rates. Moreover, in all these cases differential outcomes are determined in our analysis by domestic political coalitions. Thus we conclude that it is to be expected that governments of advanced countries with strong advanced capitalist sectors are the dominant powers in the contemporary world—*not* the EU, nor multinationals, nor transnational standard-setters, public or private.

6. *The transition to the knowledge economy has transformed the party system.* There is a rich literature on the de- and realignment of electoral politics and party systems across advanced democracies, which shows that the traditional left-right dimension has been complemented by an increasingly salient crosscutting "cultural" dimension. Positioning on the two dimensions is closely tied to occupation and location, and we provide a political economy explanation for these linkages. Broadly speaking, the knowledge economy has produced a large number of highly educated people, most of whom reside in the urban centers. As we have argued, these centers are hubs for economic and social networks based on cospecific assets, and they are the engines of economic growth. People who thrive in this

new economy typically support the entire institutional infrastructure that underpins the knowledge economy—most obviously investment in schools and education, but also public goods such as libraries, parks, culture, neighborhood development, and social services that make the urban space an attractive and secure place to live and work. Ethnic, sexual, and cultural diversity is largely seen as complements to a thriving economy, and the extensive opportunities for forming social networks with those from similar educational backgrounds do not require conformity to any particular norm set. To do well in many if not most sectors of the knowledge economy, highly educated individuals have to feel highly comfortable with diversity.

Those with lower education, working in occupations outside the advanced sectors, and typically residing in smaller towns or stagnating suburbs, by contrast, see little advantage to policies that are advantaging the urban centers, and they generally oppose ethnic-cultural diversity, which is seen as a threat to their own conformist lifestyles and a source of competition for scarce jobs and welfare benefits. This does not supplant the distributive cleavage in democratic politics, clearly, but it does add a spatial dimension to that cleavage and it does mean that there is now a large constituency for populist politics concentrated among those whose skills, occupation, and past are closely connected to the old and disappearing industrial economy.

2

Two Paths to Democracy

Industrialization and democratization were historically intimately linked in today's advanced democracies. The forging of this linkage marks the beginning of the symbiotic relationship between democracy and capitalism that is the focus of this book. This chapter seeks to explain how it came about. Although the mechanisms are different across countries, we argue that the creation of a large skilled labor force was hard to build up and sustain without the formation of democratic institutions. Although many continental European countries had effective training systems in the craft sector before the introduction of democracy, once these systems were extended to the rising industrial sector, a large unified labor movement emerged that demanded democracy. Business could have bargained with skilled unions under an authoritarian regime through centralized industrial relations, but it would have been difficult and costly to suppress demands for democracy as the industrial working and middle classes grew stronger in line with the deepening of human capital. In countries where education was underprovided relative to the needs of the industrializing urban centers, usually because of entrenched local opposition from a landed aristocracy, a unified labor movement was not a concern for the urban elites, whereas extending the franchise to middle classes keen on public goods and better educational opportunities was seen as a political lever by which industrialists could break the local monopoly on power by the traditional elites.

It may be an exaggeration to claim that a large skilled labor force is a sufficient condition for democracy; or that democracy is a necessary condition for a highly skilled labor force. But the two are strategic complements in the senses that i) it is very costly to suppress for long periods of time a highly skilled workforce with strong collective action capacity demanding democracy; and ii) democracy can serve as an effective institutional wrecking ball to break opposition among traditional elites to widespread education and to guarantee continued investment in education. It is the coupling of advanced capitalism and democracy that sets in motion the symbiotic relationship that over time creates a self-reinforcing logic, which is highly resilient to shocks.

Our account of the emergence of democracy in the advanced world stands apart from three dominant explanations, although it also overlaps with and integrates them in some important respects. One focuses on the economic prosperity and the rise of the middle classes; a second focuses on class conflict between elites and a rising working class; and a third emphasizes intra-elite conflict between the landed aristocracy and the advancing new industrial elites. All three approaches capture aspects of the democratization process in particular countries, but not in others. Class conflict does indeed seem to have played an important role in some continental European countries, but it played virtually no role in England and the settler colonies. There was a sharp division between landed and urban elites in England and France, but it played a subsidiary role in northern Europe. Rising prosperity in the industrializing urban center is clearly associated with democracy everywhere, but in some countries it was a result of democracy as much as a cause, and it does not explain why democracy took such different forms. Our account explains this heterogeneity with reference to a common underlying logic: the structure of preindustrial production and training regimes, and the pattern of early political representation. There is a close linkage between the two, also in their modern forms.

Nor does the contemporary literature seek to understand the resilience of democracy in the advanced capitalist economies—in particular after the Second World War, but also apart from Germany and Japan in the interwar period. In our long-term explanation we see the stability of democracy in advanced capitalism as embedded in parties representing economic interests that all, by and large, see themselves as benefiting from advanced capitalism even if disagreeing over redistribution. Correspondingly, we see oppositional parties as those who understand themselves to be excluded from the benefits of advanced capitalism—for example, by foreigners—as opposed to communists wishing to overturn advanced capitalism.

2.1 The Literature

Perhaps the best known hypothesis about democracy is that it is an outcome of economic development and "modernization." Commonly associated with Lipset (1959; 1960), the cross-national correlation between per-capita income and democracy is strong. There is no universally accepted explanation for the association, but Lipset emphasized the rise of a better educated middle class that was more moderate and inclined to adopt tolerant and inclusive values; Wucherpfennig and Deutsch (2009) offer an excellent contemporary survey. The thesis has been subject to much empirical research, with considerable controversy surrounding the question of whether prosperity leads to democracy or whether instead prosperous democracies are less likely to fall back into autocracy (Przeworki et al. 2000; Boix and Stokes 2003). At least in our set of countries we think it is a fair assessment that higher education and incomes have both been conducive to democracy and to making democracy more resilient. This is certainly very consistent with our argument. But it is also the case that in some countries, such as England and the United States, rises in educational attainment were a consequence rather than a cause of democracy, and the Lipset hypothesis does not explain the very different paths to democracy, which were sometimes highly conflictual, or to the particular electoral institutions that define each path. We offer a causal theory that is clear about mechanisms and also accounts for variance in outcomes.

A second approach to democratization focuses on the distribution of income instead of the level of income. One analytically compelling and empirically detailed account is presented in Rueschemeyer, Stephens and Stephens (1992, chap. 4), in which industrialization leads to working-class power. Often with left-liberal and sometimes left catholic support, this produces pressure on elites to concede political representation. And at the forefront of contemporary debate, Acemoglu and Robinson (2005) present an extension of this position with a simple but powerful model of democracy as a rational concession when the probability of a successful socialist revolution becomes too high, and when democracy offers a credible constitutional commitment to redistribution. Boix (2003) offers an equally simple and analytically driven explanation. These accounts are broadly consistent with the left critique of advanced capitalism that we discussed in chapter 1.

Yet, as Ruth Berins Collier (1999) persuasively argues, democratization is not always the consequence of elite resistance and working-class pressure.[1] She divides key periods of democratization from the mid-nineteenth century to just after the end of the First World War into those in which there was accommodation to working-class pressure and those in which labor's role was negligible or nonexistent. We will refer to the latter as elite projects or instances of voluntary extension. In this chapter we only look at the advanced democracies of the second half of the twentieth century (Australia, Austria, Belgium, Britain, Canada, Denmark, France, Germany, Netherlands, New Zealand, Norway, Sweden, Switzerland, and the United States).[2] Collier includes countries we do not cover, both in Latin America and on the Mediterranean fringe, while omitting the white settler countries that we include. Collier's classification of episodes is very similar to our own, based on independent reading of secondary sources. Collier in fact divides the cases which did not involve accommodation to labor pressure into two groups: those designed to generate political support (e.g., the UK 1867 and 1884 Reform Acts) from those which reflected middle-sector pressure

TABLE 2.1. Collier's classification with amendments

	Elite projects	Working-class pressure
Agreement	France 1870s	Denmark 1901, 1915
	Britain 1867	Sweden 1907/9; 1917/20
		Netherlands 1917
		Belgium 1918
		Germany 1918/19
Minor disagreement		Norway 1898
	(Switzerland)	
Additional cases	Australian colonies	
	Canada	
	New Zealand	
	US States	

(liberal/republican projects) in which the normalization of the Third Republic in the late 1870s is included. Because we develop a different explanation from either of these—without at all denying that they were part of the picture—we collapse these two categories in one, which we call *elite projects.*

We list these in table 2.1 (together with two minor disagreements or qualifications).[3] We additionally introduce the British white settler colonies and their successor states: the US states, Upper and Lower Canada, the Australian colonies and New Zealand. We will argue that in these states substantial moves toward democracy were voluntary extensions or elite projects, rather than institutional reforms conceded under pressure. By "elite project" we do not mean that the elite was generally united; on the contrary, it involved a conflict between different elite groups, typically between an industrializing or modernizing elite against landowners. A special case concerned the Southern states of the US: in that case, the industrializing strategy of the Republican Ascendency from the mid-1870s on reflected the failure of the North effectively to subdue the South after the Civil War: the South remained successfully hostile to industrialization, and the Republican Ascendency in consequence confined industrialization—and the push to democratization—to the North. In all these cases industrializing elites granted democracy in order to counter the power of conservative forces opposed to industrialization, and not because of pressure from the working class, as implied in power resource theory, or the poor, as in Acemoglu and Robinson, and in Boix.

Following a long line of scholarship that emphasizes party contestation over government and mass participation as defining elements of democracy (Dahl 1971; Przeworski et al. 2000), we loosely operationalize functioning democracy as a situation of competitive parliamentarism with substantial franchise (Keech 2009). The franchise in the episodes that we cover is largely male and largely white, reflecting our interest in explaining critical developments of representation in burgeoning industrialization in the late nineteenth and early twentieth centuries.[4] Very roughly, the so-called "elite projects" were earlier, designed to enable industrialization by countering conservative elites; and the "working-class pressure" later, and the consequence of the burgeoning industrialization driven initially by unified elites. In all these cases (white) male democracy was in place by the early 1920s.

We argue that a common attribute of all the cases we consider is the critical role played by the formation of human capital, which will indeed be a major theme throughout this book. It was the attempt by industrial elites to secure access to well-trained workers or to expand the supply of skilled workers—who could man and manage the machinery that made large-scale factories possible—which set in motion a process of state expansion, centralization, and class formation that proved politically transformative. In this quest for skilled labor industrial elites ran up against two constraints: traditional elites and labor unions. This is true in all our cases, but the main dividing lines differed in important ways between the elite-project countries and the working-class pressure countries: differences that are rooted in the organization of these economies and the associated system of representation *before* the onset of industrialization.

Since *national* economies grew important during the industrial revolution, what mattered before industrialization was local economic and political organization. Guided by Crouch's seminal *Industrial Relations and European State Traditions* (1993), the countries in which democratization was eventually the result of working-class pressure were organized locally on a quasi corporatist basis both in towns, with effective guild systems, and in the countryside with a widespread socially rooted semiautonomous peasantry, rural cooperatives, and/or dense rural-urban linkages (with some exceptions, such as the Juncker estates east of the Elbe, and parts of Austria).[5] Crouch notes that all of these states were *Ständestaaten* in the nineteenth century—a system in which the different estates (including organized professions) played a direct role in governing. We therefore refer to the preindustrial political economy of these societies as *protocorporatist*.

The elite-project societies, in essence Anglo-Saxon (apart from France, which we discuss separately), functioned quite differently: well-developed property markets with substantial freedom of labor mobility, towns with limited local autonomy, and guild systems which had either collapsed (Britain) or had hardly existed (the settler colonies and the United States, minus the South). We refer to the preindustrial political economy of these societies as *protoliberal*. Traditional landed elites, however, played a substantial role at the local level, where they controlled local councils to the exclusion of other groups.

France in the nineteenth century comes much closer to this liberal picture than to the protocorporatist one, despite the role of the state and Paris. Even if peasants were *enracinés* (locally rooted), they were not locally coordinated. Property markets were active. The guild system, essentially state-dominated in the ancien régime, became ineffective once the 1791 Le Chapelier laws signaled the end of state support.[6] Labor mobility was high, especially from the countryside to Paris. As in the Anglo-Saxon countries, associational life could be important; but as Philip Nord (1996) shows in his study of Republican associations in the 1860s, these were not based on shared investments in economic activities, but the coming together of individuals with similar interests. Analogously, while there were rural cooperative movements in nineteenth-century France, they were usually skin-deep and frequently run by *notables* or prefects (Zeldin 1973).

In the rest of the chapter we first explain the emergence of powerful and unified union movements in the protocorporatist economies, induced by the inherited structure of skills and production, as the key development that compelled industrial elites to accept democracy as a necessary condition for capitalism. We then explain the emergence of democracy in protoliberal countries, in which labor was weak and fragmented, as a result of elite projects to expand public goods, especially education, which were underprovided and required for industrialization. In the final section we explain why representational institutions evolved differently in the two cases. After democracy was conceded, protocorporatist countries adopted proportional representation (PR), which reflected the nature of underlying cospecific assets tying together groups across class boundaries. In the protoliberal countries, majoritarian institutions emerged to reflect elite concern with redistribution and ensuring that middle class preferences, especially for education, would dominate in public policies. Contrary to existing explanations that predict the choice of electoral institutions to be contentious, it in fact generated broad support among all the major parties (once democracy was seen as inevitable).

2.2. Democratization in Protocorporatist Countries: The Rising Pressure of a Unified Working Class

Democratization as the forced concession by elites to working class power rests on an industrially and politically unified working class. While a unified working class was true of some countries in the process of industrialization, it was not of others. Specifically, it was true of the protocorporatist Ständestaat group, but it was not true of the protoliberal societies (see table 2.2 for a summary). Since it was the protocorporatist societies which conceded democracy under pressure, we see this as a persuasive confirmation of the argument that democracy in these countries came about through working-class power against the interests of the bourgeoisie.[7] But the class power account does not explain why some countries developed strong labor movements while others did not.

TABLE 2.2. State types and working-class organization

State organization 1st half 19th century	Working class, late 19th–early 20th centuries
	Strong, coordinated industrial unions, socialist party
	Germany (also Catholic)
	Sweden
	Belgium (also Catholic)
	Norway
Protocorporatist origins	*Strong, coordinated craft unions, socialist party*
	Denmark
	Weaker, coordinated industrial unions, socialist party
	Austria (also Catholic)
	Netherlands (also Catholic & Protestant)
	Switzerland
	Fragmented craft unions, no unified working class party
	UK
	France (3rd Republic)
Protoliberal origins	US states
	Australian colonies
	Upper, Lower Canada
	New Zealand

Nor, as Ziblatt has pointed out, does it explain why democracy proved much more resilient to reversals in some countries than in others, and why democracy was voluntarily extended in the liberal societies (or, rather, extended in those societies by one part of the elite against the resistance of other parts), nor why some adopted PR and others did not.

When we talk about an industrially and politically strong and unified working class, we mean that unionization is high and that unions are organized on an industrial basis, rather than a craft basis. Thus they do not compete across crafts in terms of job demarcation, wage bargaining, or control over the supply of skills and the number of apprentices. Industrial unions in addition organized semiskilled workers (though not typically laborers). We mean in addition that the unions were closely linked to a social democratic party which saw itself as representing the interests of the working class as a whole (skilled and semiskilled factory workers, as well as journeymen, but not master artisans).

With a few differences over the interpretation of Switzerland and France, Crouch (1993), Katznelson and Zolberg (1986), Luebbert (1991), Slomp (1990), and Thelen (2004), among others, have argued that the working class grosso modo developed in a unified way in the protocorporatist countries but not in the liberal. Ebbinghaus makes a similar distinction between, on the one hand, *solidaristic unionism* (the Scandinavian cases) with encompassing unions organized by social democratic parties and *segmented unionism* (Germany, Austria, the Netherlands, Switzerland, and Belgium) with strong interlinking between the social democratic party and unions but also with religious cleavages, and, on the other hand, *laborist unionism* with sectional unions creating a party as in the UK and Ireland, the French case being one of *polarized unionism* (Ebbinghaus 1995).

These authors do not cover Australia, New Zealand, or Canada, but in the periods in question—from the 1850s to the 1890s—unions were relatively fragmented and operated on craft bases.[8] To use Marx's terminology (and with slight tongue in cheek) the working class in the protocorporatist economies became politically a class for itself.[9] By contrast, in liberal economies, the lack of either economic or political coordination led to a large number of independent craft unions; and politically labor either became a part of liberal parties or labor parties which themselves were lacking a socialist profile. Luebbert (1991) does not consider the white settler colonies or the United States, but he identifies "socialism and comprehensive class organization" with Germany, Norway, Sweden, Denmark, Belgium, and the Netherlands, while the labor movement in Britain is classified as "emphatically in favour of liberalism and trade union particularism" and in France and Switzerland "in favour of a distinctive mixture of liberalism and socialism" (1991, 166). Hence, strong or at least coherent labor movements—with industrial unions and social democratic parties standing for a unified working class—emerge in the process of industrialization in our protocorporatist group of countries. By contrast, fragmented labor movements with uncoordinated craft unionism and at most weakly organized unskilled workers emerge in liberal economies. These are semi-attached to Lib-Lab political parties in which the interest of craft workers is aligned to that of the lower middle classes against low-income groups, notably in Britain and France.

Thelen (2004) sets out comparable differences between Germany on the one hand and the UK and the United States on the other. She explains also why Denmark, despite being formally organized on craft union lines, fits closely to the picture of a unified union movement (2009). Galenson (1952) also emphasizes the integration of the union movement in Denmark through a highly centralized industrial relations system starting in 1899; Due et al. (1994) and Martin (2009) have parallel discussions of this period in Denmark in relation to employer organizations. Katznelson, comparing Germany with England, France, and the United States in the nineteenth century, draws a similar distinction for German unions. He writes:

> Compared to their American, French and English counterparts, German trade unions were less likely to build barriers between different crafts, less likely to insist on guild-type controls, less likely to fight for traditional patterns of artisan rights and practices, and, overall, less likely to insist on distinctions between skilled and unskilled workers. . . . The same emphasis on the 'arbeiter' class as a whole can be found in the very early creation, in the 1860s and 1870s, of an independent political party. Nineteenth century patterns of working class formation in France, the United States, and Germany thus differed sharply. (Katznelson and Zolberg 1986)

One additional point needs noting: apart from Scandinavia, there are also Catholic labor movements in the protocorporatist societies (Germany, Austria, Belgium, Netherlands, Switzerland), incorporated within Christian Democratic parties. But, while originally set up to blunt socialist unions, they increasingly mimicked these or cooperated in order to retain the loyalty of Catholic workers.

Why did working classes develop in such different ways? Very broadly and with many qualifications, in protocorporatist economies the combination of economic coordination and protocorporatist states pushed union movements to become increasingly industry- rather than crafts-based, with close interunion links and centralized structures; in part because of that, political representation of the working class developed in a unified way.

Three mutually reinforcing factors were behind these developments in the protocorporatist economies. Thelen (2004), noting the differences between industrial unionism in Germany and craft unionism in the United States and Britain, locates the origins of industrial unionism in the preexistence of an effective system of skill production by guilds (and cooperative rural communities) in Germany, and their absence in the United States and Britain. Hence, she argues, it did not pay unions in Germany—although initially craft-based—to seek to raise wages by restricting the number of trainees and controlling work practices because they could ultimately not control the supply. This meant that any strategy of craft control was likely to fail. Instead they (gradually) became industry unions representing both skilled and semiskilled workers, rather than the craft "aristocracy of the working class" that emerged in England. This argument extends to all the protocorporatist economies, where there was an elastic supply of skilled workers from the guild system, and the artisan sector more generally, and from the training of craft workers in rural communities.

This was the case even during periods in which guild privileges had been legally revoked, since the informal features of these systems remained in place. Galenson's analysis of the Danish case is instructive in this respect:

> The persistence of the gild [*sic*] tradition is nowhere more manifest than in the structure of the labor market. . . . When the guilds were abolished, the formerly closed trades were opened to anyone, one of the results of which was a serious deterioration of training standards. Many of the early trade unions displayed keen interest in the restoration of the old employment monopolies, and though they were not able to advocate such measures per se, they succeeded, in cooperation with their employers, in reinstituting a closed occupational system in the skilled trades through the medium of the apprenticeship. A series of laws was enacted to regulate this relationship, culminating in the Apprenticeship Act of 1937. (Galenson 1952)

As the quote from Galenson hints, effective training systems benefited both industry and artisan masters. The apprenticeship contract in general was a profitable exchange for the master—of training for cheap labor, which became increasingly skilled over the apprenticeship years. And since industry did not yet have effective training systems in place, trained journeymen were a desirable source of skills even if they would have to learn new skills and procedures in factories. And if factory work was less attractive than craft work, industry wages were higher and thus compensatory.

This argument was reinforced by a second: *ab initio* the labor markets in which industrialization in the protocorporatist economies developed were relatively biased toward skilled labor. The main reason for this was the relatively abundant supply of skilled labor available to businesses as a result of trained journeymen. Protocorporatist economies "solved" the collective action problems associated with the production of skills through guilds and rural cooperative arrangements. These skills may not have fitted exactly what new businesses wanted. But in general entrepreneurs had available a large supply of trained labor.

A further factor is the role of the state, reinforcing the long-term ineffectiveness of craft-union strategies. Assuming that companies wanted to use the skills of the available workforce but wished to control the organization of production—they did not wish either to adopt American or French techniques which ultimately implied a semiskilled workforce, nor to move toward continuing conflicts with craft workers as many UK companies did—they could typically count on state or municipal support. Nolan (1986) provides evidence of this in the German case. Founders of companies in the protocorporatist economies came from diverse backgrounds, including masters from the artisan sector as well as independent-minded professionals from the bureaucracy and army (Kocka 1986). While these were often highly entrepreneurial, they generally operated with close links in the mid- to late nineteenth century to either the bureaucracy or municipalities which encouraged formal and informal association (Nolan 1986). This was the Ständestaat institutional legacy.

As industrialization developed, therefore, businesses in many industries operated in associational ways. These were not employer associations until later; but they relied on mutual solidarity, as well as, very often, the power of the state and town government, both to keep out unions for a considerable period of time, and to impose their own organization of production. This organization was not on craft lines, but typically distinguished sharply between management and *arbeiter*, even though a substantial proportion of the latter were skilled or semiskilled (Kocka 1986; Nolan 1986). Thus when factory unionization developed seriously at the end of the long slowdown of the 1870s and 1880s and the tightening of labor markets in the 1890s, and even more so in the first decade of the new century, the non-craft organization of workforces strongly reinforced the incentives for unions to organize on industry (or factory) rather than on competitive craft lines. Not only did skilled workers not see themselves as craft workers, but, more significantly, it was difficult for unions to impose craft job controls on the workplace.

In the one case among the protocorporatist countries where unions were organized along craft lines, Denmark, well-organized employers forced a unification and centralization of the industrial relations system through massive lockouts, ending in the 1899 September Compromise. The new system resulted in a consensus-based approach to labor market regulation, reinforced by a corporatist state: "The main organization (i.e. LO and DA) were both accorded representation on the relevant councils, committees, boards and commissions, and implementation of legislation pertaining to the labour market was usually based on the principle that prior *consensus between the main organizations* was to be a prerequisite for any such measures" (Due et al. 1994, 70; emphasis in original). Although the system did not mature until the 1930s, it "shows a virtually linear development from the September Compromise in 1899."

Close linkages between the state and associational activity also mattered for the nature of research and higher-level skills acquisition. The protocorporatist economies in the nineteenth century, as Rokkan noted, were often marked by governments (sometimes royal) pressing for modernization while remaining Ständestaaten in terms of political representation. Thus, as Crouch (1993) points out, there was a more porous relation between industry and state than in the liberal economies. Via informal cartelization, governments encouraged companies to specialize in higher quality goods; and, especially in Germany and Sweden, encouraged research and training of engineers and chemists through royal foundations. Hence there was an underlying incentive for nascent businesses to use skilled labor and aim at relatively upmarket strategies. The fact of relatively skill-intensive workforces then meant that workforce cooperation, moderation of real wages, and ultimately the training process itself became important issues for business, issues which were difficult to solve without union cooperation. Thus agreements with unions which traded cooperative workforces for collective bargaining rights were attractive to both sides. But, to be credible bargaining partners to business in the supply of cooperation, unions needed to have the power to control their local affiliates within factories: hence unions needed centralized power outside the company. This was not straightforward, however, because unions, even when understanding the need for centralization, were often prevented by their locals from imposing it. This led business and business associations to pressure unions (often brutally) to acquire increased control over their members and affiliates (Swenson 1991; 2002).

For these reinforcing reasons, unions in protocorporatist economies were organizing labor on an increasingly industrial and centralized basis by the first decades of the twentieth century. In turn, social democratic parties emerged, working closely with industry unions, as parties representing both skilled and unskilled workers. There were several reasons for this. First, industrial unions had common goals in training, wages, and broad-based social insurance in these systems by contrast to their craft union counterparts in liberal economies where the exclusionary logic of controlling skills and jobs led to a worker aristocracy. Where a union was broadly representative of workers in an industry, it could reasonably believe that its interests would be promoted by the political organization of the working class—as opposed to relying on liberal parties who might support the skilled elite of the working class but not its broad masses.

The broad political organization of the class implied the possibility of mass mobilization both in the event of attack and of promoting enhanced political power and, eventually, democracy.

Second, as Gary Marks (1989) nicely argued in relation to multifarious American craft unions in the late nineteenth century, while free-riding undercut union financial commitment to a national labor party in protoliberal countries, the same argument in reverse suggests that industrial unions—each with a monopoly of an industry, apart perhaps from a confessional competitor—did not have this collective action problem. They were simply too big not to recognize their responsibility in ensuring the political success of the movement.

The German Social Democratic Party (SPD) exemplified an interaction between party and industrial unions that had this build-in expansionary logic. Lepsius (1966) shows how union and party goals coevolved in the German context of separate working-class social milieus of the early twentieth century. The SPD could organize effectively only in those milieus; hence the margin of socialist political growth was intensive—to bring unskilled workers into the party. But unions were reluctant to represent unskilled workers, still less laborers; so party policy was to ensure that they became trained and at least semiskilled. This is the exact opposite of the almost century-long agreement in the Labour Party that the party did not concern itself with so-called "industrial questions," notably about skills and vocational training; the whole issue of apprenticeships belonged to the craft unions, preeminently the engineers.

This argument is reinforced by the fact that other social groups—for example, the Catholics, as well as the Protestant farmers, the *Mittelstand*, and so on—were already organized in their own parties; in general, representative parties can best expand support intensively *within* the broad social groups they represent. A similar argument applies to other protocorporatist countries, since they were characterized by representative parties linked to broad social groups. At the same time, the German Social Democratic Party was commonly taken as a model by socialist parties in these economies. Thus in protocorporatist economies, the working class developed in a coherent and relatively unified way both industrially and politically (Luebbert 1991).

Note, however, that although the unions were kept at arm's length *politically* they were increasingly moving toward agreements with business. As figure 2.1 illustrates, the business production model based on integrated skilled and semiskilled workers required agreements with centralized unions who had control over their locals. Absent that control, as we have said, organized employers had to force centralization of unions through lockouts (Swenson 1991; 2002). Thus agreements with powerful central unions were necessary to secure the cooperation of skilled workers, and this was noticeable in the early years of the twentieth century. These agreements covered explicitly or implicitly the right of managers to organize production and the implied workforce cooperation, collective bargaining, and issues related to training and tenure; in essence, these agreements enabled industry to invest in cospecific assets with their workforces. So the period before the full incorporation of labor into the political system was advantageous to (especially big) industry: on the one hand, industry could structure agreements with unions which were underwritten implicitly by the political regime, at least for industry; on the other, the politically unified working class was kept out of effective political power and thus the possibility of advancing redistribution and social protection on its own terms. Unions therefore had two reasons to push for effective democracy: first, they wanted to pursue redistribution and social protection; second, they wanted to be a full party to the *political* underwriting with industry of the framework of industrial agreements which were rapidly developing.

By contrast, in the liberal economies, none of the three conditions above held: Absent an effective supply of skills from guilds it was feasible for craft unions to control skill supply (Thelen 2004). Absent organized employers it was difficult to pressure unions to centralize and develop strategies of cooperation. Finally, there was generally an abundant supply of unskilled labor: the result of either movement off the land due to commercialized agriculture, or immigration, or both. Hence, in the late nineteenth century, uncoordinated businesses chose one of two strategies: where it was

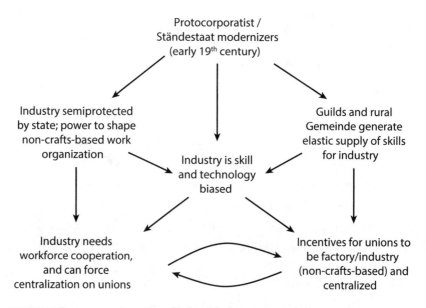

FIGURE 2.1. Protocorporatist states and industrial relations structuring.

difficult for individual companies to exclude unions, they accepted unionization for skilled workers while tending to move away from product markets which required substantial craft-skilled labor in order to compete. Or, as in the United States or France, where the political system allowed it, large companies excluded unions in part by violence and in part by developing technologies which minimized the need for blue-collar skills, and craft unions organized in small companies and in the artisan sector (Katznelson and Zolberg 1986). For skilled workers—including laborers with basic literacy and math skills, as well as higher-educated engineers, accountants, mid-level managers, and so on—employers turned to the general educational system, which went through a major expansion in the first half of the nineteenth century, fueled by government spending at both the local and central levels. In this effort, the main political constraint was not craft workers, who generally supported education for their children, but rather traditional landed elites who had no need for educated labor and saw education as a threat to their political dominance at the local level—themes to which we will return.

Thus in liberal economies unions developed along craft lines, with individual unions concerned to restrict apprenticeships, and to demarcate work by exercising tight controls on work practices, with no reason to coordinate amongst themselves apart from the promotion of a friendly legislative environment, with little in common with the goals of unskilled workers. Politically, representing the "respectable working man" by contrast to the "great residuum" of the poor, they could find a home in liberal parties. Most important, they shared with the educated middle classes a blanket hostility to redistribution to the poor. When labor parties developed, they had to balance the claims of competing constituencies. As we show below, in a majoritarian political system they did so in a manner that greatly advantaged already privileged skilled workers.

For these reasons the extension of the franchise to the working class was not dangerous in liberal economies in which the working class was split and uncoordinated, and in which the "respectable working man" had political interests not far removed from those of the expanding educated middle classes. Here neither power resource theory nor the Acemoglu and Robinson model apply. The Lipset hypothesis is supported in the sense that the skilled and educated middle classes formed a moderate constituency that made the extension of the franchise less threatening to elites, but the reason for extending the franchise in the first place was to broaden support for education and undermine the resistence of landed elites—a reverse causation logic entirely missed by the standard Lipset account.

In protocorporatist economies a more coordinated and organized working class threatened far more serious redistribution. But, paradoxically, it was where the working class reached the highest levels of organization, and was able to unite behind a socialist-reformist party and union movement, that the transition to democracy was least contentious. Any perceived organizational weakness, including divisions along ideological and/or religious lines, invited attempts by the right to thwart the transition to democracy. Even as business developed collaborative institutions with unions in the industrial relations system, the political right resisted democracy. The contrast between Germany and Scandinavia (represented by Denmark and Sweden) offers a good lens through which to understand this. We rely here on well-established research in the power resource theory tradition, and we will not belabor what others have already shown. The main point we want to make is that where democracy was largely a contest over distributive politics, a democratic constitution emerged as the result of the left being able credibly to commit to economic disruption now and in the future unless distributive goals were met. Democracy itself was not a credible commitment mechanism, as in Acemoglu and Robinson (2001)—it proved resilient only where the left was organizationally entrenched. Education was an important part of the story, as in the Lipset hypothesis, but this was by way of giving workers the power to hold up production, a mechanism not entertained in that literature.

2.2.1. DEMOCRACY BY CONCESSION: WORKING CLASS PRESSURE IN SCANDINAVIA AND GERMANY

The first major step toward democracy in Sweden came with the introduction in 1907 of universal male suffrage for the lower house and a relaxation of property requirements for election to the upper house. Conservatives had been consistently against such reforms, looking instead to Prussia and imperial Germany for a model of an illiberal regime. According to Rueschemeyer et al. (1992) the Swedish bourgeoisie supported the Conservatives, along with the upper echelons of the central bureaucracy and army, and the right was united by their opposition to enfranchising lower classes as well as their support for the monarchy and the Lutheran Church. Unlike Germany, however, the landed nobility was weak and had been gradually transformed into a "bureaucratic aristocracy" (Rustow 1955). Instead, most of the land was owned by independent farmers who constituted an important middle segment open to alliances with not only the urban middle classes but with the moderate left. As unions and the social democrats grew in strength, the independent peasantry joined in their call for universal male suffrage.

But as Rueschemeyer et al. argue, one cannot understand agrarian support for universal suffrage, and the eventual capitulation by the Conservatives, without attention to the growing organizational strength of labor. The reforms introduced by the Conservatives in 1906 were preceded by protests and industrial action, including a general strike in 1902 involving more than one hundred thousand workers (Verny 1957). The role of the unions and the political left is even more evident in the aftermath of the First World War, when mass protests and a growing fear on the right of revolutionary conditions led to across-the-board democratic reforms, including parliamentary government and universal suffrage for both houses (Verny 1957; Collier 1999, 85). The only democratic demand not met by the right was the formal abolition of the monarchy itself (Rueschemeyer et al. 1992, 93).

Unlike the right in Britain, Swedish conservatives abandoned their opposition to democracy only when it was evident that the economic and political power of the left and their allies would otherwise threaten the social peace and perhaps capitalism itself. In some measure at least, it also mattered to the calculation on the right that the police and military were relatively weak, with a conscript army that represented serious issues of loyalty if used for overt domestic purposes of repression (Tilton 1974). Rueschemeyer et al. argue that the weakness of the military itself was a function of the agrarian class structure with independent farmers and smallholders blocking the taxes needed for war fighting.

Unions and the left in Sweden may well not have been in a position to cause a revolution, and this seems not to be a necessary condition for democracy. The Danish case suggests that the key is instead organizational capacity for serious civil and economic disruption. The point is well illustrated by the Danish "September Agreement" in 1899. Although the outcome of the massive strike-lockout was in many ways a victory for employers as they sought to centralize industrial relations and reassert their right to organize work and production (Swenson 1991), it also resulted in an institutionalized recognition of unions' right to organize and to call strikes (Galenson 1952). An elaborate system of collective bargaining, rights to call strikes and lockouts, and binding arbitration was set up to manage two powerful players with conflicting but overlapping interests. The massive conflict that resulted in the compromise was clearly not a revolutionary moment in the Acemoglu and Robinson sense, but it was a milestone in the union struggle for organizational and political recognition. With all the might of an exceptionally well-organized business class levied against it, the settlement was an expression of the resiliency of the labor movement. The resulting institutions also helped entrench the organizational power of labor, and organizational entrenchment, we argue, is a necessary condition for stable democracy in protocorporatist countries. Where it is lacking, as in 1930s Germany, democracy is not a credible commitment to redistribution.

The first major move toward democracy in Denmark came with the introduction of a parliamentary constitution in 1901, and with universal suffrage (for both men and women) for both houses in 1915. In both instances it was a red-green coalition that pushed for reform against the wishes of the Conservatives (and the king). By 1913 the Social Democratic Party was the largest in terms of votes, and with the allied Radicals (formed as a splinter from the Liberal Party) they gained real influence over public policies for the first time (Collier 1999, 82). As in Sweden, therefore, the possibility of alliances with a middle class of independent farmers and smallholders played an important role, and so did the weakness of the landed aristocracy. Repression of the democratic movement under these conditions would have been exceedingly costly, if not impossible. Democracy, while deplorable from the perspective of business and the Conservatives, was better than the alternative of perpetual industrial and social conflict. And while the democratic institution was hardly irreversible, the strength of unions and the left never abated, even in the face of mass unemployment in the 1930s. Indeed, the support for the Social Democrats reached its pinnacle in 1935, with over forty-five percent of the vote.

In many respects the move toward democracy in Germany resembles the Scandinavian cases. Indeed the rise of the left was aided early on by universal male suffrage to the Reichstag. Although the parliament was merely "a façade for authoritarian rule" (Collier 1999, 103), it gave the Social Democratic Party a platform from which to mobilize voters. Already in 1890 it won nearly twenty percent of the vote, and by 1912 it gained a third of the vote and twenty-eight percent of the seats in the Reichtag (Collier 1999, 104). Despite anti-socialist laws to stem the tide of left support, unions also grew rapidly in strength. According to data compiled by Przeworski and Sprague (1986), the share of unionized industrial workers swelled from 5.7 percent in 1900 to 13.8 percent in 1910 and 45.2 percent in 1920 (76–77): faster than in either Denmark or Sweden.

Unlike its northern neighbors, however, the right was also strong, and it was united in its opposition to democracy. It is a common argument that this opposition was led by a coalition of heavy industry and the landed nobility ("iron and rye"), but Rueschemeyer et al. make a strong case, building on Blackbourn and Eley (1984), that the entirety of the German industrial elite opposed democracy, even as some endorsed collaboration in industrial relations. We do not need to settle the contentious issue of whether the business elite also aided and abetted in the Nazist takeover because our claim is only that employers outside of heavy industry preferred a corporatist arrangement— including labor-industry coordination but without the redistribution and expansionary social policies that come with democracy. Such coordination emerged well before the Nazi take-over and it continued, in a new form, under Nazi rule (Thelen 2006, chap. 5). It certainly did not require the militarism, anti-Semitism, and brutality of Nazism, but nor did it rule it out. Democracy was the greater evil and it was conceded by the German right only under revolutionary conditions in the wake of military defeat.

The details of the complex conditions that gave rise to the Weimar Republic need not preoccupy us here. The key is what most agree on: the need of the center and right to fend off a serious revolutionary threat. The war had discredited the Kaiser and the institutions of Imperial Germany, and as massive strikes broke out across the country in October 1918, revolutionary conditions were palpable with the declaration of a Socialist Republic in Bavaria. The formation of a socialist government in Berlin under Friedrich Ebert, which included the SPD's more radical splinter party, the October Revolution seemed like it might spread, and in response the industrial elite rejected the hardline position of the Conservatives, with both liberal parties offering accommodation to the SPD. The army also quickly declared its willingness to offer loyalty in exchange for cooperation with the suppression of the revolutionary insurgency. Ebert and the SPD accepted, and the revolutionary movement was put down (Collier 1999, 105–8). The democratic Weimar Constitution was adopted the following August. It is perhaps the clearest example of the Acemoglu-Robinson logic of conceding democracy in the face of a revolutionary threat.

Yet contrary to the notion that democracy is a credible commitment, it turned out to be short-lived. To understand the demise of Weimar we need to consider not only the strength of the Junkers and their alliance with big business—and the corresponding absence of a smallholding class as a potential alliance for the left—we also need to consider the declining organizational strength of the left. Table 2.3 shows unionization rates among manual workers and the electoral support for the left from the turn of the century (and after introduction of universal male suffrage, though not democracy in the German case) until the Second World War (or the end of Weimar in the case of Germany). Note that all three countries experienced an early surge in the electoral strength of the left, and this was particularly evident for the German SPD, where long-standing representation in the (powerless) lower house gave it an early edge. For awhile German unions also led the way, rising fast until the 1930s.

But unlike Denmark and Sweden, the German labor movement lost its momentum, first in terms of electoral support and then in terms of unionization. The spilt of the Social Democrats and the bitter divisions over the October Revolution, combined with rising electoral losses to the radical right, caused a twenty-percent drop in SPD's vote share and a fifteen-percent drop for the left as a whole between the beginning and end of the Weimar Republic. The economic crisis also took a severe toll on the unions. German unions did not control the administration of unemployment benefits like their Scandinavian peers (the so-called "Ghent" system), and rising unemployment caused massive exodus. In Scandinavia, by contrast, unionization was either steady (Denmark) or rising (Sweden), as union membership was seen as the surest way to be recognized for unemployment benefits and treated fairly when required to accept employment. The strength of the left was also rising in these countries during the 1930s, benefiting from a widespread perception that a unified left under social democratic control presented the only hope for recovery and political order. The Danish Social Democrats had the best election ever in 1935 running under the slogan "Stauning or Chaos" (Stauning was the beloved leader of the party and the government). In Germany the same message of order became tragically associated with Hitler and the Nazis.

It is instructive that the dwindling support for the left and for unions was roughly proportional to the opposition of big business to the grand coalition which included the SPD, the Catholic Center Party, and the two liberal parties, the German Democratic Party (DDP) and the German People's Party (DVP). After the governing parties headed by Center leader Heinrich Brüning failed to secure a majority in the 1930 election, Brüning ruled by decree while the liberal parties sought a solution that would include the Conservatives and the Nazis. The right was by now vehemently opposed to any accommodation of Social Democratic demands for social protection and redistribution, and the Weimar Republic came to an end under Franz Von Papen, who handed over the reigns to the Nazis after the fateful 1933 election (Rueschemeyer et al. 1992, 110). The power of the left proved transitory and so did business and liberal support for democracy.

Democracy in the protocorporatist countries thus initially depended on a strong and organizationally entrenched labor movement, and the defeat of fascism led to the reemergence of a powerful and independent labor movement. Democracy was enabled by advanced capitalism, but it was clearly not a necessary condition, since capitalism survived fascism and the rise of Hitler (and Dollfuss in Austria and Mussolini in Italy). Under the fascist regimes in Germany, Austria, and Italy, corporatist institutions were subsumed under the state, but they were still vehicles for coordination, which allowed industry to expand and to supply the war effort. Governments across the advanced world were motivated to build

TABLE 2.3. Left share of vote and unionization among manual workers, ca. 1900–1930s

	Denmark			Sweden			Germany		
Year	Social Democrats	Total left	Unionization	Social Democrats	Total left	Unionization	Social Democrats	Total left	Unionization
1900			14	9					6
1901	17	17							
1902									
1903	20	20					32	32	
1905									
1906	25	25							
1907							29	29	
1908				15		15			
1909	29	29							
1910	28	28	16		12				14
1911				29		29			
1912							35	35	
1913	30	30							
1914				36		36			
1917				31		39			
1918	29	29							
1919							38	46	
1920	32	33	37	30	32	36	22	42	45
1921				36		44			
1924	37	37		41		46	26	36	
1926	37	38							
1928				37		43	30	41	
1929	42	42							
1930			34		42		25	38	26
1932	43	44		42		50	20	37	
1933							18	31	
1935	46	48							
1936				46		54			
1939	43	45							
Total change	26	28	20	31	33	39	−13	−1	20
Change from peak	−3	−2	−3	0	0	0	−20	−15	−19

Sources: Vote shares are from Mackie and Rose (1974); unionization rates are from Przeworski and Sprague (1986 76–77).

institutions that would facilitate investment and growth, even if this motivation was sometimes bellicist rather than democratic. Taiwan and South Korea also grew their economies rapidly under authoritarian regimes in the intense regional cold war context. Yet, where they survived the 1930s, democratic institutions were everywhere conducive to growth and prosperity, something that is not true of all nondemocratic regimes, notably in Eastern Europe. In the context of advanced capitalism, democracy therefore does seem to be a *sufficient* condition for maintaining and expanding prosperity. And once restored after the war, the thorough discrediting of extremism—both fascism and communism—set the stage for an unprecedented era of peace and prosperity in which democracy played an increasingly important role in guaranteeing the institutions that underpin advanced capitalism. This is the topic of the next two chapters.

2.3. Democratization in Liberal States: Creating Majorities to Provide Public Goods

The mere fact that the working class in liberal societies was fragmented may explain why democracy was not strongly resisted, but it offers no positive explanation of the extension of the franchise. The Lipset hypothesis is that as education rises, so pressure for democracy grows. The argument has some limited applicability to the protocorporatist countries, as we discussed above, but not in liberal countries. In these cases the causal argument is *reversed*: under some circumstances democracy can create majorities for a range of public goods important for modernization and industrialization, including education.[10] This is particularly the case for elementary education and for sanitation, slum housing, health and town planning and other (quasi-) public goods. This path to democratization is usually the consequence of inter-elite conflict: a modernizing/industrializing elite may seek to extend the franchise to provide it with a firm majority against a conservative/landowning elite which wishes to resist the creation of such public goods (and democracy itself, of course). The working class is relatively unimportant in this story because it is fragmented; the interest of artisans and skilled workers and their craft unions is against redistribution to the masses of the poor, while in favor of education and sanitation reforms.

The argument that democratization creates a majority for public good extension has recently been insightfully developed (or revived) by two pairs of economists and a political scientist. Lizzeri and Persico (2004) argue that the 1832 Reform Act in Britain was designed to create majorities behind public good expansions in sanitation in the rapidly expanding and uncontrolled new manufacturing towns. In broader terms, but with fine-grained historical analysis, Morrison sees the 1832 Act as a conflict between Whigs (modernizers) and the dominant landowning Tory class, to generate a more reform-oriented Commons (Morrison 2011): a conflict that has roots all the way back to the late sixteenth century (Pincus and Robinson 2011). And Engerman and Sokoloff (2005) argue that the new western states of the Union in the early nineteenth century extended wide suffrage to attract settlers with families with some guarantee that they would be able to vote for education; other states then followed suit competitively.

But these arguments raise an analytic question that the authors do not address. If an elite has the political power to extend the franchise to build a majority in support of public goods, why can it not simply produce the public goods without the need for building an electoral majority? There are in our view three reasons for this. The first is that in a context of continuing struggle within the elite (between landowners and industrialists, for example), extending the franchise is easier than subsequently retracting it. Thus, if modernizers *can* extend the franchise at any particular moment in time, it may give them a long-term advantage, stymieing future attempts by, say, landowners to roll back contentious public goods. A long-term commitment by government might also be necessary for major private investments contingent on and necessary for public goods provision. Of course, traditional elites may have understood this and therefore been tempted to agree to public goods extension without franchise extension. But this points to a second and related reason for franchise extension. Traditional elites could not credibly make such promises, because of the formidable collective action problem posed by the political entrenchment of local elites in a large number of dispersed municipal governments. Unless local governments were also democratized, it would be very hard to implement major public goods programs.

Finally, and more contingent, franchise extension may also reflect the fact (for example, in the most complex and confused episode of democratization, Disraeli's 1867 Reform Act), that the "public goods modernizers" do not have a majority for the public goods but could form a majority for franchise extension with a Conservative party which believed that the new working-class electorate would be future Conservative voters. Disraeli, in other words, may have believed that franchise extension would bolster his long-term vote even if it also ensured a long-term entrenchment of public goods; and he needed support for franchise extension from modernizers who saw public goods extension as more important than future liberal government.

Thus, "public goods" democratization in liberal systems normally implies some form of elite conflict. Where that was the case (as in 1867 or in the mid-1870s in the Third Republic), democratization was not predictable—either side might have won. This doubtless accounts for the complexity of these episodes, as McLean shows beautifully for the 1867 and 1884 Reform Acts in the UK (McLean 2001). But it is not necessarily the case: the Colonial Office was in a powerful position to extend the franchise in the self-governing colonies even if the landowner class there objected. Our concern is not to provide a detailed analysis of each case of democratization but rather to suggest a general mechanism which seems to have been widely present.

The economic historian Peter Lindert in seeking to explain the rise of public education argues that "[t]he rise of voting rights plays a leading role in explaining why some nations forged ahead in education and others fell behind" (2004). His focus for predemocratic nineteenth-century laggards is on France and England, thus in line with our argument.[11] But Lindert does not argue, as we do, that this effect of democracy was also a reason for democracy.

Bentham does. As Lieberman nicely points out, Bentham's deep support of democracy did not spring from the belief that it would lead to equality (as one might have expected from the maximization of the happiness principle), but to the demolition of the "sinister interests"—the monarchy and the landed aristocracy—whose presence in government frustrated reform (2008). Interestingly, he did not believe that voters would support egalitarian policies, but rather that democracy would enable a strong centralized government to carry through reform: "Bentham's democracy . . . was served by a strong state, whose responsibilities in areas such as public health, indigence and education extended well beyond extended political conventions" (ibid., 617). Bentham was in fact a critical reference point to key Victorian reformers, politicians such as Grey and Russell, the brilliant technocratic intermediary the Earl of Durham, and civil servants such as Chadwick (MacDonagh 1977). But Bentham appears not to have explained how the sinister influences would be overturned in the attempt to extend the franchise.

We suggest that the provision of the public good of education provided a strong positive argument for extending democracy in the liberal economies. Before the extensions of the franchise, landowners and local notables had substantial political power at both national and local levels. For them, spending money on education was not only unnecessary; it also enabled those who had been educated to move where they liked, often away from the land. The precise logic of franchise extension to create a constituency for education will be spelled out in particular cases below, but for now note that it is broadly aligned with industrial interests and with more general state-modernizing interests in creating a productive economy.

2.3.1. DEMOCRACY AS A COMMITMENT TO PUBLIC GOODS PROVISION

We have argued that public goods provision was high in protocorporatist economies before democracy. Both towns and rural Gemeinde had interests in the provision of education. As more craft-oriented communities, elementary literacy and numeracy were of importance. And with the political structure to make decisions binding on inhabitants at the local level, the collective action problems behind the provision of a teacher's salary and a schoolhouse were less constraining. Both German states and the Nordic countries were leaders in promoting education, and this worked with the cooperation of villages and towns. In the area of vocational training the system was embedded in the emerging industrial relations systems and a corporatist state. In a very indirect way we may thus agree with modernization theory that education in protocorporatist countries was a precondition for democracy because it facilitated the emergence of a unified working class. But this is not true in liberal countries where the *absence* of effective education provided elites a motivation to support democratization.

In liberal economies, before the wide extension of the franchise, the landowner class controlled most political decisions in the countryside, and oligarchies were the political bodies in towns. At the national level, landowners were the dominant political class in England, as were planters in the US South, and colonial governors and landowners in the white British settler colonies.[12] The state played a larger role through prefects in France, though until the Empire they represented combinations of the aristocracy and the haute bourgeoisie, with the Catholic church (as a political actor) retaining a strong conservative influence in parts of the countryside. Only in the northeastern United States, especially New England, where landowners seldom dominated politically, were municipalities and states concerned with issues like town sanitation and education.

As industrialization developed, landowners had little interest in devoting resources to either town planning or the education or health of the poor. Even if they had a class interest in a healthy and an educated labor class (and it is doubtful that they did), a collective action problem was that it was not in the interest of local landowners to provide these local public goods—if workers in the countryside were educated they would likely have an incentive to move, and it was cheaper to rely on the production of education elsewhere. In the colonies, education mattered relatively little for landowners and they could in any case rely on some proportion of settlers having basic education. Oligarchs were equally unwilling to spend money on improving the condition and education level of the poor in towns. In France, even during the modernizing period of the Empire, developing education was difficult due to the Catholic church's simultaneous hostility to serious education and desire to control it.

Industrialization thus led to burgeoning towns and cities which (apart from a few areas) were unsanitary and unplanned, with limited effective education. As the industrial bourgeoisie grew, it understood the need for a more educated and healthy workforce; this was felt too by the middle classes who lived in towns—in addition, of course, to the poor.

From these perspectives it is useful to look at the key episodes of democratization in different liberal countries. In almost all cases accounting for democratization is messy, there are many different motivations across actors, much individual irrationality, and so on. What we can attempt as comparativists emphasizing purposeful rational action is to see if our general "public goods" framework works reasonably well to make sense of historical developments in the cases available.

2.3.2. EARLY NINETEENTH-CENTURY ENFRANCHISEMENT IN THE UK AND SETTLER COLONIES

Most colonies at the time of independence had similar voting laws as in Britain, though that meant a larger franchise (excluding blacks). Engerman and Sokoloff note that something closer to a (mostly) universal male franchise (but again excluding blacks) accompanied the setting up of new states in the west and midwest in the early nineteenth century; they argue that the motive for this was to persuade settlers that there would be a majority for supporting effective education systems, and that this would attract settlers who were keen that their families would be educated and economically successful (Engerman and Sokoloff 2005). This was, in other words, a settler selection device. Other states followed suit as they saw the danger of losing motivated workers.

If education was a large reason for extending the franchise it may be interesting to think of the continued exclusion of blacks from the franchise in this light. In some Southern states it was illegal to educate blacks. Plantation owners feared that education enhanced their ability to escape by building up marketable skills that were in demand in the North and the West. Therefore, to give blacks the possibility of building local majorities for education made little sense to the elite in the South. The underlying logic here is not unlike the opposition to education of landowners and large tenant farmers in England.[13]

A. *1867 British Reform Act.* More has apparently been written by historians on the 1867 Act than on any other episode of British history. Collier (1999) is correct in her outline of what happened: Disraeli, leader in the Commons of a minority Conservative administration, after the Conservatives had been out of power for a generation, persuaded the right wing of the party to accept substantial enfranchisement of the male population (essentially stable urban householders) on the grounds that the newly enfranchised would vote Conservative, thus giving the Conservative party a long-term majority. Collier probably rightly dismisses the Chartist movement of twenty years previously as an important influence; and few commentators saw (or see) the huge and impressive July 1867 demonstration in favor of reform—consisting mainly of middle-class and skilled workers, and led by industrialists—as seriously threatening to the privileged position of elites, let alone revolutionary.[14]

Acemoglu and Robinson take the demonstration and the ensuing 1867 Reform Act in the UK as key evidence of their hypothesis—as, at first sight, they might well. It is the first case they consider, and is set out on page 3 of their book: "Momentum for reform finally came to a head in 1867. . . . A sharp business-cycle downturn . . . increased the risk of violence. . . . The Hyde Park Riots of July 1867 provided the most immediate catalyst." Searle (1993, 225) argues that "reform agitation in the country clearly did much to persuade the Derby ministry that a Reform Bill, any Reform Bill, should be placed on the statute book with a minimum of delay.'"

Searle is one of the most distinguished historians of Victorian England, but the full quotation starts "his [Bright's] leadership of reform agitation . . ." Bright was one of the leaders of the *business* Liberals/Radicals, and, as Searle explained in his book at the start of the section headed *The Reform Crisis 1865–7* (1993, 217), his "purpose is to examine events from the perspective of those Radicals concerned with the maximisation of the interests of the business community"; indeed, the title of his book is *Entrepreneurial Politics in Mid-Victorian England* (1993). While it was certainly true that "respectable working men" were involved with the two reform organizations behind the July 1867 demonstration, the Reform League and the National Reform League were both probably largely financed by industrialists (ibid., 221–22). The whole episode of the 1867 Reform Act is of course confusing, but it strikes us as very implausible to put it in Acemoglu-Robinson terms, as a moment of revolutionary upheaval.

Our interpretation links to Lizzeri and Persico's (2004) explanation of the 1832 Reform Act. As in Prime Minister Lord Grey's account, the act was designed to change national and local government so as to have majorities for sanitation in the newly expanding and uncontrolled industrial towns and cities. Municipal reform (i.e., Municipal Corporations Act 1835) indeed followed shortly afterwards, as well as improvements in sanitation and public health in the previously inadequately represented cities. Closely following the 1867 Act, the major Forster Elementary Education Act (1870) provided for elementary education across England and the establishment of local school boards, and the Public Health Acts (1873, 1875) greatly expanded state control and local government powers over sanitation and health. The 1884 Third Reform Act of Gladstone extended the franchise to rural areas on the same basis as the urban franchise, and this was then followed by the 1888 Local Government Act, which brought in major changes in urban and rural areas which had been resisted by the landowners. As we explain in greater detail in the next section, even if the urban interests who favored an expansion of public goods achieved a majority in the parliament, they still faced the difficulty that reforms could be blocked at the local level where the landed aristocracy was politically dominant. Extension of the franchise was the only sure way to break the dominance of landed elites at both the national and (especially) local levels.

B. *1875–77 French Third Republic Constitution.* After military disaster in the war against Germany and the collapse of the Second Empire in 1869–70, the right-wing provisional government under Thiers was reelected in 1871, when it used troops to smash the Paris Commune with appalling loss of life. It was not therefore the case that the nascent Third Republic responded to the Commune by

extending the franchise: the provisional government did the opposite. But divided between Orleanists and Legitimists (and hence the
form of a monarchy) the right were unable to agree on a constitution as they had been tasked. By-election gains by Republicans led
to a compromise on a democratic constitution with universal male
enfranchisement and, more important, political freedom to organize. In the 1876 general election, the Republicans won a decisive
electoral majority, which the monarchist president MacMahon only
succeeded in strengthening when he dissolved the assembly and
called for new elections—thus sealing the fate of the presidency. The
Republicans would stay in power until 1898.

Key to the Republican mission was universal state education. In
this they had the support of otherwise rightist industrialists (Magraw
1986). This was both modernizing and politically antimonarchical,
for it sought to abolish church control over parish schools. By contrast to the Catholic priesthood in much of Germany, the French
church was ultramontane and seen as closely linked to the aristocracy. Universal manhood suffrage in free elections was a key institutional innovation to achieve school reform. And Republicans
explicitly justified the exclusion of women from the franchise by
their fear that women would be suborned by Catholic priests against
state education (Magraw 1986). The centerpiece Ferry educational
reforms establishing free education in 1881 and then mandatory state
elementary education in 1882 rapidly put this into practice. Haine
(2000) reports that by 1906, only five percent of new military re-
cruits were illiterate.

*C. British North American Act and Enfranchisement in the Austra-
lian Colonies and New Zealand.* The Colonial Office from the 1830s
on was reform-oriented, much influenced by the Earl of Durham's
report on conditions in Upper and Lower Canada (1838), calling for
"Responsible Government"—which became the Colonial Office's
formula for (more or less) male enfranchisement. He criticized the
defective constitutional system in Upper Canada, where power was
monopolized by "a petty, corrupt, insolent Tory clique." These landowners, he argued, blocked economic and social development in a
potentially wealthy colony, thereby causing the discontent which led

to a rebellion. His solution, based on advice from colonial reformers, was a system in which the executive would be drawn from the majority party in the assembly. It would stimulate colonial expansion, strengthen the imperial connection, and minimize American influences. Durham's report had been commissioned by the British government after the rebellion against British colonial rule; the rebellion had been easily crushed, but it led to reevaluation of the function of white settler colonies.

In the 1840s there was more conflict between the Reform Party in the lower house and Conservatives in the upper house. The Reform Party wanted the governor to only appoint ministers who had the approval of the lower house. In 1847 Governor Lord Elgin started making appointments according to the wishes of the lower house, injecting an element of democratic politics (Stewart 1986). Extension of the franchise was slow, however, and for a long time remained restricted to people of British ancestry with significant property holdings. But under the pressure of the Liberals, mostly at the provincial level, it was gradually extended to all males, reflecting a much slower process of industrialization than in other British settler colonies. By 1898 only four provinces still had a property franchise. Once democracy was in place, education started to expand.[15]

In both Australia and New Zealand, landowners were seen as a problem in relation to social development; and the previously standard colonial government system in which the governor appointed a legislative council, typically of landowners, which could override or veto decisions by an elected assembly, was overturned in a sequence of Acts of Parliament from the 1840s through the 1860s. The process of democratization culminated in Australia with a federalist constitution inspired by that of the United States, including a House of Representatives and a Senate elected through universal suffrage (women would get the vote in 1902).

The original settlers occupied large swathes of land, sometimes in an extralegal manner, and they dominated politics early on ("squattocracy"). Later, immigrants and the liberals fought against the landed elite by both opposing their privileged position in the upper house and by pushing for an extension of the suffrage. The conflict was in part over economic policies that would improve opportunities through education, develop towns and infrastructure, and build up industry (which also involved divisions over tariffs); in part it was also over immigration, since industrialists wanted to attract more settlers to provide labor for industrialization and build up towns, which was opposed by the landed classes because of the intensified competition for land. In this way, Australia exemplifies both arguments about public goods and elite conflict, because attracting immigrants required commitment to education and urban development (as in Engerman and Sokoloff 2005), just as these were necessary for economic development.

In New Zealand an essentially democratic constitution with universal male suffrage was adopted in 1852, also followed by an expansion of education. Local governments were obligated to provide public schooling, although in practice the local governments subsidized the church schooling system. The 1877 Education Act provided for colony-wide public education, and churches were excluded from the system. In 1891 four-fifths of the colony's 167,000 children between the ages of seven and fifteen attended school at 1255 public schools and 281 private schools. Again, as in Engerman and Sokoloff (2005), the main motive seems to have been to attract new settlers, since the economy was still overwhelmingly agricultural, and since the constitution was written in London, where raising the number of settlers was the most pressing concern. Needless to say, working-class politics played no role.

Thus, to conclude this section, an effective system of elementary education, as well as a range of other public goods such as sanitation, was important for successful industrialization. This was not a problem for coordinated or protocorporatist economies, since they could solve collective action problems through the vocational training system and coordinate at the local level. But for liberal economies it required in general a majority sufficient to override the political power of conservative higher income groups, especially landowners, who were unprepared to finance mass elementary education. But there were other members of the elite, modernizers and industrialists, who constituted important pressures for reform and saw the furtherance of democratization as a key to overcoming a conservative reaction.

The overall argument can be summarized in the following way: rising elites in liberal economies had a positive reason for extending the franchise—to build majorities behind the creation of key public goods, in particular education and sanitation. And, in addition, there was relatively little to fear, from the point of view of redistribution to the poor, from increased working-class political representation since (i) the labor movement was fractured and uncoordinated industrially and, hence, politically, and (ii) the interests of skilled workers (the aristocracy of the working class) were aligned to lower middle class voters against redistribution to the poor. Hence in liberal economies, it was no surprise that democratization was an elite project. By contrast, in coordinated economies the creation of the same key public goods was not problematic, whereas a unified working class industrially and politically meant that the political representation of labor went hand in hand with demands for redistribution to lower income groups. Again it should be no surprise that democratization was resisted by the elite.

2.4. The Choice of the Electoral System

In both protocorporatist and protoliberal countries, democratization occurred in response to industrialization and profound changes in the structure of the economy. In the former, effective training systems were built on guild and Ständestaat traditions and provided a large pool of skilled workers, which in turn led to unified labor movements with the capacity to extract democratic concessions from elites. In the latter, the absence of either guild or Ständestaat traditions led to fragmented labor movements with privileged craft-based unions but no effective training system. Here democracy emerged as the result of industrial elites compelling a reluctant landed aristocracy to accept expansion of education and other public goods required for industrialization. Democracy was the result in both cases, but the electoral institutions that emerged from these processes differed in significant ways, which will prove important to much of the rest of this book and can be understood as the result of the two paths to democracy discussed above. These differences help explain persistent variance in government policies and outcomes, which will be analyzed in later chapters, so we sketch their causes in this section.[16]

Once the shift to democracy was seen as inevitable, there were no deep partisan struggles over the fundamental economic and political institutions of modern capitalism.

In the protocorporatist countries where guilds and agricultural cooperatives were strong, employers coordinated, and unions organized along industry lines, both right and left parties ended up supporting proportional representation (PR) as a political mechanism to protect their mutual investments in cospecific assets. Where guilds and agricultural cooperatives were weak, employers poorly organized and poorly coordinated, and unions divided by crafts, the center and the right opposed PR in order to prevent risk of radical redistribution.

Countries that chose proportional representation electoral systems in the early twentieth century were the same that, historically, had had relatively negotiated forms of political decision-making: what we have called proto-corporatism. These include all of Katzenstein's small states (1985), thus also Lehmbruch and Lijphart's consociational countries (Lehmbruch, 1967; Lijphart, 1968), as well as Germany (west of the Elbe) and Northern and Central Italy, and they all had Ständestaat origins. Within these subnational communities— rural Gemeinde, as well as small and larger towns with their formal or informal guild structures, sometimes defined confessionally, linguistically, and/or ethnically—local decision-making involved consensus-based negotiation and bargaining so that different group interests (except those without possessions) could be effectively represented. This allowed the solution of collective action problems and the safe creation of cospecific assets within local and regional economic networks.

In these countries a nominally majoritarian first-past-the-post electoral system worked adequately as a representative system at the national level through much of the nineteenth century.

Constituencies were represented in national politics by local notables elected by plurality and often unopposed. With economic interests generally geographically defined, these provided for their more or less proportional representation. And, with dominant local and regional economic networks, the national level was in any case less important in regulating economic activities.

By the end of the nineteenth century, however, industrialization, urbanization, and the growth of the working class had made the system of national representation increasingly disproportional. At the same time economic networks and regulatory legislation were becoming increasingly national to reflect the accelerating growth of industrialization. We draw attention to the growth of legislation and rulemaking in vocational training and collective bargaining during the period from the late nineteenth century through the early part of the twentieth, gradually complemented by policies of social protection, from workplace injury insurance and unemployment compensation to pensions. Partially parallel is the huge growth of industry associations and unions at the national level that we have discussed, and also the development of parties from parties of notables, weakly professionalized and lacking discipline, to mass parties, professionalized and with very close relations to economic interest associations.

As regulatory politics and economic networks moved to the national level, parties in protocorporatist societies thus became increasingly professionally organized to represent local, regional, and increasingly national interests. They were "representative" parties of economic interests. Confessional parties were no exception: while Christian Democratic parties defended (within limits) the interests of the Church (though by no means always Rome) they were also, in the words of Manow and Van Kersbergen (2009), "negotiating communities" for the many different economic groups—handwork and the Mittelstand, smallholding peasants, larger peasants, Catholic unions, as well as landlords and sometimes business (see also Kalyvas 1996 and Blackbourn 1980). This reflected the fact that economic life was partially organized on confessional lines in the relevant countries.

The adoption of PR in this setting did not require exceptionally rational forecasting: once the move to the national level of industry and politics made it apparent that the preexisting majoritarian institutions of representation were producing stark disproportionalities, PR was the natural choice to restore representivity. Interest-carrying parties needed to preserve their identity to be able to continue to represent their interest or interests at the national level. The transition to PR was a means to restore a negotiation-based political system in which different economic interests were effectively represented by parties. To do this there was no obvious alternative to PR, and it was supported across the party spectrum, *unlike* democratization itself. Blais et al. (2005) show that there were no great divisive political debates on these issues (again, once democracy had taken hold).

Scandinavian and continental countries had much in common in their Ständestaat and guild backgrounds, and both ended up with PR. But their party systems diverged, and this had consequences for government coalitions and redistributive policies, as we will argue in subsequent chapters. The origins of this difference is clearly related to religion, as argued both by Esping-Andersen (1990) and Manow (2009). But we also discern a key difference in the organization of production that helped create and sustain differences in the party system. Although the evidence is tentative, in the continental countries the peasant-dominated countryside was more closely integrated into the urban economies than was the case in Scandinavia, and this had consequences for political representation (Herrigel 1995; Hechter and Brustein 1980; Katzenstein 1985).

If the formerly strongly feudalized areas (East Prussia and the Mezzogiorno, as well as the Ruhr region in West Prussia) are excluded, something like these patterns seem to be traceable a long way back in history. Hechter and Brustein use the term "petty commodity production" to describe the continental pattern in these areas and "sedentary pastoral" to describe the Scandinavian pattern, and they begin their account in the twelfth century (Hechter and Brustein 1980). While a great deal more work is needed to pin down the connections, the petty commodity production areas seem clearly related to the decentralized production regions identified by Herrigel (1995) in South and West Germany. Herrigel pointed to the most notable of these districts in Germany, but we can imagine that they were widespread on a smaller scale in the areas of Western Europe where autonomous urban centers had dominated the surrounding nonfeudal countryside.

As Herrigel makes clear, these urban-rural networks are in fact complex cospecific asset groups where producers "are absolutely dependent upon one another" and "engage in highly asset-specific exchanges" complemented by institutions that "constitute important fora to engage in negotiation and to establish understanding regarding . . . their individual and collective interests" (29). We argue that the urban-rural networks of the continental coordinated economies created political coalitions in the Catholic Christian democratic parties that connected some lower-income groups (largely peasant) with higher-income artisan and small producer groups.

In the work of Rokkan (1970), which Esping-Andersen (1990) and Boix (1998) echo, Christian democratic parties are instead a reflection of the Kulturkampf against the Catholic Church, especially over education, a struggle that led to a deep division between Catholics and other social forces on the right in continental European states. So deep was Catholic distrust of non-Catholics on the right that, though both groups were antisocialist, they were unable to join forces in a single right-wing political movement. Therefore, in the Rokkan story, right-wing parties chose proportional representation, and whenever Christian democrats participated in governments they were under the influence of the Church to choose a welfare state that would prevent the rise of socialism and promote Catholic family values.

Although Christian democratic parties did indeed emerge from the Kulturkampf, it was clearly not a sufficient condition for their creation: Christian democratic parties did not appear in either France or the then independent self-governing crown colony of New South Wales, in both of which Catholic education was fiercely attacked by their respective governments. A necessary condition for founding a highly organized Christian democratic party, we surmise, was that the Catholic adherents were already members of organized economic groups, which was not the case in either France or New South Wales.

The Kulturkampf may also have been a necessary condition for the emergence of Christian democratic parties but not for their persistence, since they remained strong long after the attack on the church had subsided. Kalyvas (1996) makes the compelling case that by the turn of the twentieth century the different Christian democratic parties were organizing themselves independently from the Church as representative parties with committees for different economic interests—as indeed they are still organized.

The reason that Catholics with different economic interests remained with a party that is Catholic largely only in name is explained, we submit, by the interdependencies of these economic interests. The rural-urban, peasant-artisan-small employer-merchant cospecific asset network acted, if our hypothesis is correct, to create a peasant-Mittelstand constituency that had an incentive to remain within the Catholic party. Another way of putting this is to use Manow and van Kersbergen's (2009) notion of Christian democratic parties as negotiating communities with a range of different economic interests in terms of income levels and hence redistribution, but also with a common interest in sharing and managing cospecific assets.

The incentive structures for unions and business in Scandinavia developed in a similar way to those in the continental economies, but a major difference with the continental economies lay in the nature of the agricultural sector. While Scandinavian peasants owned their own land and coordinated activities as in the continental countries, Scandinavian agriculture did not have the same tight links and dependency upon urban economies. Instead, the agricultural communities were tightly knit and heavily invested in cospecific asset relationships within autonomous rural cooperative frameworks. There was thus not the same logic in Scandinavia to support a peasant-Mittelstand party. Instead, the logic of cospecificity led to agrarian parties from which the occasional large landowner was excluded. In these agrarian parties, in contrast to Christian democratic parties, homogeneous economic interests reinforced cospecific assets. The economic interests of peasants, as discussed above, favored redistribution. And because of the nature of agricultural uncertainty, agrarian parties were more predisposed than the social democratic parties to egalitarianism and universality (Manow 2009).

In the liberal cases we have seen that local economies were relatively uncoordinated, with weak guild traditions and haphazard acquisition of craft skills, and farming was dominated by large farmers, so the agricultural labor force was largely a dependent one of landless workers; alternatively, in areas such as the American West, small farmers had low entry and exit costs, making embedded long-run cooperation rare.

One consequence of this pattern was that there was no corresponding push to develop coordinating mechanisms at the national level to manage investment in cospecific assets by different economic groups. Another consequence was the difficulty of building effective unions from unskilled workers, so that unions were largely craft based. Finally, because the liberal state was anticorporatist, businesses found it difficult to develop strong self-disciplining associations. This in turn meant that businesses were nervous about investing heavily in training workers in transferable skills, so this had to be left to the formal educational system. Otherwise, employers favored deregulated labor markets and in minimizing welfare and unemployment benefits for the purpose of weakening the craft unions. To circumvent job control, employers, especially in the United States, introduced technologies that reduced the need for skilled labor.

There is an important political distinction to be made between the United States and other liberal economies. In the latter, with their centralized political systems, skilled workers (Disraeli's "respectable working men") were median voters and the state underwrote legal protection for unions. But the decentralized nature of the American polity—with economic competition between states and labor law at the state level and the lack of federal or even state control over the means of violence (autonomous local police forces as well as private companies such as Pinkertons)—allowed employers a free hand to crush unions. But in both environments the consequence of these mutually reinforcing centrifugal incentive structures between unions and employers meant that there was no desire among elites or the middle classes for a political system that could give the left, relying on support from low-skilled workers, opportunities for political influence.

From this perspective it is clear that there was no pressure for PR in any of the protoliberal countries. Business had no need for a consensus political system from which an institutional framework labor market regulation and skill formation might develop; on the contrary, they saw unions as a threat to their autonomy. The split of interests between skilled workers and unskilled workers meant that the working-class representation which developed during this period paid no attention to the socialist notion of a unified working class and still less to expanding skills. Consequently, the center and right in these countries had no reason to abandon a system that effectively excluded the poor from government and focused on the interests of the median voter. They also had no countervailing reasons to favor PR in order to cultivate coordination and consensus-based decision-making.

Our central contention, then, contrary to Rokkan, is that PR and consensus-based political systems were chosen when economic interests were highly organized and when major societal framework understandings needed to be legally embedded. When that was not the case, as in the liberal economies, majoritarian systems protected the right and the middle classes against the left. In general, our claim is that the system of representation is a complement to the framework institutions of modern capitalism, and it is in particular the political guarantor of skill formation and advanced capitalism. In most existing political economy accounts the private nature of such accumulation is instead the source of distributive conflict, and growth happens in spite of, not because of, democratic politics. It is politics against markets. We do agree that distributive coalitions matter, especially in the nonadvanced sectors of the economy, but these coalitions are largely a byproduct of political institutions that were set up with very different goals in mind.

2.5. Conclusions

We have shown in this chapter the main paths to democracy in the countries that are today highly advanced. These paths correspond broadly to two different literatures: one that emphasizes the role of a strong and unified left in coercing democratic concessions from the rising industrial elite for the purpose of redistribution; and another that emphasizes the role of industrial elites in voluntarily extending the franchise for the purpose of expanding public goods required for economic development. The relevance of these factors, we have argued, are determined by differences in the early organization of the state and the economy. In countries with a liberal state, early development of flexible labor markets, and no or weak guilds, unions developed around crafts and excluded effective representation of low-skilled workers. The labor movement was therefore fractured and uncoordinated, both industrially and politically, and the interests of skilled workers (the "aristocracy of the working class") were aligned to lower middle class voters against redistribution to the poor. This also meant that there was no push to institute a proportional representation system that would have opened the door to the left. In these cases industrial elites had little fear of the working class, but they had a strong incentive to expand public goods, especially education and sanitation, required for the development of an effective labor force (in part to circumvent union control over the crafts). The key obstacles to this project were landowners and more generally conservatives who had no interest in an expansion of public goods and who held strong positions politically, especially at the local level. Majoritarian democracy in these cases essentially emerged as a means to force the landed elites to accept major public investments in education and infrastructure needed for modernization. At the same time, a majoritarian system with a strong bias toward the middle classes effectively excluded the radical left from influence over policies.

By contrast, in protocorporatist countries, the creation of the same key public goods was not problematic. These goods had long been provided locally through rural *gemeinde* and municipalities in which guilds were important, and with industrialization they continued to be supplied through a protocorporatist state and through business organizations that the state encouraged and supported. For a long time the organized artisan sector in these countries was the major supplier of skills to industry; and precisely because it monopolized the skill system, unions could never effectively control the supply of skills and therefore eventually developed into industrial unions representing a much broader segment of the working class. This unification of the labor movement was helped along by industrial employers who sought to centralize the industrial relations system as a precondition for extending the training system to industry. A unified working class industrially and politically in turn meant that the political representation of labor went hand in hand with demands for redistribution to lower income groups. For this reason democratization was resisted by the elite. It was the growing power and organizational entrenchment of the labor movement that eventually forced democratic concessions on elites. Once democracy was accepted, however, parties of the left and right supported the adoption of proportional representation, which allowed bargaining over regulatory policies that affected both business and agriculture, as well as skilled workers, who in essence shared a range of cospecific assets.

At least three important issues are raised by this chapter. *First*, theories of democratization have seldom addressed the converse shift to authoritarian regimes. Despite the focus on power in Acemoglu and Robinson, their concept of democracy as a credible commitment to future redistribution makes subsequent moves to authoritarian regimes harder to explain. Yet a fascinating fact is that it is precisely in the protocorporatist countries in which we have argued that working-class pressure generates democratization that the examples of subsequent authoritarian regression are found (Germany, Austria, and Italy). In our view this is not accidental: for, all other things equal, industry (especially heavy industry) preferred an authoritarian regime to a democratic one in countries with a politically unified working class, and it had made its preferences clear long before Hitler. When support for the left declined and unions were greatly weakened by the Great Depression in the early 1930s, important elements for the move to authoritarianism were in place. These were of course necessary conditions, not sufficient: sufficiency we know depended upon the government, the army, and the political parties. Our point is rather that the framework analysis of democratization should also be a framework analysis (in these industrial countries) for authoritarian regression.

Second, there is a perfect correlation between electoral systems and patterns of democratization: all the protocorporatist countries in our sample switched from majoritarian to PR systems in the late nineteenth or early twentieth century, while all the liberal countries maintained broadly majoritarian systems. What is interesting for our argument is that the two paths to democracy are strongly reinforced by these differences in electoral systems. The majoritarian electoral system in the liberal economies implied that the political insertion of labor would at best benefit the new median voters; and these would be white-collar or skilled workers who would share the interests of the middle classes in not redistributing resources to the poor. Such a political insertion was precisely facilitated by the lack of a politically unified working class. Moreover, because democracy was voluntarily extended, the left was not in a position to demand PR even if they had wanted it. Hence the majoritarian system reinforced voluntary extension of democracy in the liberal economies.

The electoral system equally reinforced the pattern of democratization in the protocorporatist countries, but in the opposite direction, for the PR system made the unified socialist parties key players under democracy. This was because they could represent the interest of a unified working class in parliament as opposed to being forced to focus on those of the median voter; and centrist parties would be tempted to form coalitions with them (or rely on their informal support) against the higher-income-group parties. But, given the representative nature of the societies, a majoritarian system was not an option. Hence the strategic interest of the elites in these systems was to delay democracy for as long as possible. Once democracy was inevitable, however, all major parties supported a transition to PR, just as no major party did so in the protoliberal countries. The Rokkan-Boix approach to electoral system adoption does not explain this key fact.

Third, our chapter relates to another, larger debate on the origins of post-WWII varieties of capitalism (Hall and Soskice 2001). Simplifying greatly, modern coordinated and liberal market economies are strongly predicted by what we describe here as nineteenth-century "protocorporatist" versus "protoliberal" societies. The influential position of Martin and Swank (Martin and Swank 2008; Martin 2009) also associates business coordination with the choice of PR electoral systems; and we agree that PR electoral systems reinforce business coordination. But we see PR as a consequence of business coordination, with origins of the latter in protocorporatist societies.

Finally, our approach suggests a close association between the structure of the economy and the system of political representation, including the party system. Democracy itself is closely associated with the rise of advanced economic sectors that require large numbers of skilled workers. In the protocorporatist countries this came about as a result of the emergence of a unified working class with extensive human capital needed for industrial expansion; in protoliberal counties it came about because industrial elites needed to push forward the general education system to further the industrialization process; and the form of representation depended on the structure of cospecific assets. Where strong complementarities existed between employers and workers investing in training, electoral systems with cross-class consensus-based regulation and interest-based, or "representative," political parties emerged; and where there were strong linkages between country and city, cross-class parties (in the form of Christian democracy) proved very resilient. Where such linkages were mostly absent, and where both unskilled workers and craft unions were in conflict with the interests of industrialists, centralized "leadership" parties emerged in the context of a majoritarian electoral system to appeal to the middle classes. In all cases, governments themselves became a source of economic transformation as they invested in institutions that would promote urban-based industrial development.

3

The Rise and Fall of Fordism

A central element of the argument of this book is the symbiosis between the interests of the skilled, educated workforces of the advanced capitalist sectors and their support for the political maintenance and promotion of those sectors. To these workers we should add the aspirational families who invest in their children's education so that they can join these workforces; and also other indirect beneficiaries of these sectors, notably those supplying them with services. This contrasts with the widespread assumption in the political economic literature that labor and capital have opposing interests.

In this and the next chapter, we see how this argument works in the two major technological regimes—Fordism and then the ICT era of the last quarter-century. Under Fordism the beneficiaries were the large coalition of skilled and semiskilled workers. In the information era, only the more educated and highly skilled benefited (though many were the children of Fordist beneficiaries, and, particularly in Coordinated Market Economies [CMEs] up-skilled Fordist skilled workers). This political symbiosis argument represents, in both technological regimes, a key commonality of advanced capitalism—albeit with different groups involved. The fundamental logic does not differ across technological regimes, nor across varieties of capitalism or the form of political structures. But coalitions and distributive outcomes do.

In understanding the political response to losers there are key differences between the technology regimes. Compensation to losers was relatively unproblematic under Fordism because of the technologically induced coalition between skilled and semi-skilled workers, cemented by collective bargaining. That ceased to hold in the information era. By contrast to the Fordist regime, a large proportion of the workforce—semiskilled workers—no longer had bargaining power. In this quite new social economy, we show in this chapter that the extent of redistribution and active labor market policy depended on the specific nature of coalitions which emerged in coordinated market economies under proportional representation electoral systems; and why coalitions continued to follow more redistributive strategies in the Nordic but not the Continental CMEs, nor in majoritarian Liberal Market Economies (LMEs).

More generally we outline how differences in institutions shaped initial government responses to the end of Fordism and deindustrialization. Like other advanced technologies, Fordism represents a particular organization of location cospecific assets with wide-ranging consequences for both economic and political institutions. We begin by explaining this organization, and we then turn to the forces of change that ultimately upended the Fordist equilibrium, starting in the second half of the 1970s.

3.1. The Fordist Economy

With many differences across CMEs and LMEs, the Fordist system was built on giant Chandlerian corporations, often conglomerates, which Chandler (1977) called "managerial capitalism." These giant vertical and horizontal corporations went from research and development through production to logistics and sales and marketing; hierarchical organization was a common feature. Fordist production was one part, albeit centrally important. Through the postwar period it developed out of the prewar large-scale, centralized manufacturing in megafactories, which relied on high-speed throughput technologies and incremental innovation, an extensive division of labor, and a large number of semiskilled workers. Fordism made relatively limited use of unskilled workers as well as of graduates; this was true everywhere but particularly pronounced in northern Europe, where the skill structure was partly a result of the preindustrial craft tradition, and partly a result of widespread training facilities created during the war to boost the supply of skilled workers for the war economy. Partly it was also a result of investments in a quality system of primary education, which governments of all stripes saw as a path to modernization. Almost every worker received an adequate primary school education, supplemented by some period of vocational or on-the-job training. The liberal Anglo-Saxon countries also engaged in vocational training, but they relied more than continental Europe on a combination of well-educated managers, engineers and semiskilled workers; the group of skilled workers with long vocational training attained through apprenticeships, secondary vocational schools, or some combination of the two, was less important. In most of these respects France was more similar to the Anglo-Saxon countries than to the CMEs. Still, in both systems, and in France, unskilled workers gradually disappeared from the labor force or formed a small, "flexible" segment of laborers.

Crucial to understanding the Fordist economy was the existence of strong complementarities in production between skilled and semiskilled workers—a key feature of the Fordist assembly-line technology. Because Fordist mass production relied on both skilled and semiskilled workers in a continuous production process where interruptions were costly, different skill groups made up complementary factors in the production function. As noted, Fordism took more or less skill-intensive forms, and economies of scale were important to different degrees, but in one crucial respect Fordism had the same effect everywhere: it empowered semiskilled workers to hold up production and hence potentially influence relative wages and hiring and firing decisions. This potential gave semiskilled workers a powerful incentive to organize, and it made employers and skilled workers receptive to demands from below.

The importance of complementarities in production for wage setting is set out in an overlooked article by Michael Wallerstein (1990) (although he does not explicitly discuss Fordist technology). He argues that if skilled and semiskilled workers are strong complements in production, and both groups of workers are represented by separate unions, these unions will have bargaining leverage over each other. In the absence of coordinated bargaining, both unions have an incentive to bargain first in anticipation of the other union then being forced to restrain wages to prevent the overall wage bill, and, hence, unemployment, from rising. Since neither union can guarantee itself to be the wage leader, the arrangement is inefficient, and Wallerstein argues that the solution was for unions to bargain jointly in a centralized and solidaristic manner.

In a similar vein, hold-up power over production in Fordist plants provided a strong impetus for unionization. Complementarities with skilled workers gave semiskilled workers the potential capacity of disrupting production to an extent that would not have been possible if they had been segmented into production relying entirely on skilled or semiskilled labor. The consequence was that semiskilled unions, not just skilled ones, and semiskilled groups within industry unions, were potentially powerful, and while it is common to assume that unions are powerful because they have many members, the reverse—that strong unions attract many members—is equally true. This logic implies a powerful self-reinforcing dynamic that everywhere resulted in effective recruitment of union members and correspondingly high unionization rates, peaking by the mid-to-late 1970s in most countries. Rates typically reached higher levels in relatively skill-intensive coordinated market economies, especially in systems where unions administered unemployment benefits (the "Ghent" system) and where the public sector was large (Rothstein 1992; Bryson et al. 2011), but even in liberal market economies and France unionization rates peaked out at between twenty-five percent (United States), somewhat less in France depending on the definition, and fifty percent (the UK). In such a world industrial peace was paramount, and everywhere attempts were made to reach centralized

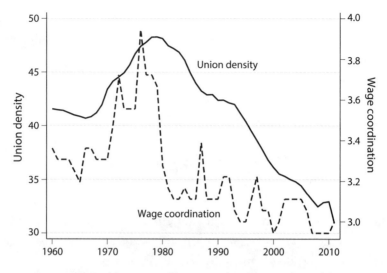

FIGURE 3.1. Average union density rates and wage coordination in 18 advanced democracies, 1960–2013. *Notes*: Union density is measured as employed union members as a share of wage and salary earners. Wage coordination is coded from 1 = fragmented wage bargaining, confined largely to individual firms or plants, to 5 = economy-wide bargaining, based on a) enforceable agreements between the central organizations of unions and employers affecting the entire economy or entire private sector, or on b) government imposition of a wage schedule, freeze, or ceiling. Thee are three intermediate values. Countries are Australia, Austria, Belgium, Canada, Denmark, Finland, France, Germany, Ireland, Italy, Japan, the Netherlands, New Zealand, Norway, Sweden, Switzerland, the UK, and the United States. *Source*: Data are from Visser (2015), Version 5.0.

national wage pacts. Even where they failed (as in Britain, France or the United States) they can be broadly understood as an expression of the technologically induced complementarity logic.

Figure 3.1 shows two measures of the industrial relations system, both from Visser (2015). One is union density rates; the other is the extent to which wages are coordinated above the plant and firm levels. Both unionization and wage coordination rise during the 1960s and 1970s and peak in the late 1970s, after which there is a secular decline. The peak average value of wage coordination of nearly 4 is equivalent to a mix of industry- and economy-wide bargaining with either central organizations negotiating central guidelines and/or key unions and employers associations negotiating pattern agreements for the entire economy. A value of 3, which is the average at the end of the period, is notably less coordinated, with industry-level bargaining

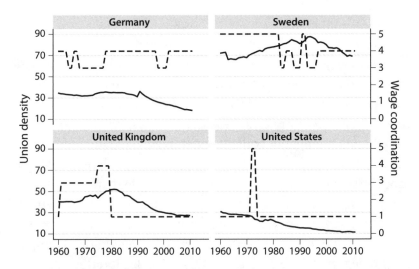

FIGURE 3.2. Union density and collective bargaining coordination in four advanced democracies, 1960–2013. *Source*: See figure 3.1. The dashed line is wage coordination.

but no or irregular pattern-setting and limited involvement of central organizations, and with some freedom of firm-level bargaining. Figure 3.2 gives a sense of the cross-national variation. Germany has modest, and, after 1980, falling unionization rates, but it has retained effective industry-level coordination. Sweden exhibited one of the most centralized and unionized industrial relations systems through the 1970s, but centralization started to break down in the 1980s and 1990s with industry-level bargaining becoming the norm after the mid-1990s. The Ghent system of unemployment benefits facilitated high unionization rates well into the 1990s, but they have since started to come down too. In Britain coordination and unionization rose through the end of the 1990s, but then collapsed. In the United States, coordination never reached sustained high levels, and unionization was much lower than in most other OECD countries throughout the period. Still, like other advanced democracies, it displays a similar cross-time pattern. Most countries in this group fall somewhere in this range, as summarized in figure 3.1. And because of high unionization rates and wage coordination, wage inequality declined sharply up until the 1980s, especially in the most centralized industrial relations systems (Wallerstein 1999; Rueda and Pontusson, 2000).

The "assembly-line logic" of unionization also applied to the organization of business. Because Fordism created extensive economies of scale in all phases of the production chain, plants became highly specialized and dependent on their suppliers and buyers. One way to manage this vulnerability through the corporate governance system was vertical integration, and the Fordist economy produced very large hierarchically controlled, multidivisional companies—most notably in the United States and the UK, where large-scale mass production was most pervasive. Alternatively, high transaction costs were managed via strong employers' associations with the power and incentives to induce cooperation among their members. In many European countries, extensive cross-shareholding, strong representation on boards by large universal banks, interlocking directorships, and well-organized employer associations already existed prior to the end of the war, and this made it easier for employers to coordinate their behavior on everything from vocational training, standard setting, and research and development. This "coordinating capacity" also facilitated the creation of centralized bargaining institutions by making it possible for many employers to act jointly in the case of industrial conflict and by increasing the capacity for the implementation of agreements with unions. Peter Swenson (1991) describes this expertly in the case of Swedish employers who used their lock-out capacity during the 1930s to force the union confederation (LO) to take control of strike funds and cut off support to militant construction unions.

The Fordist economy thus induced, often with the encouragement of governments, strong cross-class integration in the industrial relations system. But the system fostered economic integration in other ways too: between urban and rural areas, between big and small cities, and between neighborhoods within cities. While the largest and most advanced companies and assembly plants were concentrated in or near the urban centers, peripheral areas served as "feeder towns" for manufacturing inputs needed for the urban industrial machine, resulting in the build-out of a vast network of domestic freight routes. While cities were the hubs for the industrial economy, smaller towns were the spokes that kept the manufacturing wheels spinning. Unlike the early phases of industrialization, when large-scale manufacturing was almost exclusively a big-city phenomenon, in the postwar period when cities grew richer, so did the feeder towns, and city-country divisions in economic development generally diminished in the first decades after the war (Dunford and Perrons 1994).

Cities also became less internally stratified. The massive flow of workers into the cities earlier in the twentieth century had created deeply impoverished working-class neighborhoods, but rapid growth and investment in infrastructure and government services, coupled with wage compression and improvement in basic education, significantly reduced urban poverty. For all its routinization of work and life, Fordism created a straightforward transition from school to work, and for ambitious working-class youth there was a clear path to a more prosperous life than their parents' through the vocational training system. In the United States, Fordism lifted millions of blacks out of poverty, especially through migration from the South to the manufacturing centers of the northeast and midwest (even if they remained mostly segregated) (Boustan 2009). The Fordist economy was, in short, by and large a force of integration and equalization of incomes across industries, skill groups, and geographical space.

Fordism was also an economic system that for three decades fueled economic growth. The destruction of plants, equipment, and infrastructure during the Second World War meant that there were many opportunities for profitable investments. This was particularly true in Europe and Japan, where the war was most destructive and where there was consequently ample room for capacity expansion. In addition, there existed a considerable "catch-up" potential with the United States, which could be realized by incorporating, and in many ways enriching, the technologies and mass-production methods developed by American companies in the prewar period (Eichengreen 1997). Given the disorganization of international financial markets, investment was largely financed domestically, which required short-term sacrifices of consumption to spur savings and investments. This conferred another key role for the centralized wage-setting system, because wage moderation would raise profits and enable capacity modernization and expansion. With differences across the advanced economies, the intra-class coalition that underpinned coordinated and solidaristic wage bargaining thus also engendered a cross-class coalition with business. This coalition was facilitated by the understanding of unions that wage restraint in effect functioned as a national system of savings (Przeworski and Wallerstein 1982). Insofar as centralization simultaneously compressed wages, and such compression was accommodated through training, there was no sense in which a trade-off existed between growth and greater equality. Indeed, by holding back wages for the highest-paid skilled workers, the most skill-intensive and mostly export-driven firms were greatly advantaged (Aukrust 1977; Edgren, Faxen, and Odhner 1973; Moene and Wallerstein 1997; Iversen and Soskice 2010).

The cross-class coalition in the industrial relations system depended in some measure on the state playing a supportive or enabling role. Wage restraint presented a time inconsistency problem insofar as companies were not required to reinvest higher profits but could disburse them as dividends or bonuses instead (Eichengreen 1997). But they were encouraged to reinvest by tax, industrial, educational, and regulatory policies that prioritized active over passive investments. Dividend payouts were heavily taxed, and "advanced" sectors of the economy were aided through infrastructure and educational investments, and by targeting subsidies and low-interest loans to sectors where unions displayed wage restraint and where firms were willing to support apprenticeship training and invest in R&D (Katzenstein 1985).

Governments also assumed a supporting role by providing unemployment, health, and retirement programs—central institutions of the welfare state—which reduced workers' uncertainty about their future welfare and, therefore, their temptation to engage in short-termism and industrial conflict. In addition, social protection strongly facilitated the acquisition of firm- and industry-specific skills. When a worker lost his job, he could depend on a sizable income and a guaranteed package of benefits (such as health care), even if it would be difficult to find another job with the same skill profile. Due to standardized wage rates, workers could also expect to be hired back into jobs with a roughly similar pay (provided overall wage restraint created high demand for labor). Since employers in the advanced export-oriented sector depended on a well-trained workforce, they were generally supportive of such social insurance policies (Mares 2003; Estevez-Abe et al. 2001). Coupled with this insurance function was an investment function of the state: massive investment in education and training, which facilitated export-oriented production while accommodating compression of wages (Iversen and Soskice 2010).

Many aspects of government spending were therefore not necessarily a matter of intense left-right contestation. But an obvious, and important, question is how growth-enhancing policies were politically feasible, considering that governments had to commit to policies that encouraged investments in the future, whereas individual politicians tend to be concerned mostly about the next election. Investing in growth-promoting institutions and infrastructure could potentially advantage future governments and hurt the government's own electoral chances in the short run. This short-termism is not simply a matter of voters being myopic. As argued above, the provision of income protection through the welfare state was supposed to reassure unions about the future. But even if voters understood that social insurance would be desirable from a long-term perspective, the inability of current and future voters to make binding agreements with each other created a commitment problem in government spending. In other words, if public policies helped overcome a time-inconsistency problem in the industrial relations system, why did governments not inherit this problem?

There are several elements to the answer. First, the mainstream parties that emerged from Europe's experience with left- and right-wing extremism before and during the war were more inclined to emphasize economic growth and social insurance over radical re-distribution. The Cold War reinforced this pragmatism and moderation, which made "defection" for short-term distributive gains seem risky and destabilizing. Where proportional-representation electoral systems existed this was reinforced by strong incentives for party elites to seek compromise in order to form governing coalitions. Generally speaking, center parties allied with moderate-left parties to pursue policies of labor peace and social insurance financed by moderately progressive tax and transfer policies. The center and left both benefited from redistribution, and there is a strong relationship between PR and center-left governments (Iversen and Soskice 2006). But redistribution only occurred up to the point where it did not seriously undermine investment incentives or jeopardize middle-class interests. The great moderating force in the Fordist system was the interconnectedness of interests, which was rooted in the ubiquity of cospecific assets. That made it hard for any group to move forward without moving others along too, not unlike chain gangs. As we have seen in the previous chapter, one institutional expression of this interconnectedness is the delegation of regulatory policies to legislative committees with proportional party representation and close ties to the bureaucracy where the main interest organizations are routinely consulted. Any attempt by the government to usurp the regulatory powers of the committees for short-sighted partisan gain would have been met with widespread protest among top bureaucrats, unions, employer associations, and opposition parties.

More generally these positions were underpinned by voters who saw themselves as the direct and also the indirect beneficiaries of the advanced capitalist sectors of the economy, through their support of political parties and membership of unions who endorsed it.

A distinct commitment logic applies to majoritarian LMEs. Here commitments to the future came through direct appeals to a middle class including semiskilled workers, which placed strong emphasis on reputation for good economic management as a condition for voting for the incumbent. With both parties appealing to the middle, what sets one apart from the other is reputation for good governance, which is famously identified by Downs (1957) with responsible and programmatic parties. In creating such parties, leaders have to be fairly autonomous from extreme party constituencies—we have called them leadership parties—at the same time as they are constrained by a younger cohort of ambitious politicians who depend on current leaders protecting the reputation of the party, and the value of the party label, until they get a turn to govern themselves. The logic is captured in overlapping generations models where leaders have room to govern, but only with the tacit consent of future generations concerned about their own electability (Aldrich 1995; Soskice,

Bates, and Epstein 1992). We thus see the key aspect of parties to be concern with reputation and clear party labels, as opposed to large mass organizations. Just as strong brand names do not require huge vertically integrated companies, mass membership is not a prerequisite for, and may sometimes be a hindrance to, reputation-based parties. The party label is the key bond between current and future politicians, and between current and future voters.

The capacity to build up reliable party labels was undoubtedly aided by overall party-system stability. The early twentieth-century phase of mass mobilization had gradually given way to a more or less "frozen" party system characterized by stable voting blocks (Lipset and Rokkan 1967). Some societies were highly segmented or "pillarized" by religious and other divisions, but no pillar could reasonably aspire to become hegemonic (Lijphart 1977). Once clear party labels were established, competition for an increasing pool of "swing voters" could focus on reputation for good governance—an outcome that Slovik (2013) has elegantly shown is sustainable. This reduced the incentives of parties in PR systems to try to buy off each other's constituencies through populist tax cuts and deficit spending. In majoritarian systems, stable voting blocs with a smaller cohort of swing voters likewise facilitated centrism and focus on "valence issues" of competence and proven ability to improve a majority's material situation. Party-system stability and a focus on growth also helped build cooperative relations with unions and employer associations on which the government depended for labor peace, wage restraint, and the provision of public goods such as constructive involvement in vocational training systems.

From the perspective of unions, as long as the Fordist economy gave them bargaining power and resources to recruit members, both majoritarian centrism and proportional representation with center-left coalitions guaranteed that future governments would not move radically against their interests. Insofar as parties owed some of their electoral success to the efforts of highly centralized organizations of capital and labor (the latter in particular), governments also had an incentive to consult and involve labor organizations in the preparation of new legislation and to seek their consent in its implementation. This simultaneously brought powerful unions onboard, but it also limited policy flexibility—themes that are pervasive in the neo-corporatist literature dominating intellectual debates in the 1970s and early 1980s (for prominent examples, see Schmitter and Lehmbruch 1979 and Goldthorpe 1984). In effect, the existence of disciplined unions and employer associations helped mainstream political parties to credibly commit to the consensus policies of the postwar economy. Social Democratic and Christian Democratic parties featured the best-developed links to organized interests, and it is therefore not surprising that they brought support and were seen as reliable coalition partners by center parties.

In addition to these domestic political-institutional conditions, the international trade and monetary regime gave governments an important measure of fiscal and monetary policy autonomy by cushioning currencies against speculative attacks and by permitting governments to restrict and direct the international flow of capital. Likewise, GATT only brought down trade barriers slowly and allowed many exemptions to help European countries build their own industries (Ruggie 1983). Non-tariff barriers were particularly dense in services where European governments argued that special considerations—such as financial stability, an encompassing system of public transportation, and country-wide postal service—justified heavy state regulation and exclusion of foreign competition.

Public utilities were widely considered natural monopolies that required state ownership or tight regulatory control, and in areas such as telecommunication and postal services there was also arguably a national-security interest in keeping foreign firms at bay. Regulation or nationalization of banking and insurance were considered necessary to protect markets against mass bankruptcy and to allow governments to steer the national economy in the event of a crisis. Protected service markets could also be used more directly as an employment buffer against business cycle swings, stabilizing the economy and facilitating the government's commitment to full employment. Finally, protection of services against competition was seen, rightly or wrongly, as a means to ensure universalism in service provision and as inherently inseparable from the goal of modernizing society by extending telephone, postal, transportation, and other services to rural and less developed regions. Infrastructure, broadly construed, was a precondition for industrial development, and the future depended on the spread of industry. By combining economic growth and full employment with some measure of social justice, regulating and sheltering services from international competition became part and parcel of the European growth model.

Seen in combination, the policies and organizational commitments that characterized the Fordist economy played to the strengths of the political platforms of the center and the moderate left. As we discussed in the previous chapter, and will consider in more detail below, Christian Democratic parties represented cross-class alliances of skilled, semiskilled and even professional and business groups, and their continued relevance in a secularizing world can be understood in part as a result of the cospecificity of skill investments in the Fordist economy and the complementarities in production that we have described. At the same time, Social Democracy as an ideology perhaps best captured the essence of the fortuitous combination of equality and growth characterizing the Fordist economy, and while Social Democracy was largely a working-class phenomenon, it was very supportive of both intra- and interclass compromises. For the most part, so were middle-of-the-road nonreligious center parties. We see this as a major foundation for the strong popular support of center and center-left parties, as illustrated in figure 3.3. On average, these parties secured close to fifty percent of the vote up until the 1990s; and one might well have added here some parties to the left of Social Democracy, although communist parties were for the most part shut out of government. While the political right strongly opposed any infractions on the private ownership of the means of production—Swedish wage-earners funds were vigorously opposed for this reason (Pontusson and Kuruvilla 1992)—and while the right was critical of redistribution, for the most part liberal and conservative parties adopted platforms that were supportive of major swaths of the Keynesian welfare state. Distributive conflict existed but it could be bridged by cross-class commonalities in interests.

We hasten to add that we do not want to romanticize the Fordist era. Highly routinized production processes were mentally and

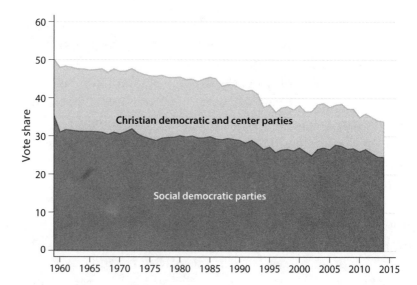

FIGURE 3.3. The vote shares of social democratic and center parties, 1960–2013. *Note*: Vote shares are calculated by country-year and then averaged for 20 advanced democracies. *Source*: Authors' calculations based on Armingeon et al. (2016).

physically exhausting, especially when combined with piece-rate pay systems that paced and wore down workers. Many industrial workers aged prematurely or developed disabilities, and welfare state services, while increasingly encompassing, were themselves standardized and impersonal (Kitschelt 1994). The centralized top-down command structures that characterized all aspects of the system—from vertically integrated companies and centralized union confederations to a limited-access corporatist state—also shut down rank-and-file participation, and they were at least partly to blame for the widespread outbreak of wildcat strikes and protests in the "hot summer" of 1968. Educated youth with lofty ideals of participation and individual autonomy found little to like in this standardized and conformist society. Perhaps most important, it was a highly gendered system, where opportunities for women to establish independent careers were severely limited (Orloff 1993).

Nevertheless, Fordism was a system that produced economic growth and generally reduced occupational and geographical inequalities. For those in the lower half of the skill and income distribution, Fordism served as a huge socioeconomic escalator. Most people could look forward to a life in relative material welfare without deep worries about poverty as a result of unemployment, illness, or old age: a huge leap forward compared to their parents' and grandparents' generations. Their own children could reasonably expect to do even better, attending school for longer and having more occupational choices and opportunities for career advancement. From a contemporary viewpoint, gender—de facto blocking most women from serious careers—was a huge failure of the Fordist system. But viewed in the rearview mirror and in a long-run historical perspective, Fordism was a relatively solidaristic system, where democracy and capitalism were both mutually reinforcing and socially encompassing.

3.2. The Fall of Fordism

There appears to be a long-run U-shaped evolution in wage and/or pre-fisc income inequality in a majority of OECD countries: first a decline from 1920s until the middle of the century, followed by a sharp increase starting in the late 1970s. It also appears that periods of compression have been characterized by smaller differences in inequality across countries, while periods of rising dispersion have been marked by greater differences. The long-run pattern for the United States is illustrated in figure 3.4, using the Gini and 90/10 percentile differentials in wages for full-time male workers. While no consistent series exist that extend further back in time, available data suggest that the downward-sloping trend that is so clearly visible from the 1930s to the 1960s can be traced all the way back to the 1920s, which marks the breakthrough of Fordism. Data for other countries are in line with this pattern. For example, Ljungberg (2006) finds increasing compression of wages in Sweden from the 1910s until the 1980s. Top income shares follow a very similar trajectory for a large number of countries (Piketty and Saez 2006). In addition, new production technologies and deindustrialization have produced a divergence in unemployment security between core and peripheral workers (Kalleberg 2003; Emmenegger et al. 2012).

We have argued that the drop in inequality until the 1970s is closely linked to the rise of Fordism and the associated rise of

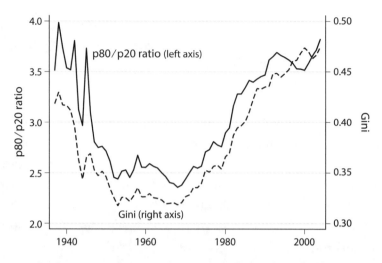

FIGURE 3.4. Male wage inequality, 1937–2005. *Notes*: The data are for all employees in commerce and industry aged 24–60 above a minimum threshold ($2,575 in 2004). Excluded are government employees, agriculture, hospitals, educational services, social services, religious and membership organizations, and self-employed. *Source*: Kopczuk, Wojciech, Emmanuel Saez, and Jae Song. 2010. "Earnings Inequality and Mobility in the United States: Evidence from Social Security Data since 1937." *The Quarterly Journal of Economics* 125 (1): 91-128. Data downloaded from http://www.columbia.edu/~wk2110/uncovering on April 27, 2018.

unions and centralization of industrial relations and expansion of the welfare state. By the same token, the sharp bifurcation in wages and labor market insecurity in the 1980s and 1990s was at least in part a result of the breakdown of complementarities between skilled and semi- or unskilled workers following the widespread application of new information and communications technology, which are strong substitutes for semiskilled routine tasks (Autor et al. 2006). New technology also greatly increased productivity in manufacturing, and as markets for consumer durables were gradually saturated and demand shifted toward services—a shift accelerated by the outsourcing of services that previously were provided in-house—the industrial labor force dropped sharply (Iversen and Cusack 2000). Figure 3.5 shows that industrial employment as a share of the total civilian employment was nearly cut in half between 1970 and 2010. In several countries, industrial work went from being the occupation of a near-majority to just one occupation among many.

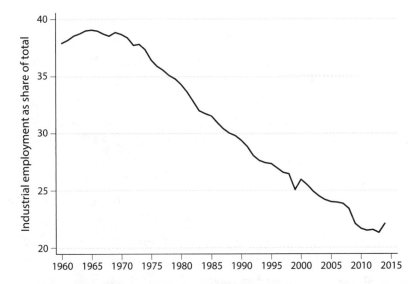

FIGURE 3.5. Average industrial employment as a share of total civilian employment in 18 advanced democracies, 1960–2014. *Source*: OECD (2016), "Labour Force Statistics: Summary Tables," OECD Employment and Labour Market Statistics (database).

We will discuss in the next chapter how major reforms to the financial system, stronger competition policy, mass investment in higher education, and corporate governance reforms set the stage for the rise of new knowledge-intensive industries. Here we underscore how new technology and deindustrialization contributed to the breakdown of centralized wage bargaining and the decline of unions, and we will consider initial responses of different governments to this breakdown. As less-skilled workers became increasingly segregated into a growing tier of low-productivity service sector occupations—especially in low-end personal and social services—the complementarities between high- and low-skilled workers unraveled. In both fragmented and industry-based industrial relations systems, this has meant a severe loss in the power of semiskilled workers' unions and of semiskilled workers within more encompassing unions, and unionization rates have in most countries fallen dramatically because unions failed to replace losses of industrial workers with new members in services. Kristal and Cohen (2013) estimate that almost half the rise in wage inequality in the United States from the levels in the 1980s is due to the decline of unions and the inflation-adjusted minimum wage. By the same logic, effective protection for semiskilled workers has declined with the ebb of Fordism and with deindustrialization, exacerbating the inegalitarian effects of greater wage dispersion. The exception are unions representing public-sector municipal and state workers where jobs were still relatively protected (Bryson, Ebbinghaus, and Visser. 2011). The collapse in overall union membership is captured in figure 3.1.

The changes in the industrial relations system had immediate—or what we will call first-order (Hall 1993)—consequences for both macroeconomic policies and policies of social protection and compensation . In the former arena we see an across-the-board transition to much more restrictive ("monetarist") policies. In the latter arena, we also see deregulation of low-skill labor markers everywhere. But compensation through the welfare state has varied across countries due to differences in political and economic institutions.

3.2.1. RESPONSES TO THE CRISIS OF FORDISM: MACROECONOMIC POLICIES

As we have already argued, with the uncoupling of skilled and semiskilled interdependencies solidaristic wage bargaining also declined, and in countries such as Sweden and Denmark highly centralized bargaining systems were abandoned, while attempts at centralized pacts in countries such as Britain and Italy failed (Flanagan, Soskice, and Ulman 1983; Iversen 1998). The changes are evidenced in the decline in the wage coordination measure in figure 3.1. With this decline in coordination, the macroeconomic capacity for wage restraint also dropped. Although the most centralized systems weathered the first oil crisis in 1973 remarkably well, more fragile systems saw sharp increases in wage inflation, and after the second oil crisis from 1978–79 inflation was a pervasive problem across all advanced democracies. Even more troubling was the simultaneous increase in unemployment. Between 1973–79 and 1979-85, unemployment rates Europe-wide rose by half and in some countries, such as Belgium and the Netherlands, they more than doubled. At the same time public debts had risen everywhere, and they exploded in Belgium, Ireland, and Italy, raising immediate questions of fiscal sustainability. The combination of unemployment and inflation was not supposed to happen in the Keynesian orthodoxy of the day, and a new approach was called for.

Where centralized bargaining and continuous consultation between the peak associations and government could no longer be relied upon for wage restraint, there was a pressing need to anchor inflationary expectations—to signal the unions that monetary policy would be nonaccommodating, implying that excessive wage demands would mean additional unemployment and not just inflation—by adopting an exchange-rate commitment and giving the central bank the independence to pursue it. Exchange-rate commitment (in one form or another) generally came first, in the 1980s; central bank independence followed in the 1990s (see figure 3.6); but the two were part of the same macroeconomic policy realignment. In addition, a credible commitment to exchange-rate stabilization and monetary nonaccommodation presupposed a solution to the fiscal problem; otherwise, central banks might come under pressure to inflate as a way of rescuing governments from their own debt liabilities. Pegging the exchange rate could only bring interest rates down toward German levels and reduce debt-service costs if fiscal policy was also controlled.

This goal was accomplished in two ways. First, in countries where deficit spending had been a problem, budgetary processes were centralized and rationalized—usually by concentrating budgetary powers in the finance ministry, making the budget more transparent, and imposing an ex ante hard budget constraint (Hallerberg 2004, Von Hagen and Hallerberg 1999). Top bureaucrats in the finance ministry are often recruited from central bankers, who also frequently move into careers in the financial sector, all sharing a conservative macroeconomic outlook (Adolph 2013). By aggressively signaling to the market, and to unions, that macroeconomic policies were now targeting inflation and balanced budgets rather than full employment, governments made a sharp policy break from the past.

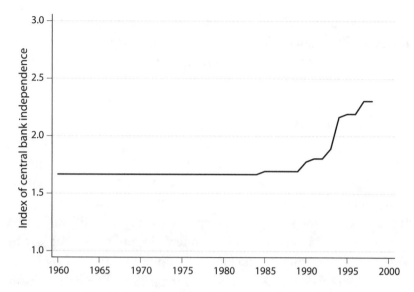

FIGURE 3.6. Central bank independence in 18 OECD countries, 1960–98. *Source*: This is essentially an index of common indexes of both political and economic independence of the central bank by Freitag (1999), as recoded in Brady et al. (2014).

Second, the European Monetary System (EMS), the Single Market, and the Maastricht Treaty contributed to this shift in many countries. To be sure, the implications of European integration have been complex, even contradictory. For some it has been seen as a way of introducing the chill winds of competition and intensifying the pressure to deregulate and eliminate the excesses of the welfare state, while for others it has been seen as a way of halting the race to the bottom. What is important here is that integration supported labor market decentralization. By eliminating capital controls and making realignments more difficult, the EMS solidified the exchange-rate commitment and the credibility of the nonaccommodating monetary policies needed to restrain wage demands in more decentralized labor markets. By making central-bank independence and fiscal retrenchment conditions for qualifying for monetary union, the Maastricht Treaty reinforced the credibility of that macropolicy stance. And the advent of monetary union itself, which handed the reins of monetary policy to a European Central Bank with unparalleled independence, residual doubts about the new direction of monetary policy waned.

While decentralization in the industrial relations system was thus accompanied by a robust tightening of monetary and fiscal policies, it is important to note that it did not lead to institutional convergence. In all CMEs where skilled workers and employers have large investments in cospecific assets—firm- and industry-specific skills in particular—wage coordination was reestablished at the industry or sectoral levels, although with a much more marginal role for semiskilled workers (whether organized independently or as part of industry unions). The continued importance of unions in these European countries is explained in part by the fact that skilled workers continue to be co-owners of major production assets, which are irreplaceable for employers. This is much less true in countries such as Britain and the United States, which have therefore also seen a more complete collapse of coordination and union membership, with an attendant sharp rise in inequality.

3.2.2. RESPONSES TO THE CRISIS OF FORDISM: SOCIAL PROTECTION AND COMPENSATION

The extent of support for, and redistribution to, the losers of the decline of industrial Fordism, what we might refer broadly to as the vulnerable sector of ACDs, depend on two related factors: (i) the degree of movement between, and economic distance across, the two sectors (labor market segmentation); and (ii) the incentives in the party system to form coalition across the two sectors.[1] Segmentation matters, because if the middle class fears that they, or their offspring, could end up in the vulnerable sector, they are more likely to support policies that will support and protect workers in that sector. Conversely, the more segmented the labor market is, the fewer the opportunities of moving out of the vulnerable sector through upskilling, and the less the risk of falling into this sector, the less the likelihood of political support. This logic can be captured in a simple insurance model where the long-term risk of ending up in the vulnerable sector is determined by the transition probabilities, and where middle-class support for redistribution (and related social insurance) is a function of this risk as well as the "distance" in terms of income and welfare between the two sectors. The Fordist industrial economy can be understood as one where segmentation was relatively low in the sense that skilled and semiskilled wages were not too far apart, where unemployment tended to be relatively similar across groups, and where intergenerational mobility between the two was relatively high. This is not true in the knowledge economy: a theme we pick up on in chapter 5 where we consider the electoral consequences of this growing divide.

A key question for our entire understanding of the role of democratic politics in redistribution is the extent to which governments have stepped in to compensate and assist workers who have been adversely affected by deindustrialization and technological change: the people who make up the vulnerable sector of modern capitalism. (As we have seen in chapter 1, the included middle classes have been able to keep up with the general advancement of the economy, and in the next chapter we argue that they have in fact been the driving force behind the new economy.) To answer this question, we pick up on the division of democratic institutions in ACDs that we analyzed historically in chapter 2 as two paths to democracy.

The critical question for redistribution toward the vulnerable sector is whether there is an incentive to include this sector in the governing coalition. Our argument, building on Iversen and Soskice (2006), implies that this depends on the party and electoral systems. In a PR multiparty system where each class is represented by its own party, there is an incentive for the middle-income party to ally with the low-income party, because the size of the pie to be divided rises with the wealth of those excluded from the coalition. Majoritarian two-party systems are different, because the middle might end up with fewer benefits and higher taxes under a center-left government where the left has taken over, whereas lower benefits are likely to be partially offset by lower taxes if the right takes over in a center-right government (under the assumption that redistribution cannot be regressive).

This model implies that redistribution to the vulnerable sector is only possible in PR multiparty systems. Yet there is an important differentiation within these systems that speaks to Esping-Andersen's (1990) distinction between social democratic and conservative welfare states. Following Manow (2009) and Manow and Van Kersbergen (2009), if parties under PR represent more than one class it opens the possibility for governing coalitions that excludes *both* the left and right. The historical example is Christian democratic parties, because they represent multiple groups, including skilled workers, technicians, and upper-middle-class professionals and managers. They are different from "cross-class" parties in majoritarian systems because they do not need to win elections by appealing to the "median voter," and they can instead allow group differences to be bargained out inside the party. Using the terminology from chapter 2, they are representative rather than leadership parties. Because these parties need to accommodate different interests, they tend to set aside divisive issues of redistribution and focus on their common interest in social insurance. But this "centrist" bias also means that they can often govern with other center parties without having to make compromises with the left. We would thus expect the interests of low-end workers to be far less well represented in *both* (liberal) majoritarian *and* PR electoral systems with strong Christian democratic parties.

We can illustrate this logic with some numbers from the OECD's Social Expenditure Dataset for the post–1980 period (roughly the start of the rise in labor market inequality).[2] If we assume that the vulnerable sectors are hit harder by adverse economic changes or "shocks," and if all countries have been exposed to the same structural shocks, and if we control for unexpected growth and "automatic" spending increases due to demographic shifts, we can compare government spending across the three types of political systems: LMEs with majoritarian institutions, CMEs with PR and strong Christian democratic parties, and CMEs with PR and weak Christian democratic parties. This division corresponds to Esping-Andersen's (1990) three worlds of welfare capitalism.[3] The results are illustrated in figure 3.7 using a "typical" shock, here defined as an exogenous change that causes governments to increase spending by one standard deviation of all spending changes (the detailed results and estimation procedure are described in appendix A).

Consistent with the notion that inclusion in the governing coalition is critical, we find that PR countries with weak Christian democratic parties respond much more aggressively to shocks than other countries. For total social spending they increase outlays at twice the rate of majoritarian countries, and although other PR countries are

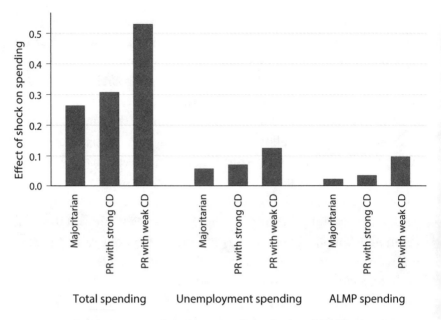

FIGURE 3.7. The responsiveness of governments to adverse shocks in different political systems. *Notes*: Figures are based on results in table A1 in appendix A and show the estimated change in government spending as a percent of GDP resulting from a "typical" exogenous shock, which is defined as a change that causes governments to increase spending by the equivalent of one standard deviation of all spending changes. *Source*: OECD Social Expenditure Statistics. Online Database Edition.

also more responsive than majoritarian countries, this is true to a much lesser degree. In fact, the most striking finding is that PR countries with strong Christian democratic parties are not notably more responsive to shocks than majoritarian countries. When it comes to being attentive to the needs of lower-skilled and more risk-exposed workers, it is clearly essential that representatives of these workers are regularly included in legislative bargains, and such inclusion is typically not the case when the center can govern on its own (with or without right-party participation).

Looking across policy areas, the differences between PR countries are somewhat muted for social-insurance-type spending like unemployment, but it is more pronounced when we consider active labor market programs (ALMPs) that are more targeted toward vulnerable workers. In the latter policy area, governments in PR countries with weak Christian democracy increase spending almost three times more than governments in majoritarian countries. Of course, since spending on unemployment and ALMPs are only a fraction of total spending, the effects of a typical shock on spending as a percent of GDP (measured on the y-axis) are also smaller.

These results highlight the importance of coalitional politics for distributive outcomes. During the "Golden Age" of welfare state development these differences were hidden behind high levels of wage compression, shared job protections, and employment-related social insurance. When production technologies bind together skilled and semiskilled workers, as was broadly the case under Fordist production methods, semiskilled workers can "free-ride" on the bargaining strength of skilled workers. This is still true to some extent—labor markets in all coordinated market economies are more integrated and equal than in liberal countries—but the contrast to the Nordic countries in terms of deliberate government policies of compensation has now become very striking.

The lack of direct compensation to losers in LMEs and CMEs with strong Christian Democracy does not mean that there are no salient differences between these varieties. All CMEs feature highly developed vocational training systems, which have broad political support and enable firms to compete effectively in high value-added international niche markets. The resulting high demand for specific skills is also associated with an institutionalized school-to-work transition, where workers at the lower end of the ability distribution have strong incentives to work hard in secondary school to get into the best vocational schools or to get the best apprenticeships (Estevez-Abe et al. 2001). This in turn raises skills at the low end, which supports the pursuit of a more compressed wage structure by unions through the collective wage bargaining system. In general skills systems like the United States, by contrast, there is a well-known bifurcation of the high school population between those students who expect to go on to college, and therefore have strong incentives to work hard to get into the best schools, and those who are academically disinclined and expect to leave the formal educational system during or right after high school. For the latter, there are few opportunities for acquiring additional skills, and they end up in the post-Fordist world in relatively poorly paying jobs with little prospect for advancement. LMEs do exhibit high investment in general skills, which also serves as insurance against labor market insecurity, but it has been difficult to secure political support for extending public higher education into the lower middle classes—an important fact that we argue in chapter 5 is one reason for the spread of populist sentiments in countries like the US and the UK. Because of the center-left bias of the Scandinavian model, lower-end access has been expanded at a much higher rate. Christian democratic PR countries fall in between, as we would expect from the centrist political system that tends to be more encompassing than the center-right majoritarian systems characteristic of LMEs (Iversen and Stephens 2008).

The last paragraph highlights a key difference to Esping-Andersen's conjecture that the welfare state undermines markets and the interests of business in general, including the advanced sectors of the economy. In this view the welfare state is fundamentally the result of a class struggle (Korpi 1983; Stephens 1979); it is "politics against markets," as succinctly captured by the title of Esping-Andersen's 1985 book. If true, this has consequences for how we understand economic advancement. "Social institutions," writes Dani Rodrik, "can be treated 'just like' any other determinant of comparative advantage" and "more generous social welfare systems will be associated with lower competitiveness" (1997, 45). We instead see the core institutions of social protection found in both the conservative and social democratic welfare states as complementary to the functioning of the advanced sectors of the economy.

So far as redistribution toward the vulnerable sector goes, this does not involve the institutional framework that supports the advanced sector. As we spell out in the next chapter, this institutional framework covers a wide range of areas, including vocational training and higher education, technology transfer and innovation systems, regulation of skilled labor markets and industrial relations, corporate governance and markets for corporate control, those aspects of the welfare state relevant to advanced capitalism (its insurance but not redistributive functions), trade, competition and intellectual property policy, and the macroeconomic regime. As we will argue, all governments have an interest in effective institutional frameworks: this is not generally an area of partisan division. But redistribution toward the poor, and, in general, the protection of workers in the vulnerable sector of the economy, is not part of the institutional framework of advanced capitalism. Political constraints limit such redistribution.

3.2.3. RESPONSES TO THE CRISIS OF FORDISM: SECOND-ORDER EFFECTS

Borrowing loosely from Hall (1993), the policy responses of governments discussed above may be thought of as first-order effects of the decline of Fordism and the breakup of intra- and cross-class alliances in the industrial relations system. They are the expressions of the nature of existing political parties and the coalitions they engender given existent political institutions. But those who are shut out of effective representation in the political system feel alienated from the system and become subjects of mobilization by new parties. These parties are often created by charismatic leaders and tend to have fragile party organizations with ideologically incoherent voter appeals. Populism of this sort may thus be seen as the opposite side of the coin of the decline of traditional social and Christian democratic parties: as a second-order effect. Figure 3.8 illustrates the point, adding the vote shares of populist parties to those of traditional social and Christian democratic parties. By and large, as Fordism declined the gap in support for traditional parties was filled by an increase in support for populist parties.

In fact, figure 3.8 understates the real changes, because populist parties have been suppressed in majoritarian systems, where it is much harder to form successful third parties. And, in fact, it is in majoritarian LMEs that populist sentiments are most widespread and intense. This is because in these countries the semiskilled working class is largest, and there are few opportunities for upskilling through intra-firm training (as opposed to countries such as Germany and Sweden) at the same time as the political system largely fails to compensate losers (as opposed to countries such as Denmark and

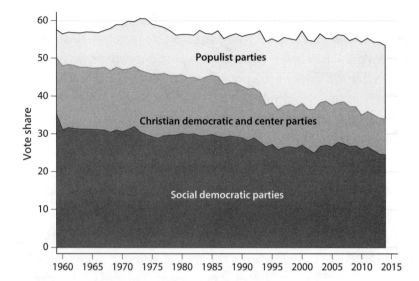

FIGURE 3.8. Voter support for populist parties. *Notes*: Vote shares are calculated by country-year and then averaged for 20 advanced democracies. Populist parties are those coded as "right-populist" or "protest" in Amingeon et al. (2016). *Source*: Authors' calculations based on Amingeon et al. (2016).

Norway). Measured as a set of values, populism is much more widespread in majoritarian systems like the United States and the UK, as powerfully illustrated by Brexit and Trump's election. In fact, we will show in chapter 5 that the extent of populism is highly dependent on the entire educational system and the extent to which it offers the losers of the transition to a knowledge economy opportunities to restore their status: not through direct monetary compensation but through acquisition of new skills and, above all, better educational opportunities for their children. Where such opportunities are few, losers feel trapped and turn away from established parties and toward new populist ones.

3.3. The Advanced Sector and the Symbiotic Relationship

We conclude this chapter with a bridge to the next: the rise of the advanced, knowledge-intensive sectors of the modern economy. Our key claim is that, despite the rise of populism, there exists a

symbiotic relationship between business and democratic governments, where the latter set up or sponsor an institutional framework
which enables firms in the advanced sector to develop and carry
forward their comparative advantages. We see the provision of the
conditions in which advanced capitalism can flourish as a central
function of governments in these countries. Again, this institutional
framework covers a wide range of areas, including vocational training and higher education, technology transfer and innovation systems, industrial relations, corporate governance, trade, competition
and intellectual property policy, and the macroeconomic regime. It
also includes those aspects of the welfare state relevant to advanced
capitalism: namely its insurance rather than redistributive functions.
But unlike the Fordist economy, there is nothing that binds together
the interest of the main social classes. A majority gains, and a small
minority gains a great deal, but a large minority loses.

The 1980s was the starting gun for a series of reforms that ended
up greatly benefiting the advanced sectors and the knowledge
economy in general. We discuss these reforms in detail in the next
chapter. What is critical to note here is that advanced capitalism
has always been underpinned by political support from an educated majority of the electorate. Under Fordism, that core con-
sisted of high school graduates and a substantial number of workers
with additional vocational training—in some countries involving
multiyear school- and/or firm-based training. In the knowledge
economy the core has shifted to those with college degrees, with
a continued role played in some countries by those with long vocational degrees and firm training. The industrial working class
was by no means to be excluded from the advanced sectors of the
knowledge economy, since many of the children of formerly industrial workers were part of what we will see was the massive rise in
participation in higher education starting in the 1980s. But, from
then on, as new generations entered the economy, what changed
was the uncoupling of the distributive interests of more-educated
and less-educated workers and the stark separation of life experiences and support for the institutions of advanced capitalism between the two groups.

Appendix to Chapter 3

ESTIMATION AND DETAILED REGRESSION
RESULTS FOR FIGURE 3.7

We use a modified version of a method pioneered by Blanchard and Wolfers (2000). The core idea is to use year dummies to estimate the effects of unobserved common shocks on policy variables, while at the same time differentiating the direction and strengths of these effects by distinguishing countries on key political-institutional variables. The original model requires nonlinear regression, but it turns out that it is complicated to produce the correct standard errors using Stata's nonlinear procedure (as in Blanchard and Wolfers). We have done this in a separate paper (Iversen and Soskice 2014), and the results are consistent with the ones reported here.

Here we use a simpler two-stage procedure that can be estimated using linear OLS. In the first stage we regress changes in government spending against a complete set of year and country dummies, plus controls, in order to identify the average effects of shocks in each year on spending. We use these results to construct a "shock" variable (for each of the dependent variables), which is simply the magnitude of the estimated time effects in each year. In other words, we use average policy changes as a proxy for the extent of the shock in each year. These shocks can be both positive and negative.

In the second stage we regress spending against the shock variable and its interaction with our political-institutional measures (PR with weak and strong Christian democratic parties). The comparison group is majoritarian countries. Only two cases in our sample exhibit change on the institutional variables. Italy introduced a majoritarian system in 1994 before switching back to PR in 2006, and New Zealand went from a SMD majoritarian system to a PR-dominant system in 1994 (with the first election under the new system in 1996). Because there is a possibility of heteroskedasticity and serial correlation in the errors, we use panel-corrected standard errors with correction for first-order serial correlation as recommended by Beck and Katz (1995). The specific procedure in Stata is xtpcse, using AR-1 correlated errors.

To take account of unobserved heterogeneity across countries, we use country fixed effects, and we also include a set of controls designed to remove nondiscretionary components of spending decisions. One is unexpected growth, which is defined by the difference between the rate of GDP per capita growth in a particular year minus the average rate of growth in the previous three years. The logic is that governments make budgetary decisions using GDP projections that are based on recent growth trends, so when growth is unexpectedly high or low it affects the denominator of the spending as share of GDP measure. In addition we control for the "automatic" effects of demographic changes by including variables for (the first difference in) the share of the population who are under fifteen or who are over sixty-five.[1] Like the growth data, these data are from the OECD.stat online database. Finally, we include a control for "automatic unemployment disbursements," which are the benefits the unemployed receive "automatically" because of the income replacement rates that are "on the books" at the time they are laid off. By including a control for spending "mandated" by replacement rates that were in place in the year before the shock, we focus attention on the discretionary elements of the budget. The replacement data are from Vliet and Caminada's (2012) updated version of Scruggs's (2004) widely used dataset.[2]

We also tried to include measures for economic openness (imports plus exports as a percent of GDP), female labor force participation (as a percent of the working age population), and voter turnout. None of these register a significant effect, and leave our substantive results unaltered. They have been omitted in the regression results reported below.

Finally, there are two technical issues that we need to address. Since the shock variable is estimated rather than observed directly, the estimate of the effect of shocks will contain measurement error. Such error, however, will always bias the results downwards, never upwards. So using the estimated shock variable will give us a conservative (or lower bound) estimate of the true effect. More precisely, in the simplest form the true model is

$$\Delta y_{it} = \alpha_{PR} \cdot s_t + u_{it}$$

where s_t is the true shock and α_{PR} is the parameter on either of the PR dummies. But we estimate s_t by $\hat{s}_t$; then we estimate

$$\Delta y_{it} = \alpha_{PR} \cdot \hat{s}_t + \alpha_{PR}(s_t - \hat{s}_t) + u_{it}$$

with the error term now augmented by the measurement error.

Assume $\hat{s}_t = s_t + \varepsilon_t$ (which we can in principle derive from the Stage 1 regression as the unbiased difference between the estimated and true value of the parameter s_t). Then:

$$\Delta y_{it} = \alpha_{PR} \hat{s}_t \, d_{PR} + \alpha_{PR}(s_t - \hat{s}_t) d_{PR} + u_{it}$$

$$E\hat{\alpha}_{PR} = \alpha_{PR}\left(1 - \frac{\sum \hat{s}_t (s_t - \hat{s}_t)}{\sum \hat{s}_t^2}\right) = \alpha_{PR} E\left(1 - \frac{\sum_i (s_t + \varepsilon_t)\varepsilon_t}{\sum \hat{s}_t^2}\right) \rightarrow \alpha_{PR}\left(1 - \frac{\sigma_\varepsilon^2}{\text{var } s}\right)$$

So the estimated effect of PR (with or without a strong CD) underestimates asymptotically the true effect. The same proportionate (asymptotic) bias is true for the other PR effect.

The second issue is that in estimating the first stage against a full battery of country and time dummies, the procedure consumes $N + T$, or 45 (in average) degrees of freedom. In principle these need to be subtracted from the actual number of observations (393) in estimating the standard errors for the second stage. This gives us 439 instead of 483 degrees of freedom and introduces a small error. Specifically, if the reported standard error of any reported coefficient, α is $se_\alpha = se_a/\sqrt{484}$, the "true" standard error is $se_\alpha^* = se_a/\sqrt{439}$ so that each reported standard error should be multiplied by $se_\alpha^*/se_\alpha = 1.05$. Since this does not affect any of the reported significance levels, and since the two-stage procedure biases the coefficients downwards, we report only unadjusted results.

Table A3.1 shows the regression results from the second stage of the estimation, which are the basis for figure 3.7 in the main text.

We might add that the general results presented in table 1 are confirmed if we use a nationally specific shock variable in a non-linear setup. The shock variable in this analysis is deindustrialization,

TABLE A3.1. Regression results for the effect of shocks on government policies

	Total social spending	Spending on unemployment	Spending on ALMP
Shock	0.78***	0.68***	0.51***
	(0.12)	(0.12)	(0.12)
PR with weak CD * shock	0.74***	1.24***	1.53***
	(0.26)	(0.32)	(0.27)
PR with strong CD * shock	0.12	0.24	0.25
	(0.16)	(0.24)	(0.27)
Unexpected growth	−0.15***	−0.24***	−0.44
	(0.01)	(0.03)	(0.19)
Share population under 15	0.52***	—	—
	(0.17)	—	—
Share population over 65	0.30	0.43***	—
	(0.17)	(0.02)	—
Automatic disbursements	0.69***		
	(0.11)		
N	493	483	397
Adj. R-squared	0.59	0.64	0.27

Key: *: p<.10; **: p<.05; ***: p<.01 (two-tailed tests)
Note: These are the results from the second stage estimation described in the text. Country fixed effects have been omitted.

defined as the annual drop in industrial employment as a share of the working age population, incorporated into a nonlinear model. The results are reported in Iversen and Soskice (2014). This analysis also shows that our common shock variable, as defined above, is fairly highly correlated with the deindustrialization variable, measured as annual means (.64).

Knowledge Economies and Their Political Construction

Even in the tumultuous century since the end of the First World War, arguably the greatest "shock" to advanced capitalist democracies has been the ICT revolution—though the economist's jargon use of "shock" is hardly a good description of the exponential development since the Second World War of computing and the electronic transfer of information. It is certainly the greatest technology regime change since the so-called "scientific revolution" based on huge corporations, with its subsequent metamorphosis into Fordism, which began in the late nineteenth century.

We argue in this and the next chapter that the ICT revolution illustrates very well the underlying hypotheses of the book: first, that advanced capitalist democracies have been remarkably resilient in the face of major shocks—even given the rise of populism, neither advanced capitalism, nor advanced democracy, nor the autonomy of the advanced nation state, are under attack. Second, that the advanced capitalist democracies face political opposition from groups who (i) feel that they and their children are left out of and excluded from the benefits of the "American Dream" (or equivalent), especially if they feel "others" (notably immigrants) are benefiting in their place; *and* (ii) can organize (or be organized) politically. Third, apart from small isolated groups—for example, the Occupy movement (themselves typically potential winners of the knowledge economy)—effective political opposition is in no way socialist, nor is it concerned to destroy or take over advanced capitalism; this is consistent with our basic argument that *advanced* capitalism should be analyzed in terms of the basic complementarity at the *national* level of the interests of advanced capital and the more skilled part of the population, and the many other groups who in turn benefit from the more skilled—and not in terms of the conflict between capital and labor (as in Piketty or Streeck, to cite particularly prominent recent accounts).

In 4.1, we sketch out the massive changes in economy, polity, and society which have stemmed from the (painful) emergence of the knowledge economy. Thus, we take a quite different perspective than the many commentators who see these changes as exogenously driven by a new liberal hegemony, or by globalization, or by the resurgence of capitalism, or some interrelated combination: in our analysis we locate the driver squarely in the massive change of technological regime, *enabled* by the set of policies that allowed this change to take place. Moreover, short of major political dislocations, advanced societies are likely only a partial distance from far greater technological breakthroughs. If the scientific revolution is dated to the last decades of the nineteenth century and lasted until the 1970s, the information era has only seriously been underway since the 1980s or 1990s, or for perhaps three decades.

Knowledge economies did not spring spontaneously from the ICT revolution. In 4.2 we argue that knowledge economies have been enabled by a different political economic framework from that which supported Fordism. We describe this framework as "embedded knowledge-based liberalism." By contrast to those who attribute these changes to ideational drivers or to the forces of advanced capitalism concerned to roll back redistribution, the welfare state, and collective bargaining, we rehearse the basic argument of the book and how it might apply to the information era (in section 4.3) and show how the shift of the political economic framework through

the 1980s and early 1990s was taken deliberately by democratically elected governments in order to strengthen the economy and
further their own careers (4.4). In 4.5 and 4.6 we explain in some
detail how the framework change to embedded knowledge-based
liberalism in the 1980s and early 1990s provided the foundations for
the knowledge economies to flourish: a process very far from completed. We highlight the emergence of winners and losers from this
ongoing construction, and how it has engendered new geographical
(big city versus peripheral areas) and educational (graduate versus
non-graduate) cleavages—cleavages that we will examine in depth
in chapter 5.

Our basic argument is that democratic governments have a strong
political incentive to respond to technological shocks by pursuing
policies—regulatory, educational, and macroeconomic—that will
further the economic benefits of these shocks to a majority of voters,
generating in the process a pivotal constituency that supports a continuation and deepening of policies on the same path. As we saw
in the previous chapter, this in no way implies that those adversely
affected by technological change will be compensated. Instead, winners are rewarded, and despite populist reactions to this dynamic,
winners (including "aspirational families") outnumber losers, which
is usually what matters politically. In the face of major shocks, and
the technological regime change generated by the ICT revolution
has certainly been such a major shock, advanced capitalist democracies are therefore resilient.

More specifically, in support of our theory of the resilience of
advanced capitalist democracies, we make five basic points:

(1) In response to massive technological change, the political
decisions setting up the institutional framework change to permit
embedded knowledge-based liberalism were taken through the
1980s and early 1990s by democratic governments in the advanced
democracies. This process inevitably developed at different paces
in different advanced economies. But policies represented—with
many qualifications, and very broadly—decentralizing and liberal-
izing measures as well as skill-enhancing policies designed to take
advantage of the greater power that information technology put into

the hands of small skilled groups and educated individuals in the interest of improving economic efficiency and competitiveness. In no way can this shift be understood simply as a *consequence* of new technology. Governments could have protected the status quo and shut down its adoption, as did the Soviet Union until close to its demise (indeed, we believe, partially causing its demise). Likewise, policies in many current middle-income countries are not conducive to technological progress because they protect hierarchically organized oligopolies and their insider labor forces (Schneider 2013).

(2) We show that, given this framework change, the construction of knowledge economies took place primarily through the education, location, and career choices by (especially) young people, and through related choices by knowledge-based companies, including multinationals, tied together by skill clusters and social networks. These choices certainly led to increased inequality (though with important differences across advanced economies), including increased income inequality as a result of skill-(higher-education) based technological change and increased wealth inequality: most notably through house price increases in big successful cities. We will argue that it makes little sense to think that these complexes of developments of micro decision-making reflected advanced capitalism acting as a *political force*, as Piketty suggests when he discusses capital reasserting itself, the "fundamental inequality" of $r > g$, or government rolling back the egalitarian *"trentes glorieuses"* (the three decades after the Second World War) under the weight of global competition for capital.

(3) Our analysis shows how the construction of knowledge economies built up complexes of specialized knowledge resources at the national level in the advanced nation-states. Because these knowledge resources have been embodied in colocated skill clusters of well-educated workers and researchers, companies cannot (at all easily) move them across locations: knowledge-based capital is the reverse of footloose. Hence, since the early 1990s there has been a profusion of FDI of knowledge-based foreign multinational enterprises (MNEs) tapping into these knowledge resources through subsidiaries and vice versa. From that perspective the construction

of the knowledge economy has reinforced the national knowledge base: instead of Friedman's flat earth (Friedman 2005), there is a highly uneven topography of knowledge competences in skill clusters across the advanced world (Iammarino and McCann 2013, Overman and Puga 2010, Storper 2013).

(4) As we saw in the previous chapter, redistribution in many advanced economies did not increase to compensate for increased market inequality. But we will argue that that was the consequence of democratic decisions: in particular, hostility by old middle-class voters to the poor and by disinterest among the rising middle classes to the plight of the declining old middle classes. By and large, moreover—as we have shown in the previous chapter—in those advanced economies in which there was effective protection for full-time workers in labor markets, employment protection changed little: established workers ensured that their conditions did not worsen.

(5) We show how the construction of the knowledge economy and the creation of winners and losers has led to geographical (big-city versus peripheral areas) and educational (graduate versus nongraduate) segregation of advanced societies. In chapter 5, the political construction of populism is seen as a consequence of this emerging social cleavage.

4.1. The ICT Revolution and Societal Transformation

The slowly gathering technological regime change brought about by development of information and communication technologies is arguably the most profound and continuing—and probably accelerating—shock (or set of shocks) to impact the advanced capitalist democracies in the past century: in terms of economic consequences, more so even than the Second World War and the financial crises of the 1930s and 2000s. Starting with the first commercial computers in the late 1940s and propelled by the discovery of the microprocessor in 1971 and the development of the internet in the early- to mid-1990s, we will argue that it precipitated the painful and at times conflictual transformation of the advanced world from Fordism into contemporary knowledge economies.[1] It has brought with it a whole range of further technological breakthroughs in the life sciences and biotechnology, in robotization and artificial intelligence, virtual and augmented reality, as well as in materials and nanotechnology, in sensor technology and mobile and cloud computing, and these have all fed on each other. Even so, short of major social or political dislocations we are likely only in the early stages of greater technological change (Rosenberg 2006; Brynjolfsson and McAfee 2013), which we discuss further in chapter 6.

This continuing process has already generated massive social, educational, locational, economic, organizational, and political change, if the contemporary world is compared to the post–Second World War decades. It has notably led to the empowerment of women in a way unimaginable in the 1950s and 1960s, even less imaginable at any earlier stage in recorded history. In addition, more than half of young people (and a greater proportion of young women) now go through some form of higher education, contrasting to the elite-driven postwar world in which only a small minority went to university. And large successful growing cities attracting skill clusters and young professionals and innovative companies as well as high value-added services have reversed the suburbanization movement of earlier postwar decades (Glaeser, Kallal et al. 1992).

But if this is a period of massive change it is also a period of massive dislocation. As we discussed in the previous chapter, it has generated major increases in income and wealth inequality, which marks an unwinding, and then a reversal, of the movement toward equality of the postwar decades (Atkinson and Piketty 2011). There are many differences in the pace and form of this reversal across advanced economies: the exceptional rise in the share of top incomes to which Atkinson and Piketty have drawn our attention has been primarily confined to the United States and UK. The rise in market, but not always in posttax, Ginis is universal.

The great rise in higher education has been accompanied almost necessarily by a major cleavage between graduates and nongraduates, and (as we will see later) this and its translation into a locational cleavage has been a main driver of the development of populism: that, over time, younger graduates were increasingly associated with successful expanding cities (skill agglomerations) while many nongraduates, even with skills and high school education, felt "left behind" in smaller, less successful, peripheral communities (Goodhart 2013).

There has also been significant growth in poverty, especially in the United States and the UK, to a lesser extent in continental Europe, notably Germany, and to a lesser extent still in Scandinavia. The term the "precariat" has been coined by Guy Standing (2011) to refer to this growing army of the "undeserving poor," living on benefits seen by the employed as unreasonably generous. In the next chapter we discuss how such hostility toward the poor is part of the emerging populist ethos that has taken root in the "old" middle classes: those mostly semiskilled workers who did well in the Fordist economy but who have been losing out in the new economy, often forced to accept lower-paid jobs and diminished benefits. This is a nastier, darker side of these massive societal changes.

In summary: the contemporary advanced world is in most economic, social, and political ways radically different from the Fordist era and the postwar decades; and, in many respects, unrecognizable to earlier generations. In addition, while these great changes have produced many winners, they have also created many losers. Our underlying hypothesis is that the main driver of societal transformation has been the technological regime change facilitated by the ICT revolution, but this change has involved complementary political change that permitted the shift to take place and is the result of deliberate choice by ambitious politicians.[2]

In pushing this argument, we reject the notion that globalization was the driving force. To the contrary, globalization was enabled by decisions of governments to liberalize trade and capital markets, which in turn fueled investment in locally rooted technology clusters, and, in the case of short-term financial capital movements, signaled a credible commitment to balanced budgets and nonaccommodating monetary policies (especially when accompanied by independent central banks). Nor was it driven by the collapse of the Soviet Union, or the consequent development of the transitional economies of East Central Europe and the rise of the extraordinary manufacturing capacity of East Asia and China. We broadly see the causation as going in the opposite direction: that it was direct and indirect effects of the politically enabled ICT revolution which caused both. Had they not happened, we believe industry in the advanced world would have become automated and robotized at a much slower pace. Capitalism was reinvented by democratically elected governments.

4.2. The Embedded Knowledge-based Liberal Framework

The causality of these changes requires closer scrutiny. It is tempting but wrong to conceptualize this great transformation in a technologically determinist way—as coming about *simply* as a direct if prolonged result of the (exogenous) technological shock of the information technology revolution. We argue in this section that a major set of strategic and at times conflictual political decisions in the advanced democracies were necessary to create the radically different institutional political economic framework that brought about the gradual collapse of Fordism and the construction of knowledge economies. We will refer to this as the "embedded knowledge-based liberal framework": partly in homage to Ruggie's (1982) insight that liberalism is embedded in national institutions, and partly as an abbreviation of the wider set of interrelated strategic directions linked to knowledge-intensive production.

First, strategic—and contentious—political choices were and remain necessary in enabling this technological transformation through institutional reforms. Second, these strategic political choices were made by democratically elected national governments in the advanced economies in a context of potential winners and losers from the collapse of Fordism emerging from the mid-1970s on. Indeed, the key strategic choices of *regulated liberal globalization and mass higher education* were made in the 1980s and early 1990s in most of the advanced economies.

To understand these choices we begin by setting out what is meant by regulated liberal globalization and mass higher education. These we argue might be seen as the key "public goods of advanced capitalism" and were and remain needed to convert the ICT revolution into knowledge economies. The logic bringing about these public goods will become clearer as the modus operandi of the knowledge economy is set out below, but a brief preview of the explanation will help the reader navigate the chapter.

Realizing the benefits of information and communications technology lies in enabling educated and skilled workers, with individual access to computing power and to the internet, to take necessarily *decentralized* decisions. Monitoring is difficult and the "product" of effort is hard to define ex ante. Since individual decisions need generally to be consistent with wider corporate strategies, themselves operating under greater uncertainty and with less central direction, this in turn typically requires complex processes of joined-up colocated decision-making within a company operating in a particular specialized area. To be available to move to other such specialized companies, and for other specialized companies to be able to tap into that specialized area of knowledge, both skilled workers and companies (or their subsidiaries) need to locate in the geographical proximity: hence skill clusters. The implication of this is that specialized knowledge competences are geographically distributed in larger or smaller agglomerations across the advanced world, producing sophisticated and differentiated goods and services, either as final products or as inputs into other goods and services developed elsewhere in other knowledge locations. Thus, knowledge economies make up a radically specialized advanced world of geographically distributed skill clusters, often in large agglomerations of smaller skill clusters. In this advanced world, knowledge-intensive companies are complex portfolios of domestic and foreign direct investments: "capital chases skills" in a contemporary business school metaphor.[3] Multinationals play a central role in tapping into multiple skill clusters and tying together complementarities of knowledge (Cantwell and Iammarino 2003; Iammarino andMcCann 2013; Whitley 2010). Rugman (2005, 2012) argues that many of these knowledge-intensive multinationals operate primarily within their own triads (North America, Europe, and East Asia), so that globalization across the advanced world may not well reflect their geographically ordered portfolios.

The cost of moving embedded knowledge in the advanced world is highlighted by the difficulty of MNCs in integrating knowledge from their FDI subsidiaries into their core activities. The only way to accomplish this is to have their own highly educated workforces physically move to and from their subsidiaries on a regular basis. These "core-MNC employees" have to absorb the tacit "integrating" skills to enable the relevant knowledge complementarities to be captured. Indeed, one hypothesis is that Rugman's important "triadization" finding is explained in part by the need for sufficient proximity between MNC core and subsidiary to enable physical travel on a regular basis.

"Footloose capital" may move fairly costlessly across the "flat earth" (in Thomas Friedman's metaphor) of the nonadvanced world, but the advanced world is one of many valuable peaks of specialized knowledge, the knowledge being embedded in the social networks of colocated, highly educated, and relatively immobile skill clusters. It is in these skill clusters that the value-added of advanced knowledge-based capitalism is dependent. Companies within these skill clusters can of course be bought and sold, but the value-adding resources are much more immobile: largely because they consist of high-skilled workers who are themselves dependent on other high-skilled workers. Patents and intellectual property is only an exception to this in the rare cases in which it is not complementary with tacit knowledge—as is the case for some pharmaceutical patents.

All this comes with major regulatory changes toward greater openness, both in terms of trade—including sophisticated high value-added services—but even more so in terms of capital mobility. Many of these changes took place in the second half of the 1980s (including the Single European Act). Thus, we have a different understanding of what is often seen as an ideational or ideological move to liberalism, and away from the regulated "Keynesian" international environment of the postwar decades. But in our interpretation this goes far beyond deregulation (it frequently involved flexible reregulation) to whole transformations of the educational environment, including mass university participation.

Our claim is that this shift reflected the desire by governments to promote their knowledge sectors. To accomplish this governments have had to undertake a wide series of reforms that reconfigure the political economic infrastructure. We need to be clear about what the "public goods" of advanced capitalism are—namely, the political/institutional framework rules and conditions which make such a knowledge world possible—before we look more carefully at why democratic governments adopted them. Most fundamentally the new framework has depended on the following set of conditions (in comparison to the Fordist era):

(1) *Higher education:* a massive transformation and upgrading of education, most notably of higher education and research. Figure 4.1 shows the share of a younger (25–34) and older (55–64) age cohorts with higher (tertiary) degrees from 1990 to 2015. The effect of transformation was already apparent in 1990, with much higher education levels among the young, and continued investment in higher education has more than doubled the education levels in the population as a whole over a twenty-five-year period—reaching more than fifty percent in younger cohorts in many countries.[4] The generational gap in education is, we will see in chapter 5, partly to blame for a growing populist cleavage in politics, but it is important to keep in mind that older generations are linked to younger ones through family ties, and if we include upper secondary education, well over fifty percent of the electorate in all ACDs has a longer education. Adding "aspirational" families to middle-level education to the university-education the welfare of a large majority is thus tied to the continued expansion of the knowledge economy.

(2) *Decentralized competition across the advanced world:* an across-the-board decentralization of decision-making in terms of both corporate strategy and employee autonomy, permitting the opening-up of product markets across the advanced world in response to the radical geographical specialization of goods and services. Compared to the highly centralized, vertically integrated, and hierarchically organized companies of the Fordist era, the organization of companies in the knowledge economy are rooted in clusters of highly skilled workers working with complementary

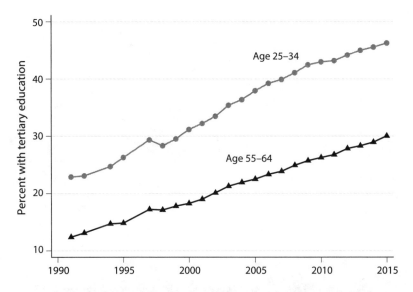

FIGURE 4.1. Percent with tertiary degrees, 1990–2015, by age group (25–34 and 55–64). *Note*: Population with tertiary education is defined as those having completed graduate education, by age group. *Source*: OECD, Education at a Glance, population with tertiary education (indicator). doi: 10.1787/0b8f90e9-en Accessed on August 13, 2017. Graphs are annual averages for 19 advanced democracies: Australia, Austria, Belgium, Canada, Denmark, Finland, France, Germany, Ireland, Italy, Japan, Korea, the Netherlands, New Zealand, Norway, Sweden, Switzerland, the UK, and the United States. For some years data are missing for some countries (the minimum number of observations is 13), but the graph looks almost identical whether the sample is restricted to the minimum number with continuous annual observations.

and often very specialized technologies in geographically confined spaces. The opening-up of these skill clusters across the advanced world or triad to foreign direct investment (FDI) by knowledge-intensive companies has both been responding to and aiding this radical geographical specialization of knowledge competences. Capital controls and restrictions on FDI access have been eased, as captured in figure 4.2, and this has led to an exponential increase in the stock of FDI as percent of GDP, from about twenty percent in 1990 to about 120 percent in 2013, which has intensified national and regional specialization. Only the most knowledge-intensive firms can set up foreign subsidiaries (Helpman et al. 2004), and while MNCs benefit from local knowledge clusters they also contribute knowledge to these (Coe et al. 2009; Greenaway and Kneller 2007).

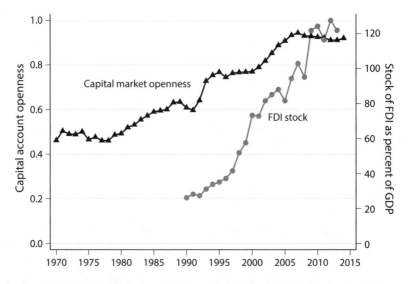

FIGURE 4.2. Capital market openness and the stock of FDI in advanced democracies, 1970 (1990) to 2014 (2013). *Notes*: FDI stock is the sum of outward FDI stock, the value of the resident investors' equity in and net loans to enterprises in foreign economies, and inward FDI stock, the value of foreign investors' equity in and net loans to enterprises resident in the reporting economy. Capital account openness is a summary measure of four measures of openness to cross-border capital transactions: (i) the absence of multiple exchange rates; (ii) lack of restrictions on current account transactions; (iii) lack of restrictions on capital account transactions; and (iv) no requirement to the surrender of export proceeds. The index is normalized to a range between 0 (minimal openness) and 1 (maximal openness). For both measures the graph shows averages for 19 advanced democracies: Australia, Austria, Belgium, Canada, Denmark, Finland, France, Germany, Ireland, Italy, Japan, Korea, Netherlands, New Zealand, Norway, Sweden, Switzerland, the UK, and the United States (Korea is missing from capital openness measure). *Sources*: FDI stock: OECD International Direct Investment database. Capital account openness: Armingeon et al. (2016) based on Chinn and Ito (2006, 2008).

The "public goods" created by education and investment—here referring specifically to open-access fluid skill clusters—reinforced decentralization of decision-making for highly educated and skilled individuals, at the same time reorganizing hierarchical knowledge-intensive companies into (something more resembling) federations of horizontal units. Just as decentralization enabled the transformation from the standardized goods and services of the Fordist world into dynamic highly differentiated product markets, so it enabled increasingly educated individuals to pursue correspondingly nonstandardized careers. In relation to knowledge economies, *globalization* refers primarily to highly skilled workers and knowledge-intensive companies, regardless of national origin, combining and recombining within the national boundaries of these economies.

(3) *Regulated liberalization.* The advanced world has also seen a pervasive rise in regulation; we follow Levi-Faur, Jordana, and Kaletsky in seeing this as integral to the knowledge economy, and an increasingly major qualification to a simplistically Thatcherite perspective (Jordana and Levi-Faur 2004; Levi-Faur 2005; Kaletsky 2010). Reregulation mirrors a radical decline in the efficacy of contracts in moving from the standardized world of Fordism (with standardized goods and services, including well-defined employment, insurance and financial contracts, with limited complexity and customization, and limited future uncertainty) to knowledge economies with a multiplicity of goods and services, with complexity and variety, and with radical uncertainty, in which networked products and their externalities become important. The simple standardized contracts in the private sector, and the correspondingly simple rules set by public bureaucracies through administrative and hierarchical decision-making, were no longer effective for many sophisticated modern activities. This is most notably the case as a result of financialization: the interaction between financial systems and the macroeconomy has become increasingly complex; and this has led to further waves of regulation.

Specifically, attention should be drawn to three related strategic political choices in particular regulatory policy areas:

(4) *Financialization.* An implication of the radical destandardization of careers and of company organization and decision-making (decentralized competition) and the increase in uncertainty which has accompanied this shift, has been the need for a transformation of the financial sector, and also the insurance sector, from one which provided standardized financial products to individuals and companies to one capable of generating complex, customized, risk-bearing and risk-insuring assets. This shift is reflected in the IMF's measure of financial development (figure 4.3), which is defined as "a combination of depth (size and liquidity of markets), access (ability of individuals and companies to access

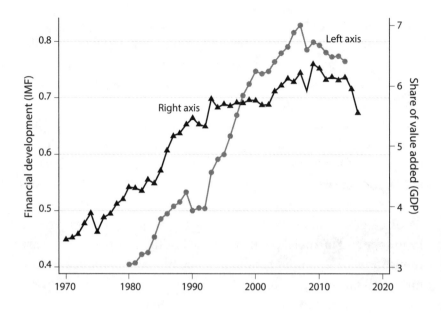

FIGURE 4.3. Financialization of advanced economies, 1970–2015. *Notes*: Line with circles shows IMF's index of financial development; line with triangles shows the average share of value added (in percent) accounted for by finance and insurance, for 19 advanced economies: Australia, Austria, Belgium, Canada, Denmark, Finland, France, Germany, Ireland, Italy, Japan, Korea, the Netherlands, New Zealand, Norway, Sweden, Switzerland, the UK, and the United States. *Source*: Svirydzenka (2016). OECD (2017), "National Accounts at a Glance." Value added by activity (indicator). doi: 10.1787/a8b2bd2b-en. Accessed on August 15, 2017.

financial services), and efficiency (ability of institutions to provide financial services at low cost and with sustainable revenues, and the level of activity of capital markets)" (IMF 2016, 5). The index closely tracks the expansion of finance and insurance in total output, also shown in figure 4.3.

As with every element of the complex institutional framework discussed here, many different interests have been involved in the development of financialization; Lapavitsas (2014) notably analyzes it as reflecting the power of capital. Without question it has had problematic consequences, including financial crises (discussed in 4.7 below). What we argue here is that—for all its problematic consequences, including financial crises and whoever were the key actors in its political promotion—financialization is a necessary part of the knowledge economy, and it is indirectly supported by a majority in the electorate for this reason.

This is not simply a matter of demand for more complex financial products by firms to hedge against uncertainty in an economy that is simultaneously more decentralized and globalized; it is also a matter of educated workers demanding easier access to credit as they pursue increasingly "nonlinear" careers with more frequent changes in jobs, house purchases, flexible mortgages and savings, time off for retraining and additional schooling, and moves back and forth between work and family (especially as child birth is delayed among high-educated women), as well as complex retirement and partial retirement choices. Because of the implied volatility in income, access to credit markets serves an increasingly important income-smoothing function that is not adequately addressed by the social protection system.

(5) *Macroeconomic management:* as discussed in chapter 3, there has been a widespread move to central bank independence combined with inflation targeting or membership of the Eurozone. In addition, apart from the prolonged zero lower bound in the post-financial-crisis world when fiscal policy activism replaced or at least augmented monetary policy, governments have adopted some form of "consistent fiscal framework." This usually includes delegation of budget-setting power to a finance ministry with veto power over individual spending ministries, as explained by Von Hagen and Hallerberg (1999) and Hallerberg (2004).

These developments can be seen as a consequence of three concerns: first, as discussed in the previous chapter, where wage bargaining is to some degree coordinated, but not fully centralized, as in most of the advanced economies of northern Europe, central bank independence and inflation targeting generates wage restraint. Related, it is arguably easier to fine-tune modern economies through short-term interest rates than through fiscal policy. And it is certainly true that after the macroeconomic turmoil from the ending of Bretton Woods to the early 1990s, the period from then until the financial crisis in 2007, the so-called Great Moderation, was marked by very low amplitude output-inflation movements (even if this partially masked the large financial cycle which was building).

Second, given the requirement of open financial markets, and hence the absence of controls on capital movements, fixed exchange rates are problematic since markets can bet against them with little risk: the two effective options are therefore flexible rates or membership of a common currency. With floating rates, an independent central bank must provide the monetary policy anchor to stabilize exchange rates and prevent the build-up of inflationary pressures. The need for credible commitments to a low-inflation environment is itself an additional motivation to give up capital controls. In a currency union like the Eurozone, the common central bank sets policies for all, and it cannot be beholden to any government.

Third, in an advanced world in which product market competition is through variety and innovation, and in which knowledge-based companies are frequently networks of international subsidiaries, inflation and exchange rate movements are particularly costly and low inflation targeting (or at last equal inflation across advanced economies) offers some guarantee of exchange stability (as well as by definition low inflation). The data for inflation rates in relation to the adoption of inflation targeting is shown in figure 4.4 for four countries with high inflation in the 1980s (see chapter 3 for more on central bank independence).

(6) *Product market competition* and *cooperative labor.* The above "public goods" of advanced capitalism in the information era are different from those complementary to the more organized, hierarchical, and centralized world of Fordism. But two further (key) requirements are highly significant in the knowledge economy era, even if they also held (less effectively at least in the UK and United States) under Fordism. These are that product markets operate under conditions of strong competition; and that the framework of labor markets and industrial relations ensures that workforces behave cooperatively. In the previous chapter, we considered changes in the industrial relations systems, especially the decline of unions in LMEs and continued coordination in a more decentralized system in CMEs; here, we highlight production market competition (which of course also constrain unions). Competition policies are set at the national level as well as the European and international levels (if we

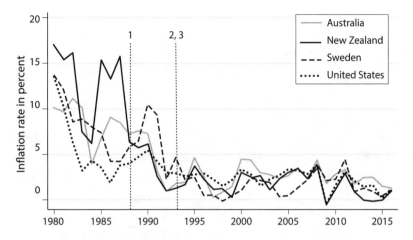

FIGURE 4.4. Inflation rates before and after adoption of inflation targetingl. *Notes*: Dates inflation targeting was first adapted: 1) Reserve Bank of New Zealand, April 1988; 2) Sveriges Riksbank (Swedish central bank), January 1993; 3) Reserve Bank of Australia, March 1993. The United States had no formal inflation target over most of this period but did adopt a target of 2 percent in January 2012. *Source*: IMF, International Financial Statistics and data files. Downloaded from https://data.worldbank.org/indicator/FP.CPI.TOTL.ZG?locations=AU&page on April 24, 2018.

include trade). In the EU, competition policy has emerged as one of the most important functions of the Commission, with a powerful Commissioner for Competition (even if its highly technical nature draws little attention in the social science literature) (Cini and Mc-Gowan 1998; McGowan 2010). In the United States, antitrust law, of course, builds on the Sherman Act of 1890 and the Clayton Act of 1914, but there is broad consensus that consumer-centered competition policies have been notably strengthened since the late 1970s, marked by the publication of Robert Bork's *The Antitrust Paradox* in 1978 (see Hovenkamp 2015).

The OECD has developed an economy-wide indicator of the strength of product market regulation, beginning in 1998 and updated every five years (the latest at the time of writing is 2013). According to this measure, product market competition policies are much stronger on average in ACDs than in the emerging economies included in the study, and they have been notably strengthened over time with convergence to a highly procompetition regulatory framework by 2013 (see figure 4.5).[5] There is every reason to believe that

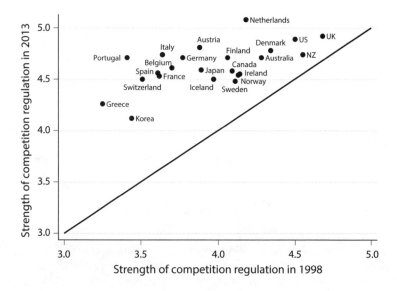

FIGURE 4.5. The strengthening of product market competition policies in ACDs, 1998–2013. *Notes*: The index of strength of the regulatory competition framework varies between 0 and 6, with 6 being the most pro-competition framework. The specific indicators used for the index are listed in footnote 7. First observation for the United States is 2003, not 1998. *Source*: Koske et al. (2015)

this change is a continuation of a trend dating back to the 1980s, with falling barriers to trade and FDI, privatization of state enterprises, and opening of network sectors to competition. Thus, Koedijk et al. (1996) found that while continental Europe had been slow to adopt competition reforms compared to Britain or the United States, such reforms were well under way in 1990, and the OECD data show almost complete convergence since then.

A key reason that maintenance of competitive markets became, and remains, so central is that the more easily companies can dominate markets through network externalities, as in communications or social media, the more important is flexible but tough competition regulation. In the Fordist economy, large vertically integrated companies sometimes attained very dominant positions in the domestic economy—in some cases spurred by governments that were eager to promote "national champions"—but they were almost invariably constrained by open trade and international competition. Modern MNEs based on technologies with strong network externalities,

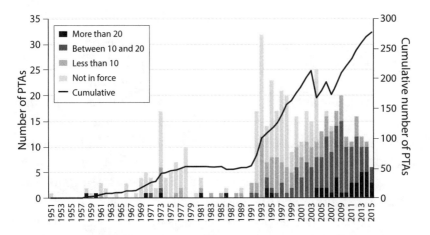

FIGURE 4.6. Number and depth of trade agreements, 1951–2015. *Notes*: The solid line shows the total number of preferential trade agreements (PTAs), while the bars show the number of provisions in each agreement. More provisions imply greater depth. The figure covers all trade agreements worldwide, but the majority of high-depth agreements occurs between advanced economies, especially in Europe and North America. *Source*: Hofmann, Claudia; Alberto Osnago, and Michele Ruta. 2017. "Horizontal Depth: A New Database on the Content of Preferential Trade Agreements." Policy Research Working Paper, No. 7981. World Bank, Washington, DC. © World Bank. https://openknowledge.worldbank.org/handle/10986/26148. License: CC BY 3.0 IGO.

such as Facebook or Amazon, can potentially attain dominant global market positions. Technological disruption can and does sometimes upend such market dominance—as in the case of Microsoft's web browser—but preventing it in the first place speeds up technological change (Koedijk et al. 1996; Bourlès 2013).[6]

Across-the-board trade liberalization, although it is no longer sufficient to guarantee competition, makes it harder for companies to establish entrenched monopolistic or oligopolistic market positions. Trade liberalization is a global phenomenon, as illustrated in figure 4.6, but the agreements with the most extensive free-trade provisions and greatest impact have been between advanced democracies, especially in Europe (the creation of the internal market) and in North America (NAFTA). Complaints by the current US administration notwithstanding, all of these agreements are still in force, and the Trans-Pacific Partnership Agreement (TPP) has been substantially retained (now called the Comprehensive and Progressive Agreement for Trans-Pacific Partnership) even without formal US participation (but with Trump hinting that the United States may rejoin).

Our claim is that conditions (1) through (6)—*mass higher education, regulated liberal globalization, financialization, monetary macroeconomic management, effective product market competition* and *cooperative workplaces* in the advanced economies—constitute the broad institutional framework necessary for the ICT revolution to lead to knowledge economies. There is an implicit, more complex necessary condition, that the economy is already a technologically advanced economy and that the state will in fact make the technological investments needed for it to retain its technologically advanced status; or, in very rare circumstances, can build or help to build it up from scratch, as with South Korea or Taiwan. We will see in more detail later in this chapter—when we explain the operation of the knowledge economy—how all these different parts tie together. For now, we are simply noting that it would be difficult to imagine how a knowledge economy would work without—at least very loosely— such an institutional framework, in addition to advanced technological capabilities. For example, it is notable that the Soviet Union arguably had the centralized scientific computing expertise in the 1970s and 1980s to evolve into a knowledge economy, but could not pay the necessary political price in terms of a decentralized institutional framework; indeed, it was felt necessary to maintain prohibitions on personal computers until the late 1980s (Curtis 2006).[7] Without politically initiated reforms economies stagnate, even when they possess the necessary technologies and know-how.

4.3. Recapping the Basic Argument

In this section we address why and how this massive institutional reconfiguration came about as a result of a series of political decisions. Our explanation is that it reflected the democratic choice of autonomous governments across the advanced capitalist democracies, designed to further the political careers of politicians while simultaneously promoting economic growth. The "exogenous shock" of the information revolution created opportunities, but these could only be realized through institution-building by a strong state. The shock is thus a test of our fundamental argument that democracy is conducive to the advanced knowledge economy.

It is useful to briefly recap our fundamental hypotheses:

(1) Advanced capitalism is organized on a national basis, and, labor-skill intensive, it generates directly and indirectly a large educated and skilled workforce whose regeneration and upgrading is necessary for maintaining the dynamic resilience of advanced capitalism. Because this workforce is relatively highly skilled and educated (depending on the technology regime in place), and hence normally developing skills specific to the employer and co-employees, it is in a bargaining position—even if not necessarily collectively organized—to gain relatively high incomes. (An obviously unstated assumption is what might be called the "nonslavery" requirement: one could theoretically imagine a world in which any income above a subsistence level was taxed away by the state, so that there would be no incentive to vote for the promotion of the knowledge economy. Or to be even more fanciful, laws that required you to work for a particular employer and allowed employers to punish you for not working hard enough.)

Critically, from a political economic perspective, this skilled workforce constitutes an electorate whose broad interest is in the maintenance or regeneration of the infrastructure needed for making advanced capitalism competitive: the "public goods of advanced capitalism." This extends to electoral support or underpinning from many other economic sectors of society, beyond the obviously advanced capitalist sectors, which derive their income from the demand generated by the advanced sectors; these include many sheltered service sectors. And it is underpinned by an increasingly important "aspirational" electorate, deeply concerned that they and their children benefit from the advanced economy.

(2) This educated and well-rewarded workforce, as well as this wider aspirational electorate, also drives demand for innovative goods and services and thus is critical to the dynamic resilience/survival of advanced capitalism (contrast this to the technological failure of economies throughout history based on de facto slave

labor, with the status of wealthy landowners depending on the extent of their land and the number of their slaves, such as under the Roman Empire; the demand for innovation is here very limited, despite the high level of culture and intelligence of the elite). It also reinforces their electoral interests.

(3) These voters are generally "decisive" voters and regard a party as electable when they see its leaders as capable of and credibly committed to making the right strategic decisions in relation to the maintenance of advanced capitalism. Basically, this presupposes that mainstream parties build up a reputation for good economic governance, and parties have an incentive to do so in order to capture the group of decisive voters. As we noted in the previous chapter, reputation-building within parties is possible when younger generations of ambitious politicians can hold their leaders accountable and ensure that they invest in the party label, which is critical for future electoral success.

(4) The essence of democracy is not equality or redistribution. It is instead that the decisive voters—whether they include lower middle or upper middle classes—want to secure a more or less constant share of the productive capacity of the economy for themselves, which is enabled by education and via social transfers largely paid through taxes by those at the top. If this "fundamental law of democracy" holds, the middle classes have a strong interest in promoting the knowledge economy, even when it creates disproportionate gains at the top. Concern for the poor is limited to the extent of the middle classes (or their offspring) being concerned about becoming poor themselves. For those who have acquired the necessary skills to benefit from the knowledge economy, this is a relatively minor consideration, and the interests of the poor are therefore rarely well-attended-to.

(5) It is generally very costly (if not often de facto impossible) to relocate the core competences of a knowledge-based company (or of a knowledge-based subsidiary) since they are based on the locational cospecific skills of the colocated workforce built up over a considerable period of time; hence the maintenance/renewal/ upgrading/regeneration of a country's advanced capitalist system reinforces national "ownership" and national access to its particular

collection of knowledge competences: that in turn both underlines the limitations of advanced companies using the threat of exit, and it enhances the autonomy of the national government in an advanced capitalist democracy. Moreover, were it not the case and were advanced knowledge-based companies easily able to relocate where they chose, the argument for a national government to invest in the educational, research and other resources necessary to sustain national advanced capitalism would be much more limited.

Hence *colocation* is critical to the survival of advanced capitalism, since advanced capitalist systems can only operate within an effective infrastructure which typically requires public funding. Conversely, for governments to have an incentive to invest in infrastructure requires that the advanced capitalist workforces, in which governments invest and from which advanced companies derive their value added, are geographically sticky and not footloose.

Thus we have argued in the book—in this chapter in the face of technological regime change—that advanced capitalist democracies are generally resilient in the three senses that: (i) strategic political change to reinvigorate advanced capitalism is a democratic choice, and (generally) seen as in the interest of decisive voters; (ii) that its reinvigoration reinforces both advanced capitalism and democracy; and (iii) that the colocation and cospecificity underlying advanced capitalism reinforce the anchoring of particular knowledge competences nationally and thus reinforce national democratic autonomy. It is in these senses that advanced capitalist democracies are typically resilient in the face of shocks. Thus we will argue that the autonomous democratic nation-state—which acts as the framework for advanced capitalism—does not hang on against all odds, but is positively reinforced by advanced capitalism, which in turns owns much of its dynamism to democracy. This is what we have called the symbiotic relationship.

(6) The elements above of our theory are fully sufficient to analyze the political construction of the knowledge-embedded liberalism framework largely taking place in the 1980s and early 1990s. And this framework has enabled knowledge economies to develop rapidly through the quarter-century or so since the early 1990s.

(7) An important part of a general theory of advanced capitalist democracy is to understand the conditions under which political opposition and discontent may grow. We set these conditions out now as part of the general theory in the next chapter. To anticipate, we argue that, at a deep underlying level, many people see something like an implicit social "contract" that citizens who behave properly in an advanced economy will benefit from it. And there are two elements to this implicit contract which make it quite congruent to our general analysis of advanced capitalism. First, just as we see advanced capitalism as being *nation-based*, so too is the implicit contract. It sees citizens of the advanced nation in question (at least those who have behaved "in the right way") as those entitled to the benefits. Those who are seriously poor, or dropouts, are not seen as "deserving"—they have not behaved in the right way. Second, just as we see advanced capitalism not as a compromise between capital and labor but as something more like a joint project, so those held responsible for breach of the implicit contract are not advanced capitalists but the government and established politicians; either this represents incompetence by the government, or their inability to control the borders and let immigrants take what should be "ours," or their favoring the undeserving poor or ethnic minorities, or simply having their fingers in the pie: in any case it is the established politicians (the establishment)—who are in control—who are guilty of the breach of the contract, and not the capitalist system (Hochschild 2016).

We have seen in the previous chapter that the collapse of Fordism caused many with a good secondary education to lose out in terms of both jobs and wages—what economists call the hollowing out of the middle. But governments have the capacity to compensate and provide new opportunities for these workers, and in particular to open the educational system to their children and bring these into the stream of wealth created by the knowledge economy. The problem is that democracy does not guarantee that politicians have incentives to do so. Losers may simply be left to lose, as we saw in the previous chapter, and this will be perceived as a breach of contract by those who cannot even aspire for their children to do well.

Until the 1990s, this social contract of the upward moving escalator was not questioned. But as the knowledge economy got underway, through the quarter-century after 1990, while many (most) big cities in the advanced capitalist democracies transformed themselves into high value-added agglomerations with graduate-intensive workforces, many other smaller communities, with lower levels of education, were left behind. Later in this chapter (in 4.5) we will see how this geographic and educational segregation has been caused in a major way by the development of the knowledge economy. The politics of the rise of populism is then discussed in the next chapter.

4.4. The Political Construction of the Embedded Knowledge-based Liberal Framework

In this subsection we look more closely at the construction of the embedded knowledge-based liberal framework. The three most common explanations are, first, that it represented the power of ideas, second the power of capital, and third the imperatives of new technology. As will have been evident from the main argument of the book, we take a different position: here it is seen as a set of interrelated strategic choices by the democratically elected governments of the advanced economies, which can be modeled as in Simmons and Elkin (2004) as a strategic complementarities game (see figure 4.7). The larger the number of advanced nation-states that chose embedded knowledge-based liberalism (weighted by their share of the output of advanced countries), the higher the payoff from adoption to remaining nonadopters because the scope for specialization in high-value-added production is scaled up. If the payoff to the nonadopter with the highest payoff is always positive, then the game is initiated once new technology makes reform sufficiently attractive, and this will lead to a cascade of changes beyond a certain tipping point. There were, of course, hiccups in this process, and adoption was far from conflict-free; nonetheless, all the advanced states eventually chose to adopt some version of the knowledge-based embedded liberalism framework. In terms of figure 4.7, the process gets underway because governments in both Britain and the

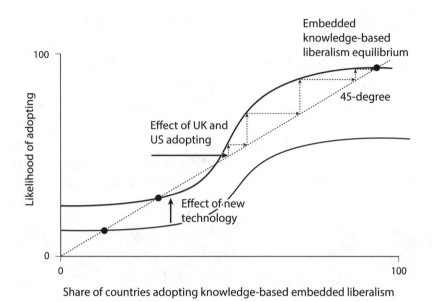

FIGURE 4.7. A strategic complementarities game of reforms

United States, representing a large share of output among advanced countries, decide to reform their institutions to overcome serious impediments to growth in those countries (thick horizontal arrow). This was enough to tip the balance in favor of reform in other advanced countries, setting off a cascade (dashed arrows) that is very consistent with the evidence presented above for the strengthening of competition policies (i.e., convergence over time to a more pro-competition regime). The effect of technological change is to make reform more attractive (shown as an upward shift in the curve in figure 4.7), but the transformation to a new equilibrium requires deliberate government action and would not have occurred without such action by the early adopters.

Our emphasis on democratic choices in response to electoral demands stands in contrast to the concept of *global liberalism* in much of the literature. Clearly the government policies that led to the new economy represented a large ideational shift (almost by definition), but they were not the *consequence* of ideas. Ideas are not (usually) conjured out of thin air; and there was a clear material basis behind these choices, reflecting the need, in response to electoral pressure for economic progress, for a massive decentralization of decision-making, which ICT required if it was to be effectively used, and if countries were to remain competitive in advanced sectors. The choice to institutionally accommodate the ICT revolution translated into election-winning strategies. Thus the story is not ideational, at least in the sense that ideas were the exogenous drivers of the adoption of this transformed political economic framework. Nor did these choices represent the reaction of *capital* to the egalitarian postwar decades, stifling or "suborning" democracy in the process, as Piketty and Streeck, in different ways, suggest. Quite to the contrary, the political power of capital has eroded over time, and in 4.7 we discuss why capital has not been in a position to impose threats on the elected governments of the advanced economies to bring about the changes it desired against the will of business. (As we develop at greater length below, in the most clear-cut case of change—namely, Thatcher in the UK—British business and finance was alarmed by and opposed to her proposals.)

4.4.1. THE ELECTORAL INCENTIVE

It is difficult to underestimate the importance of electoral incentives in driving political parties to institute economic reforms that push forward the advanced sectors. Massive investment in higher education, financialization, liberalization of trade and FDI, inflation-targeting, and strong competition rules were all ultimately instituted or reinforced to address middle-class demands for improvement in living standards. Our argument is not that democracy produces advanced capitalism, but that it can sustain and spur growth of the advanced sectors in a context where parties compete to be perceived among a majority as effective economic managers (even as they clash on issues of distributive politics). This is an equilibrium in ACDs, because the more voters cast their vote based on government reputation for good governance, the greater the incentive of parties to build up such reputations; and the more parties emphasize their reputations, the greater the incentive for voters to base their vote on reputation for good governance.

A large empirical literature that speaks to this issue is on "economic voting." The idea is that voters reward governments for good economic performance and punish them for bad performance. This can be based either on past performance ("retrospective voting") or expectations about future performance ("prospective voting"), or a combination, where past performance is used to predict future performance. The literature also distinguishes between "sociotropic" and "egotropic" (or pocketbook) voting, where the first is based on aggregate performance and the latter on personal economic outcomes.[8] In Lewis-Beck and Stegmaier's extensive recent review of the literature (updating and largely supporting the seminal 1994 piece by Nannestad and Paldam), they find that most evidence supports prevalence of sociotropic and retrospective voting, with the key consistent finding being that governments are held accountable for economic performance such as employment and income growth. This result holds across advanced democracies and institutional contexts (Lewis-Beck and Stegmaier 2014), and it seems to have only intensified with the decline in mass parties (Dassonneville and Hooghe 2017). The combination of rising employment opportunities and income growth is almost entirely due to investments in the advanced sectors of the economy; so, to us, this is strong evidence that electoral politics provide political parties with incentives to perform.[9]

An obvious limitation of this research is that in an equilibrium where mainstream parties behave as responsive reputation-based parties, policies to promote the economy become valence issues that will not show up as economic voting, since governments cannot be differentiated in equilibrium.[10] It is only when governments deviate from such behavior that we can empirically detect economic voting, even if such voting is ubiquitous. Evidently this does occur frequently enough to be detectable in voting behavior, but the economic voting literature may well underestimate the importance of electoral incentives to perform. Comparative work have shown that valence issues such as competence, integrity, and reliability are at the forefront of voters electoral calculations (Clark 2009; Abney 2013).

This suggests examining the content of what most voters expect from their government. Yet, most of the political economy literature ignores the valence nature of many economic policies and focuses on distributive issues instead. For example, there may be a broad bipartisan agreement on the need to expand the university-educated labor force, but most research focuses instead on the differences between the center-left and center-right in their relative emphasis on expanding access to higher education versus deepening the quality of such education. Important as these differences are, they do not capture the symbiosis between democracy and advanced capitalism that we are interested in.

Public-opinion scholars and organizations tend to compound this problem, because they are typically interested in uncovering disagreement in attitudes, not agreement. A well-designed survey question is one that creates variance across response categories. Again, in political economy this variance is typically about differences in distributional preferences. But there are exceptions. The latest ISSP survey on the role of government (carried out in 2005/6) include a few questions about policies with broad implications for the advanced sectors, which turn out to be valence issues. One is about education and reads:

> Listed below are various areas of government spending. Please show whether you would like to see more or less government spending in each area. Remember that if you say 'much more', it might require a tax increase to pay for it. Government should spend money: Education.

Respondents' answers are coded in five categories from 1 ("Spend much more") to 5 (Spend much less). The results for sixteen ACDs are shown in panel (a) of figure 4.8. Note that fully seventy-one percent of respondents (light gray bars) say they prefer more or much more spending on education; only three percent (dark gray bars) say they prefer less or much less spending. This pattern generally holds for all countries (support for more spending in the Scandinavian countries is lower than the mean, likely because these are also the countries with the highest current levels of spending).

Another question gauges respondents' support for government policies to assist industries developing new products, which can loosely be seen as support for public investment in R&D (panel b). Here, eighty-four percent say they favor or strongly favor such

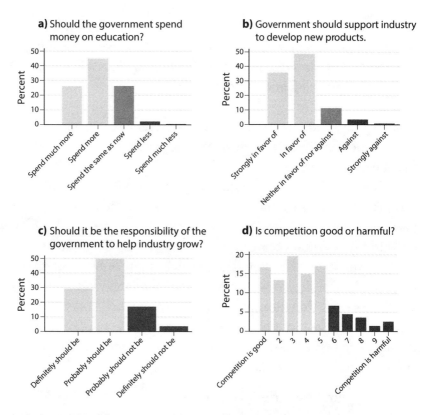

FIGURE 4.8. Support for government intervention in economy, by policy area: (a) *Should the government spend money on education? Notes*: Number of observations: 22689. Countries: Australia, Canada, Denmark, Finland, France, Ireland, Japan, South Korea, the Netherlands, New Zealand, Norway, Portugal, Spain, Sweden, Switzerland, and the United States. (b) *Government should support industry to develop new products. Notes*: Number of observations: 22403. Countries: same as in (a). (c) *Should it be the responsibility of the government to help industry grow? Notes*: Number of observations: 22123. Countries: same as in (a). (d) *Is competition good or harmful? Notes*: Number of observations: 57646. Countries: same as in panel a) but including the UK, Germany, Italy, and Israel; and excluding Denmark, Ireland, and Portugal. *Sources*: (a–c) ISSP, Role of Government IV, 2006; (d) World Values Survey, 1981–2014.

policies, and this result is backed by a broader question about whether it should be the responsibility of governments to help industry grow (panel c). In this case, seventy-nine percent say it should be.

Finally, the World Values Surveys include a question about another key government policy: competition. Here, eighty-one percent answer on the "good" side of the middle when asked whether competition is good or harmful. There is clearly a broad understanding of the economic benefits of competition, even if competition has negative connotations when it comes to interpersonal relations.

For some of these answers, there may well be an element of "cheap talk" (despite reference to the need for a tax to pay for new spending that accompanies the first question), and the wording of the question allows for some nuances in interpretation. On balance, however, we think these responses are indicative of the broad support for policies that promote the knowledge economy. Also note that this support extends well beyond the group of highly educated, and in that sense it implies a large number of aspirational voters. We see the data as an individual-level window into the preferences that underpin the ubiquitous finding discussed above, that voters vote for (against) governments producing good (bad) macroeconomic performance. Such public preferences are a major political foundation for the government-initiated policy changes we discuss below. A majority of voters expects governments to provide what we have called the "public goods of advanced capitalism" since they see their welfare depending on them.[11]

One issue related to voter preferences that has attracted much attention in both the economic voting literature and in the public opinion literature is the role of information. People may simply not have the necessary information to hold governments responsible. From a political economy perspective such lack of information could be explained by incentives for individuals to be "rationally ignorant." Yet, in Lewis-Beck and Stegmaier's (2014) reading of the evidence, people have "a good deal of knowledge about the economy . . . and they employ this in their economic vote." Public opinion scholars such as Bartels (2008) are less sanguine and conclude that many voters end up supporting policies that are ill-aligned with their economic interests despite declaring that they want to advance these interests (what Bartels calls "unenlightened self-interest"). Lack of information may also in part explain Gilens's (2005, 2012) finding that, for most policy areas where preferences differ, those with high income and education get their way far more often than those with middle and low income.

Other studies that extend the analysis to non-US countries are more cautious. Elkjær (2017) using Danish data finds that the middle and upper income classes appear equally influential, and the middle class is far more influential than the affluent when examining ISSP data for a broad sample of advanced democracies. The Elkjær finding is important because it may suggest an important limitation of the Bartels's and Gilens's methodology. Whereas their data (as well as the Danish data) are used to examine correlations between preferences for policy change and actual policy change, the ISSP surveys ask about preferred levels of spending, which are correlated with levels of actual spending. This matters because it is plausible that governments reflect the preferred mean level of spending or redistribution of middle classes—or coalitions between these with lower or higher classes—even as fluctuations of spending around these means are better aligned with expressed preferences of the affluent. Elkjær and Iversen (2018) show that this is largely due to those with high education and income being better informed about the changing constraints that affects fiscal policy—which could be a function of the standard business cycle and automatic stabilizers—even as they have little influence on spending *levels*.[12]

Our own reading of the comparative evidence points to two broad conclusions. First, in areas that have to do with promotion of the advanced sectors and economic growth, people have enough information to reward and punish governments for performance, and voters tend to agree on what the desirable policies are. In assessing Gilens's evidence, it is important here to note that, in three-quarters of the policy issues, middle- and high-income voters agree on the direction of needed change. Second, on issues of distributive politics, low-educated and low-income voters often lack the information to reliably vote their interests (at least as predicted by political economy models). For the educated middle classes, however, their interests appear to be well-attended to in public policies, and they have for the most part been able maintain their relative position in an expanding economy, as we showed in chapter 1. Thus, the median disposable income makes up a more or less constant share of average disposable income over time—what we have referred to as the fundamental law of democracy.

4.4.2. THE BRITISH REVOLUTION

The UK is indeed an exemplar case, and it is an early adopter that helped set in motion the cascade of reforms we outlined in the discussion of the network game above. After discussing the British experience, we will briefly consider three additional cases: two are CMEs, Denmark and Germany, and one is the distinct case of France. Together with the UK (and related LME cases) they capture the range of reforms that occurred in the aftermath of the transformation in Britain (and the United States).

Already in the mid-1970s, the minority Labour government with Callaghan as Prime Minister and Healey as Chancellor had rejected the protectionist position of the left-wing unions and left-wing members of the government (Tony Benn and Michael Foot) as a means to preserve employment in Fordist manufacturing sectors. When Thatcher came to power in 1979, it was accepted by the incoming Conservative government that a major change in economic strategy was necessary to enable the UK economy to face international competition effectively. There was considerable agreement politically in the Conservative leadership that this required both more effective management and more control over shop-floor unions. At the same time, it was agreed that a stable and much lower inflation rate was needed.

On these questions, the center and right of the Labour leadership (including Callaghan and Healey) were also agreed. But there was a major dispute within both parties about how these changes were to be brought about. On the one hand, the so-called "wets" inside the Conservative party (most notably Prior) believed the UK should move toward a German-style consensus or corporatist system. Thatcher did not believe this would work, probably correctly, since she doubted that the Confederation of British Industry (CBI) leadership would be able to impose policies on the CBI membership— indeed, the CBI leadership had been unable to deliver on price restraint, which it had offered the government in the mid-1970s (with members of the CBI board breaching the agreement).

Instead, Thatcher maintained that companies should face both a competitive international and national market environment and the possibility of hostile takeovers; and this required inter alia that the government got rid of the web of protective relations which enabled financial institutions in the city to maintain profitability in a sheltered environment. Equally forcefully, she pushed for anti-union legislation, to weaken the ability of unions to take industrial action, and she rejected the implicit understanding that the government would intervene to prevent a major company going bankrupt (though the government did in fact intervene to prevent the bankruptcy of the British Motor Company). This new competitive framework included major programs of denationalization. Finally, the Thatcher leadership endorsed a monetarist macroeconomic policy in which the central bank set the growth rate of the money supply, "allowing" unions to set the inflation rate but now with the understanding that unemployment would rise until inflation had come down to the rate of growth of the money supply.

What is relevant for our argument is that the debate on the direction of change in the economic framework took place largely among politicians. There was, as is well known, considerable resistance to these measures by unions; but once Thatcher had won the internal government argument, and Prior (initially Secretary of State for Employment) had been dispatched to the Northern Ireland office (a graveyard for politicians), Thatcher moved successfully against the unions. She said of Prior—with heavy Thatcherite irony—that "he had forged good relations with a number of trade union leaders whose practical value he perhaps overestimated." The dominant establishment wing of the CBI was deeply opposed to many elements of Thatcherite policy; Sir Terence Beckett, the CEO of Ford UK, and also the Director-General of the CBI, called in his keynote speech to the CBI annual conference in 1980 for the CBI to engage in a "bareknuckled fight with the Government." Thatcher was able to brush this attack aside, and made clear her distaste for corporatist relations with business. Equally she brushed aside the widespread opposition in the City to the Big Bang. And she proceeded to support the Single

European Act in 1986 designed to create a single internal market in the then EEC.

Nor did the adoption of embedded knowledge-based liberalism reflect the partisan color of governments. Not only in the UK did the Callaghan Labour government preceding Thatcher espouse key elements of it, just as Labour did under Kinnock and then Blair, who almost completely signed up to the Thatcherite agenda. But, more sharply still, Roger Douglas, the finance minister in David Lange's New Zealand Labor government in the early 1980s pushed through a radical economic liberalization program in the highly protected and subsidized NZ economy; here the opposition to liberalization was from the outgoing populist prime minister of the defeated National (i.e., conservative) party, Rob "Piggy" Muldoon—again, as in the UK, backed by large portions of the NZ business community as well as NZ unions. The same is true in the United States, where Reagan soundly defeated both Carter and Mondale, who favored nationally negotiated pacts between labor, big business, and the government, to fight inflation and unemployment.

4.4.3. REFORMS IN CMES: DENMARK AND GERMANY

It is our contention that the shift toward the knowledge economy has been facilitated by a set of broadly similar reforms that have allowed economic agents to take advantage of the economic possibilities opened up by the ICT revolution. But the precise character of these reforms differs depending on the existing economic and political institutions. In this section we discuss the transformation of two distinct CMEs, Denmark and Germany, and how they are similar and different from the British case.

A. Denmark. It is no accident that Britain led the reform process in Western Europe, because the country was rapidly falling behind most of the rest of Western Europe on almost every economic indicator. Real economic growth during the 1970s was a full percentage point below Germany's, unemployment was rising fast, and inflation was accelerating in wake of the first oil crisis, whereas in Germany it was quickly brought under control (sixteen- versus four-percent inflation in the second half of the 1970s). Despite falling domestic demand, British competitiveness and trade balances were deteriorating at the same time as government debt was accumulating. Again, both major British parties broadly agreed that drastic reforms were required, and such reforms were made politically feasible by the decline of union membership and the political marginalization of British industry. Democracy, in other words, induced reforms against the will of both business and labor (narrowly construed).

Perhaps the country that came closest to the UK in terms of deteriorating economic conditions at the end of the 1970s was Denmark. Suffering from a "British disease" of rising inflation and unemployment, chronic trade deficits, and growing debt, a conservative government coming to power in 1982 (led by Poul Schlüter) embarked on a set of economic and institutional reforms. As in Britain, one of the first policy shifts was to adopt a nonaccommodating monetary policy, by simultaneously tying the Danish currency to the deutsche mark and removing capital controls (yielding in the process virtually all policy-making power to the central bank). The target was semiskilled unions and public-sector unions, which were both seen as a source of inflation because of their influence in the centrally coordinated wage bargaining system ("solidaristic wage policies"). The shift in monetary policies was complemented by restrictive fiscal policies, themselves facilitated by a more central position of the finance ministry in the budgetary process (see Iversen 1998 and references therein for a more detailed account).

In combination, these policy changes greatly constrained public-sector unions because no government, national or local, was willing to raise taxes to finance wage increases, nor to drive up relative prices on public services where these were partially financed out-of-pocket (such as daycare). There was simply no appetite for higher taxes or copayments in the electorate. The macroeconomic policy shifts also reduced the power of the large union of semiskilled workers (SID) by facilitating a more decentralized wage-setting system that gradually became organized by bargaining cartels in which semiskilled unions were junior partners (Ibsen and Thelen 2017), and by moving to a minimum wage system for semiskilled workers (in the old centralized system their actual wages were set directly).

While the new Danish bargaining system differed from the German because of the continued, while diminished, role of semiskilled and public-sector unions, it nonetheless shared fundamental features of an industry- or sector-based coordinated bargaining system operating in a strictly nonaccommodating macroeconomic environment. With the shift inflation was brought under control and competitiveness and the trade balance gradually restored. In very broad strokes, but with important differences in the institutional details, a similar shift occurred later in Sweden (the macroeconomic policy changes were not complete until the early 1990s).

Successive center-right governments also embarked on reforms of credit and insurance markets, which had been heavily regulated until the 1980s. Capital account restrictions on capital inflows were abolished, and restrictions on bank lending and the regulatory separation of banking and insurance were lifted. This made it easier for new firms to get access to finance (often in foreign markets) and to hedge against risks, and it also allowed individuals much greater access to consumption loans and mortgages. The effect was to restore demand and (near) full employment, even as it also boosted real estate prices to the point where a bubble emerged in the mid-1980s (and again in the 2000s). In addition to financialization, publicly regulated utilities were privatized or deregulated, notably in telecommunication, and competition policies in a range of markets, including public services, were introduced or intensified. These changes were partly to comply with the rules for membership in the EC Internal Market, itself a commitment to competition, but it was also designed to encourage innovation, expand choice in public services, and contain inflationary pressures in the labor market.

While initially controversial, these reforms were largely endorsed and even furthered under subsequent center-left governments, notably those led by Poul Nyrup Rasmussen from 1993–2001. Privatization of public assets was continued, and the commitment to the hard currency policy, cross-cycle balanced budgets, and deepening of trade and financial liberalization was strengthened. The main innovations came in the areas of labor market polices, education, and social policies to facilitate a better work-family balance and to encourage upskilling (Campbell and Pedersen 2007). Labor market policies were shifted decisively toward activation with tighter time limits on unemployment benefits, but also guaranteed offers of re-training or work, as well as paid leaves for educational purposes—all designed to facilitate labor market flexibility while maintaining (re) employment security and social protection (a combination of poli-cies known as "flexicurity").

The state took a leading role in this transformation by modern-izing the large public sector, but it is important to understand that the policies were helped by a historically heavy involvement of em-ployers and unions in the training and unemployment systems, and as a result they were implemented with considerable consultation and coordination, in contrast to Britain, at the state, local and re-gional levels (Kjær and Pedersen 2001; Martin and Thelen 2011). Flexicurity also cannot be understood without acknowledging that job protection and long tenure rates never became an important feature of the Danish labor market, unlike the Germany case. There were consequently no entrenched insider interests that could block greater flexibility and upskilling.

Another key element in post–1980s reforms was massive expan-sion of educational opportunities at all levels—preprimary, voca-tional, and higher education. The share of twenty-four- to thirty-four-year-olds with tertiary education shot up from less than twenty percent in 1993 to over thirty percent in 2001, and this expansion was continued under subsequent governments regardless of parti-sanship. It currently stands at close to fifty percent, with more than half of the younger generation getting college degrees. Spending at other levels of the general education system, notable preprimary education, has also increased in line with entry of women into the labor market, and in the area of continuing vocational education and training, public money has been complemented by (decentralized) collective agreements and continuous negotiation involving unions, employers, and municipal and regional governments (Campbell and Pedersen 2007) that set aside money earmarked for retraining. In the Danish case upskilling has become, in many ways, a substitute for solidaristic wage polices (Ibsen and Thelen 2017).

This educational revolution happened to different degrees in all ACDs, and it is a critical ingredient of the shift toward the knowledge economy. Yet, what is distinctive about the Danish case, and also the other Nordic countries, is the success in bringing up the bottom. As measured by the OECD adult literacy test from the late 1990s (OECD 2000), the Nordic countries were essentially indistinguishable from liberal market economies in the top five percentile, but scores averaged about forty percent higher in the bottom five percentile (Iversen and Stephens 2008). This difference has been shrinking over time according to the latest adult literacy test from 2011/12 (OECD 2016), but that survey also highlights the across-the-board advances in the Nordic countries for skills that are used intensely in the new economy: what OECD calls "proficiency in problem solving in technology-rich environments."[13] The Nordic counties take four out of the six top spots on this measure (OECD 2016, figure 2.16), and we will argue in the next chapter that the broad acquisition of such skills in the new generation is an important element in limiting the spread of populist values.

The high level of technology literacy is coupled in Denmark and other Scandinavian countries with high-speed internet access, itself a result of public infrastructure investments, to create a propitious environment for innovation and knowledge-intensive technology and helping to grow firms in biotech, ICT, and cleantech industries. A particularly vibrant metropolitan area for the new economy is the Øresund Region, which has a population of nearly four million (including Copenhagen and Malmö) and accounts for more than a quarter of the combined Danish and Swedish GDP (equivalent to about half of the Danish GDP). With twelve universities and about a hundred and fifty thousand students, this high-tech corridor supports thousands of leading-edge companies in ICT, cleantech, and life sciences—mostly small and medium-sized enterprises, but also such established names as Haldor Topsøe, Coloplast, Novo Nordisk, and Lundbeck (not to mention global giants like Google and IBM with a strong local presence). At the end of the 1970s this was a depressed area, and it would have been hard to predict its current status as one of most successful economic regions in Europe. Indeed, it would have been inconceivable without the range of reforms we have briefly outlined above.

B. Germany. In many respects the German model was institutionally well-positioned to take advantage of new technological opportunities at the beginning of the 1980s. Unions were organized on industry lines and skilled workers in the export sector were firmly in control of these. The German central bank was highly independent and deliberately targeting the collective bargaining system to give unions and employers, especially in the wage-leading metalworking sector, a strong incentive to refrain from inflationary bargains. Wage restraint was also facilitated by a well-functioning 3.5–year vocational education and training system that kept successful exporters supplied with a highly skilled workforce. The ICT revolution changed the content of training, clearly, but it did not render the VET system redundant.

Yet, in important respects, the German model faced deeper challenges than the Danish, and, in some respects, even the British. What is sometimes referred to as the "Bismarckian" welfare state was associated with an increasingly bifurcated labor market with benefits tied to full-time employment, and high job protection for full-time workers arguably stifled labor market flexibility. Subpar public daycare and preschool options impeded, and continues to impede, women's entry into the labor market, and the financial system was geared almost exclusively toward lending to established businesses, with limited access credit by startups and individuals. Compared to other European countries, including Britain and Scandinavia, employment in high-end services has also been trailing. More than other ACDs, Germany's economy is dependent on the industrial sector.

And yet significant changes have taken place, beginning with the financial and corporate governance system. The German banking system is highly unique due to the combination of commercial banks that have traditionally financed large companies, and the publicly owned savings banks—Landesbanken and Sparkassen—that have dominated retail banking and acted as house banks for small and medium-sized enterprises (jointly with the cooperative credit unions: a third tier of the system). Since the 1980s, however, the lines between the tiers have blurred and both commercial and savings banks have increasingly engaged in investment banking, raising competition in the financial sector. Equity markets have also somewhat increased in importance as a source of firm finance, and access to foreign capital has been greatly facilitated by capital account liberalization. These changes have been helped along by both competition policies at the EU level, and, from the mid-1990s, by consecutive "Grand Coalition" governments (CDU/CSU/SPD) that have overhauled the financial and corporate governance system to promote competition, securitization, international lending, and improved access for startups to risk-willing capital. Public-owned banks including the Landesbanken and Sparkassen have lost their public finance and increasingly compete with commercial banks for business outside their traditional local lending markets.

The most important effect of these changes has been the sale and purchase of financial products on international markets, notably stocks, bonds, and real estate in the United States and UK, but also in the European periphery. An underlying driver of this trend, as we discuss later in the section 4.6, on the financial crisis, is the huge current account surpluses of the export-oriented Germany industrial sector. In this sense the competitiveness of the German industry has fueled the growth of the German banking sector, at least until the financial crisis. Financial services are still underperforming the UK, United States, and France in terms of value added and employment, and the control over private lending by savings banks and credit cooperatives has reduced consumption and labor market flexibility by inhibiting life-cycle changes in employment and education (even as this has also helped avert housing bubbles). Credit to the household sector remains very limited compared to the rest of Europe. Still, competition in the financial sector is higher today than in the past, and the insider power of banks in companies has diminished with changes to corporate governance that restrict the number of seats on boards, improve accounting transparency, and strengthen minority shareholders.

In the labor market a major impetus for reforms was German unification, which caused widespread unemployment (at the peak, nineteen percent in the east and ten percent in the west) and rendered generous unemployment and pay-as-you-go pension benefits unsustainable. The Harz reforms limited the duration of earnings-related unemployment benefits and severely cut long-term replacement rates as a tool to encourage workers to seek employment outside their previous occupation (Hassel 2010). This has greatly expanded part-time and temporary employment in services, and the continued employment protection for full-time workers has encouraged companies to engage in continuous upskilling of their core workers (while leaving those without full-time employment with few options).

The reform of the unemployment benefit system can be seen as part of a broader effort at employment activation. The early retirement schemes that were introduced in the 1980s to cope with redundancies have been scaled back, and the contribution-based pension scheme has been partially replaced by individual plans. The employer contribution-based system significantly added to labor costs, especially at the lower end of the pay scale, and it compounded problems of transitioning young people from the school system into employment. In response, benefits were first cut under the Kohl government and the transformation was carried forward under the social democratic Schroeder government, which reduced contribution rates and introduced private pension schemes in a major 2001 reform that has proven to be a boost to the equity market and private pension providers.

The broader vision of changes in the German model was laid out in "Agenda 2010," which in addition to the Harz reforms relaxed employment protection rules for smaller firms, cut sickness and other contribution-based benefits, and reorganized the Federal Employment Agency to reduce the influence of unions in the administration of unemployment system (such as criteria for suitable new employment). The changes were implemented without much input from the social partners, and sometimes in direct opposition to these, cutting through conflicts between large and small employers and between unions representing different industries and occupations (such as the well-publicized clash between IG Metall and the chemical union over pensions, which the latter won).

Changes have also occurred in the celebrated German vocational education and training (VET) system. The traditional apprenticeship system is still an important route to skilled employment for many young people, and almost all large firms as well as most of the Mittelstand participate in the system. At the same time many small and medium-sized firms have opted out, just as they have opted out of the collective bargaining system. Among firms with less than fifty employees only a minority now train, and the average firm participation rate dropped from thirty-four to twenty-five percent between 1985 and 2005 (Busemeyer 2009, 41). Demand for apprenticeships tend to outstrip the number of places, and many young people have been going through "preparatory" vocational schools from which they often transition directly into work without a proper certificate. This excess demand has been a source of recent reforms. Shorter two-year apprenticeships have been introduced, and while this is not meant to replace the dual apprenticeship system, it is increasingly filling the demand for intermediate skills. In addition, the content of regular 3.5-year apprenticeships have become more differentiated (Busemeyer and Thelen 2009), and in many cases, in research-oriented firms, their skill-level and theoretical content has been progressively increased.

Of even greater long-term consequence has been the growth in the higher educational system. The number of new entrants into tertiary education has risen continuously from the 1960s, when it was reserved for a small elite only, and in 2011 it exceeded the number of entrants into the VET system. In terms of the secondary tracking system, the number of students placed in the academic track has doubled from thirty to sixty percent between 1990 and 2012 (Baethge and Wolter 2015). Correspondingly, the share of twenty-five- to thirty-five-year-olds with a tertiary degree has increased from about twenty percent in the early 1990s to thirty percent in 2015. While this is below the ACD average (see figure 4.1), it is still a large increase that has been essential for the expansion of industries and occupations relying heavily on abstract and analytical skills (Baethge and Wolter 2015).

This shift has been enabled by a greater share of the educational budget committed to tertiary education—from twenty-two to twenty-seven percent between 1993 and 2014—which has in turn been a response to two reinforcing trends. The first is that industrial production has become increasingly digitalized, decentralized, and dependent on workers with high cognitive and analytical skills, causing demand for employees with university or technical university (*Fachhochschulen*) degrees to rise, while VET training has become relatively less important. The second trend is that the number of employees in services has far outpaced the number of VET apprentices. This reflects the growing bifurcation of services into low-skilled occupations and, increasingly, occupations such as financial services, IT, life sciences, and education that require higher educational degrees (Baethge and Wolter 2015). In short, rising demand for the college-educated has outpaced demand for VET trainees in both industry and, especially, services.

As in Demark and the UK, the transformation of the German economy has been associated with a revival of large cities and the clustering of innovative firms and high value-added services. The city state of Hamburg is a case in point. Home to some of Germany's heavy industry after the war—chemicals, steel, and shipbuilding—it suffered greatly from deindustrialization in the 1980s, with high levels of unemployment and population decline, but since the 1990s it has made a remarkable comeback and now has the highest GDP per capita of any German city with *The Economist* rating it the most livable city in 2017. The revival has been centered around a diverse set of innovative service industries in finance, life sciences, ICT, cleantech, media and creative industries, as well as trade (it is home to the second largest container harbor in Europe). In many ways Hamburg resembles the Øresund Region and is built on the same raw material: an expansive cluster of high-educated workers supplied by more than a dozen universities and technical universities in the region as well as from around Europe.

Both the Danish and German models have thus undergone major changes designed to accommodate and facilitate the transition to the knowledge economy. Many of the changes have been contentious, but they have largely been embraced by both the political center-left and center-right. The main opposition comes from organized losers among employers and unions; yet these have not been able to veto changes that democratic governments keen to push forward the economy want. The result are major changes in macroeconomic policies, wage-setting, social policies, competition policies, and, above all, training and education. At the same time, broad institutional and political differences persist, setting these countries apart from each other and from Britain and other LMEs. Germany's institutions continue to favor full-time skilled workers, and increasingly also professionals, and reforms have not been as effective as those in Denmark at integrating those at the lower end of the skill and income distribution, or in temporary or part-time employment. In the next chapter we look more closely at the consequences of these differences for the emergence of a populist cleavage in electoral politics.

4.4.4. FRANCE

The deterioration of growth across the industrialized economies which gathered pace in the second half of the 1970s led to intense debates about the role of government, involving political leaders, and generally played out in the electoral arena. This period corresponded to the slow beginning of the collapse of Fordism and the OPEC oil price shocks. In France the debate and the policy changes were sharp. Zysman's seminal *Governments, Growth, and Markets* (1983) covers several countries—most notably, France—and sets the stage for understanding these changes.[14] The French political economy since the 1950s had attached high importance to the role of the state; this both reflected the weakness of the French economy in the immediate postwar years, and the exceptional ability of top civil servants and politicians (typically from the same top educational background) who played a major role in detailed decisions on major investments through state control of key banks. On this, both leading socialist and Gaullist politicians shared a similar belief that the private sector required considerable state supervision (and vision) to achieve major innovations.

Thus French strategies to react to the slow collapse of Fordism involved increased involvement by the French state in reconfiguring large companies to make them more competitive. Just as British business and financial leaders saw Thatcher's reforms as against their interests, so, not surprisingly, did the French private sector. Anglo-Saxon readers may raise eyebrows at the widespread nationalizations of leading manufacturing companies by Mitterrand when he became president in 1981 in a socialist-communist alliance. While ambiguity doubtless colors many of Mitterrand's strategic moves, this major maneuver conformed to the Gaullist idea of the *grande politique industrielle* of creating great industrial clusters, including the supply chains (*filières*) which had come apart during the Giscard-Barre period of liberal economic policy in the turbulent second half of the 1970s; nor was it a million miles from the idea of the Japanese vertical *Keiretsu*. It is true that it did not represent a direct policy of radical liberalization, but it was exactly intended to arm national champions with the competitiveness and innovative capacities needed to succeed in increasingly competitive world markets.

In any case, it took place within an electoral debate of deep concern over French industrial policy; it was part of the Socialist program during the presidential election; it was large-scale and serious political experimentation in a very unclear climate; and its goal was to create innovative and competitive national champions.

The whole development fits well in our basic argument. The government was deeply concerned with restructuring large companies to face increased world market competition as the ICT revolution gradually got underway, which went directly against the perceived interests of French advanced capitalism. And it was very clear to Mitterrand that he needed, electorally, the reputation of being capable of responding to the needs of the advanced sectors in France.

As we know, the experiment failed; and from the mid-1980s the French government moved to give their leading corporations much more freedom to work out their trajectories, and by the late 1980s to denationalize them. But this did not mean either that the government ceased to be interventionist, or not to be continuously concerned about their competitive and innovative capacities (Hancke 2002). Much of the discussion in French political and administrative circles has concerned ways of making the advanced sectors of the French economy more competitive and innovative.

This is as true of the most recent presidential election in 2017 as it is of earlier ones. Macron was capable of winning not because of the support of established parties but because he had built a reputation for economic competence, and whether or not voters liked his policies on deregulation of labor markets he was the one candidate in the first round who was seen as economically competent (and clean). Macron's victory is remarkable in another way because he soundly defeated Marine Le Pen in the run-off election. Chirac did the same to her father in 2002, but this time was different because of the continued division of France into winners and losers in the transition to the knowledge economy, and because Marine Le Pen had shed the fascist and anti-Semitic overtones of her father and cultivated a more mainstream, if strident, populist image. In that sense, the last French presidential election highlights the new cleavage in electoral politics that accompanies the transition to the knowledge economy; it is one we will revisit in the next chapter. It also highlights how the electoral arena is a major driver of policy change, as we have argued. The shift did not originate with business or unions or think tanks or the intelligentsia—it originated with broad electoral discontent with the stagnation of the French economy and the emergence of a political entrepreneur with a message of hope, reform, and economic progress (in contrast to Le Pen).

4.5. The Socioeconomic Construction of the Knowledge Economy

In this section we move from the macropolitical level to the micro-level of production and social organization and show in greater detail how the knowledge economy has been constructed from bottom-up. We will concentrate on the formation of skill-clusters, which are the backbone of the new knowledge economy, and will show how these clusters have been formed around decentralized social and economic networks, which are concentrated in the advancing cities with few linkages to small towns or rural areas.

4.5.1 CHANGING SKILL SETS

Fundamental to our analysis of the development of the knowledge economy, as well as to the reactive development of populism, has been the dramatic changes in skill sets described in the previous sections. As was noted, advanced economies have gone from an educational world in which, in the 1950s, the great majority of children had left school before sixteen, and only a small elite—and a tiny proportion of women—went through higher education, to the contemporary situation in which around fifty percent of young people—and closer to fifty-five percent of young women—graduate. We will explain below how and why this was so closely linked to the decentralization of knowledge-based organizations and skilled-biased technical change; and how, in turn, this has been associated with both big-city agglomerations and "left-behind" communities.

There have of course been a wide range of technologies through which ICT has operated (and developed) in addition to computing itself: these include biotechnology in the widest sense, and the extraordinary changes across the life sciences, nanotechnology, materials, laser and sensor technology and robotics, as well as the cloud, computer security, mobile communications, and, increasingly, artificial intelligence. And there have been major complementarities between these different technologies. But at the heart of this wider technological—and social and economic—revolution is the semiconductor chip operating as a so-called "general purpose technology" used in transforming most social and economic activities (as electricity had been since the late nineteenth century).

In thinking about how skill sets work in the knowledge economy, four factors are of key importance from a political economic perspective: first, "returns" (in the most general sense) to these developments have operated through individuals with their skill sets and their *relations* to other individuals with their skill sets. Second, these relations between individuals develop over *historical* time—the relation between individual A with skill set a and individual B with skill set b depends for its effectiveness on the history of the relation between A and B: two randomly chosen individuals with skills-sets a and b respectively can seldom substitute for an A and B with the relevant historical relationship. Third, geography matters in these historical relationships: at the most fundamental level these relationships are *geographically embedded*, and A and B require to be physically colocated at least for periods of time, either in companies or other organizations, and/or in social networks and skill clusters. Exactly why physical colocation has been so important is not completely clear, although we shall put forward some hypotheses (revisited in the final chapter, on the future); in any case, this is central to the whole way in which knowledge economies have developed as urban agglomerations in particular nations (our advanced capitalist democracies). Fourth, what we might think of as historically and geographically embedded relational skill sets of those participating in knowledge economies are *reconfigurable* in relation to technological and market "shocks" as well as to new information about employment opportunities: here the roles both of learning competences in higher education and of colocated relations within social networks, skill clusters, and companies are of importance.

Thus, to summarize, individuals with particular skill sets relating to other individuals with particular (perhaps differentiated) skill sets; where the relation has typically developed historically over time; where the relation takes the geographically embedded form of physical colocation; and where these skill sets are reconfigurable: this framework is critical to our analysis of the development of knowledge economies. And, to anticipate slightly, we will argue that the *geographical segregation* it has led to between the beneficiaries of knowledge economies in big-city agglomerations and those less skilled in left-behind communities, with those less-skilled lacking *reconfigurability* because they are nongraduates, and absent from relevant social networks and skill clusters, is a major element in understanding the development of populism.

We now look in more detail at how the ICT revolution has directly and indirectly led to changed skill sets and, more generally, changed organizational structures within and between knowledge-based companies. We dig a bit more deeply to understand the last paragraphs, and look first at the skill sets and company organization structures of those who have broadly benefited from the knowledge economy, typically graduates in big-city agglomerations:

1. *Analytic skills and decentralization.* A short preamble: the ICT revolution might have gone in two radically different directions in generating social and economic transformation. In a hugely cited book, *Labor and Monopoly Capitalism: The Degradation of Work in the Twentieth Century,* written originally in 1974, Harry Braverman argued that the computer would lead to mass deskilling and, in effect, the centralization of economic power (Braverman 1998). But in fact transformation has gone in a radically decentralized direction, as the individual console has put greater and greater computer power in the hands of the individual. Our approach is not technologically deterministic: it could be plausibly answered that Braverman could have been right had the development of computing remained under central control, either by governments (as it might have been in the Soviet Union) or by great corporations with monopoly control over product and labor markets. In our perspective, it was the fact that ICT developed most powerfully in advanced democracies (especially the United States) where—as we have argued—it paid democratic governments to promote competition in order to further advanced capitalism. (And, of course, it was no accident that ICT developed most powerfully in advanced capitalist democracies: had communism controlled the advanced world, it is plausible to imagine that Braverman's vision would have been correct.)

Given that ICT developed in a competitive environment, with Osborne then IBM and Microsoft developing the hardware and software for personal desktop and portable computers, individuals have had individual access to computing power. A workforce with the ability to use this power has grown exponentially as a result, and given the ability of individuals to use computing power to make decisions, the most direct incentive for individuals was to invest in education, then, notably and quickly, higher education, in order to acquire the analytic ability to use computing in ever more sophisticated ways.

2. *Relational skills; horizontal organization of decision-making.* It is possible that a single person could use his or her analytic capacity to harness the powers of a computer to bring a product to market and for it to be sold without any need for the person to communicate (share information, negotiate, etc.) with anyone else. But even for academics using a computer to produce articles this is difficult— discussions with coauthors, research assistants, and other academics, persuasive interactions with heads of departments to establish the value of the article, and so on, are usually necessary. Most nonacademics are engaged in much more "cooperative" endeavors (eventually leading in one complex form or other to some good or service being put together and sold), where a group of employees or coworkers all use computers individually, as does the person or organization buying the service or product. For such interaction to be highly productive most have high analytic skills, and relational (sometimes called social) skills—discussing, critiquing, negotiating, strategizing, persuading, hand-holding, emotional support (and perhaps sometimes blackmail)—are generally central to such endeavors.

There is a high incentive to acquire relational skills, but they are difficult to signal. For most people a critical point for acquiring relational skills is at university, for young people interact as adults together in a wide range of situations for an extended period. Arguably, therefore, a major reason for hiring graduates is not just the analytical skills they have acquired through learning, although these are important, but also that university is seen as important for most people in the process of learning how to acquire sophisticated relational skills.

3. *Physical colocation over historical time.* An intriguing question is why physical colocation appears to be so important to relations between employees (including managers) in knowledge-intensive companies and organizations. Related, why does it appear important in knowledge-intensive businesses (KIBs) that this takes place over historical time? Take the latter question first: many (probably most) elements of relational skills, at least in important work relations, depend on a degree of trust and reliability—strategizing about

the future, negotiating, and persuading are obvious examples. But in the language of game theory, there is often "incomplete information" about whether or not someone who claims to be reliable or trustworthy or concerned about others actually is so. Even if it is not always put in these terms, de facto this depends on reputation. Under some circumstances a new employee may be able to bring with him or her a reputation for (say) trustworthiness and reliability—usually because they already know existing employees from social networks they all belong to, or because they have worked with the new employee in a previous company; and such a history may be why the new employee is hired, especially if the relevant existing employees have good reputations with other employees and managers. Otherwise, and common for most, the new employee has to build up a reputation over time in a company through trustworthy and reliable behavior; moreover, once such a reputation is acquired, then, whether it is true or not, it normally pays the employee to go on behaving in such a way.[15]

Why is physical colocation important? Could a KIB consist of employees who regularly need to solve problems or take joint decisions together who simply work individually on the internet in different parts of the world, meaning that the KIB has no physical existence? Such an idea has often been mooted by futurists: employees live in beautiful Scottish glens or wherever and communicate over the internet. Indeed, such an idea is suggested by Thomas Friedman's *The Earth Is Flat* (2005), a book almost as widely cited as Braverman's. We will show that the ICT revolution has generated almost the opposite pattern in the topography of the knowledge economy, with knowledge competences geographically embedded in individuals in big-city agglomerative peaks. Although not sufficient, the physical colocation of employees in companies (or their subsidiaries) is one key to understanding why. This is an empirical claim, and the future may hold different possibilities, which we take up in the concluding chapter.

There has been little academic discussion that we are aware of as to why physical colocation of employees for KIBs, almost all centered in cities, might be important. For some types of advanced activities, such as lab research or medical procedures, there is clearly a physical need for teams of researchers or doctors to be working in the same location, just as Fordist plants required employees to be physically present because they were working on the same physical object. But for many activities that are carried out via linked computers, that is not the case. It would certainly seem quite possible in the contemporary information era for individual employees in many activities to be located anywhere on earth with easy communication with each other through rapidly expanded online conferencing capabilities.

We believe again that game theory can shed light on this question, via contract incompleteness: in a great many moments in time employees will be working together on one or more unfinished often complex projects, each making project-specific or cospecific contributions, and from which the company or the employees together have not yet appropriated the benefit. If the company has no physical existence, consisting simply of employees and owners plugged into the internet wherever they choose to be, it is typically not easy for the company to tie employees into low-cost enforceable legal agreements to ensure he or she will carry out what needs still to be done by them; the temptation in a nonphysical, virtual world to misappropriate work is very high; and employees—scattered around the world—may well have similar concerns about owners. If employees and managers are colocated, by contrast, the incompleteness of contracts is less problematic: it is easier to see what employees are spending their time doing. Moreover, there is generally a significant cost involved in starting a new physically located job and hence a cost to losing one.

In addition to effective network monitoring there is an aspect of physical presence that is very hard to pin down precisely, but which is deeply rooted in human evolution. Evolutionary biology and psychology have uncovered a multitude of ways that we are driven by subconscious processes to express emotion—fear, anger, spite, joy, admiration, warmth, etc.—and to convey related signals of (dis)honesty, (in)sincerity, (dis)approval, etc., through complex body language, context, and even airborne chemical molecules (Ekman

2004; Lacoboni et al. 2005). These signals may be very difficult to pick up through electronically transmitted voice or video, which also offers much greater scope for manipulation. A smile may come across clearly on the computer screen, but not the nervous tinkering with a button that give away insincerity. This is especially true because signals can be exchanged repeatedly through frequent interaction in diverse contexts when people are colocated. Evolutionary biologists, neuroscientists, and social psychologists believe, based on much indirect evidence, that emotions and the capacity to send complex subconscious signals through direct interaction confer an evolutionary advantage in making, and inferring, credible commitments and producing human cooperation and trust (see the edited volume by Barkow et al. 1995 for examples). The more frequent the interaction, and the more diverse the settings, the easier it is for people to develop mutual trust and reputation for honesty.

4. *Skill clusters: risk, specialization, reputation, product variety.* KIBs vary significantly in their degree of market risk. But there is a general argument implying they are likely to operate in a riskier product market environment, and that employees in KIBs are likelier to operate in a riskier labor market environment. The general argument (above) is simply that ICT puts more power into the hands of small groups of highly educated employees. Assume such a small group is itself a KIB: then it in general pays the group to specialize either in creating new products (or product varieties or customized products) or new processes or both, as opposed simply to reproducing existing products (Nahapiet and Ghoshal 1998). It pays the (small decentralized) group to specialize, because it has the group solving-problem capacity to do so, and because by differentiating their output they can generally gain a higher profit. Evidently, specializing in this way, and competing in markets with new types or varieties of products, there is a possibility that the group will not succeed in making a market, and hence this is a more or less high-risk area. In some cases, the risks may be relatively low; this is the case where the company has a high reputation for developing new or customized or more sophisticated products (including services) in an area where an established market already exists for the products

of the company in question. This may be the case for many German Mittelstand companies, where tenure of employees is high and skill sets can be reconfigured within the company.

But it is not easy for a higher-risk group to survive if its tenure rate is low, and if its employees are physically colocated, without being in a geographical environment in which there are other similar high-risk groups requiring employees with broadly similar specialist skill sets. This is because the cost of moving physically is high (especially if children and partners with different specialty skill sets are involved). Consequently, a precondition in general for a higher-risk company to survive is that it is located in a *skill cluster*. A skill cluster is a physical environment with a set of companies and highly educated individuals all focused on the same broad set of specialized skill sets, and with both relevantly specialized skilled individuals and companies colocated in the same relatively close physical environment.

Skill clusters thus have key functions: they enable individuals with suitably high prior education to specialize within broad areas (and perhaps quite narrowly); and they enable companies to assemble groups of workers prepared to engage in relatively risky activities in the knowledge that other jobs will be available within the skill cluster, given the number of companies and the probability that some are increasing their workforces as others are shedding labor. Insofar as they constitute social networks, they generate information about job vacancies (Holzer 1987; Pellizzari 2004), and they also act as carriers of reputations about reliability as well as the nature of individual skill competences. Both workers and companies are likely to do better as a result (Montgomery 1991).

Thus, not only are companies and individuals embedded in skill clusters, but the embedding is reinforced by the cost to a relevantly skilled individual of leaving a cluster which "carries" his or her reputation. The same is true of companies.

5. *Social networks: assortative mating and clusters of skill clusters.* Skill clusters are themselves embedded within and across broader social networks of the highly educated; these seem of critical importance for our understanding of the knowledge economy, and big-city agglomeration.

Meeting partners occurs often at university. Given the high lifetime income of graduates, assortative mating (being more likely to choose partners of the same educational background the higher the level of your education) has become a phenomenon of central importance as participation in higher education has risen. But partners do not necessarily choose similar careers. Thus, partners, if they are following or likely to follow different careers, will want to settle in urban areas with wide enough skill clusters to accommodate both partners. The direct effect of assortative mating is thus that couples are likely to favor settling in cities with more skill clusters. This favors the growth of big cities.

This dynamic is reinforced in two ways: first, going to university in a big city means less concern in choosing partners in any particular profession (or potential skill cluster). Second, equally important, and complementary to assortative mating, students tend to join together with friends and their partners in social networks; there seems good reason to believe that this constitutes a highly valuable resource subsequently in people's careers in terms of contacts, new jobs, and perhaps career opportunities (as well as being central to satisfying human needs for friendship). Social networks, of any size and diversity, need large cities to provide the wide enough range of skill clusters.

We can see how assortative mating and social network formation magnifies the inegalitarian effects of skill-biased technological change that economists have identified. By pairing people at similar skill levels and embedding them in complementary social groups, household income by education is becoming increasingly stratified. Assortative mating in the Fordist economy was less prevalent because careers tended to be highly gender segregated and stratified, and social networks were far less important for careers or as a source of insurance.

6. *Patterns of specialization and knowledge-intensive MNEs.* The advanced economies have long been marked by patterns of specialization, underpinned by varieties of capitalism. These have increased (typically based on preexisting patterns) and become more geographically focused, especially in the form of skill clusters in

large urban conglomerations. As we see it, the dramatic increase in knowledge-intensive FDI between the advanced economies in the 1990s and 2000s can be explained by the increased variety permitted by decentralization noted above, and by the associated fragmentation permitted by specialized skill clusters. As Cantwell and others have noted, knowledge-intensive MNCs have developed networks of subsidiaries within the triad, not to cut costs, but to tap into advanced skills and associated technologies complementary to their core technologies and products.

But the return on skill sets has also been degraded by the ICT revolution in important ways. So we now turn to the effect on the skill sets of those who may not have benefited from the knowledge economy:

7. *Downgrading of physical skills for ICT enabled tasks.* Most notably, physical skills are unnecessary for the range of higher value-added tasks which require analytic and relational skills, and which have been made possible by ICT.

8. *Downgrading or elimination of routinizable tasks.* As Autor, Manning, and others have noted, a wide range of routinizable tasks and occupations have been downgraded or eliminated by a range of combinations of ICT-related technologies, notably automation, artificial intelligence, robotization, sensor technology, mobile communications, and cloud-computing, as well as others (see Autor, Levy, and Murnane 2003; Autor and Dorn 2013; Goos, Maarten, and Manning 2007). This has been a far from straightforward process—even leaving behind the social problems—as it has required many related institutional and legal changes (for example, in regulating driverless vehicles). Thus far, it has been argued, a significant proportion of those affected have had low- to middle-level skills (high school completers but nongraduates) and low- to middle-level incomes, but not the unskilled or very-low-income workers who are often engaged in activities involving contact with others (e.g., social care, food service, etc.), which are difficult to codify and computerize.

9. *Job elimination: outsourcing, immigrants, and import competition.* All the above changes to skill sets have been the direct and indirect result of new technologies within knowledge economies. But

many jobs, especially in manufacturing industry, have disappeared as a result of outsourcing and import competition. There is a dispute about the effect of immigration on domestic jobs, but in (nearly) all these cases it is not graduates who have suffered but those with less education. And the putative cause is that domestic jobs have been replaced by foreign workers with the same broad level of education as those who have lost their jobs. High-educated immigrants, on the other hand, mostly serve as complements to resident workers with high education, allowing skill clusters to expand and thrive (see Ottaviano and Peri 2012; Borjas 2013). So we can think of this "external" shock as complementing the technology regime shift rather than challenging it. We return to this below.

4.5.2. DYNAMIC DRIVERS OF THE KNOWLEDGE ECONOMY: BIG-CITY AGGLOMERATIONS

In this subsection we sketch how knowledge economies have grown through the process of agglomeration of certain cities into high value-added metropolitan areas with substantial graduate populations. This process has mostly happened from the early 1990s on, after the sharp decline of big industrial cities in the wake of the collapse of Fordism in the late 1970s and through the 1980s. There is still no complete agreement about why some urban areas have grown as a result of the technological transformation into successful and wealthy knowledge-economy cities with substantial graduate populations, while others have not. But where a city had ab initio a range of professional service sectors and strong universities it has typically grown into a major cosmopolitan metropolis. Size is not necessarily everything: what were originally just university towns (Chapel Hill or Austin in the United States, for example, and York, Norwich, or Brighton in the UK) with an initial range of higher value-added service sectors, can also become on a smaller scale graduate agglomerations, sometimes referred to as "smart cities." By contrast, those cities or towns which had been prosperous in the Fordist era largely on the basis of single industrial sectors have found survival and growth much harder. Thus Baltimore, Cleveland, Cincinnati, Akron, and Detroit, as well as many more mainly industrial smaller towns, contrast with what are now highly skilled agglomerations like New York, Boston, Chicago, Washington, San Francisco, and San Diego.

A. Participation in Higher Education. The most intuitive starting point of understanding the agglomeration process in "successful" cities is growing participation by young people in higher education. As we have seen, the ICT revolution has generated two main reasons for deciding to participate in higher education: the incentives to acquire analytic and relational skills. Conversely, with arguably more effect on women than on men, physical skills are no longer important. We have suggested a further set of reasons for choosing universities in a particular metropolitan area. This is that expected access to well-paid and/or rewarding careers takes place through skill clusters of graduates, themselves embedded in social networks of graduates.

A study by Winters (2011) of decisions to migrate into US metropolitan areas to participate in university education captures indirectly the importance of graduate social networks and skill clusters by ranking the metropolitan areas by the proportion of graduates in the city population in 1990. He shows that the higher the proportion of graduates in the city (in 1990), the larger the probability that an in-migrant in 1995 had come to enroll in higher education and the smaller the probability that those who left in 2000 had come there to be enrolled in higher education. By contrast the probability that in-migrants in 1995 had *not* come to enroll in higher education was unrelated (not statistically significant) to the graduate percentage, while the probability that out-migrants in 2000 had *not* come (originally) to enroll there in higher education was significantly positive. (Winters also notes interestingly that the bulk of in-migrants for higher education into a "smart city" come from within the state in question; so, of relevance to our subsequent discussion of populism, this geographical segregation between successful and left behind cities may be widely spread across the United States.)

In equilibrium, a higher in-migration for the purpose of education and the lower outmigration of graduates will lead to a concentration of the high-skilled in cities, which is what has happened. Across advanced economies, urbanization and education is strongly related (Glaeser and Resseger 2010; Caragliu, Del Bo, and Nijkamp 2011). Measured by PISA scores, educational performance is also higher in urban areas, after controlling for socioeconomic factors, which likely reflects a higher wage and social premium on having a good education (OECD 2013).

This illustrates another example of a strategic complementarities game, since cities with a high density of graduates increase the incentives of individual graduates to move to, or remain in, those cities. More specifically we have this game as consisting of a range of interrelated decentralized decisions as follows:

First, in the knowledge-economy companies, employees with cospecific skills colocate in these companies (or research facilities, or whatever are the relevant departments or offices of companies). If in addition we assume that the company (or sector) is innovative, then tenure may be relatively short (as the company may both have to ditch projects and also hire new workers with different skill sets), and, as the cost of moving is typically high for employees, a skill-cluster equilibrium may develop where those with skills relevant to the sector live in the same broad area, and companies also locate in the same area. This is greatly reinforced by the de facto impossibility of a company relocating with its workforce; if the company's value-added is largely embodied in the workforce, then it will be unlikely to relocate. Hence the skill cluster of companies working in the innovative sector in question, and those with the skills relevant to the sector, will both live and work or establish their operations in the same broad geographical area.

Secondly, a significant proportion of those who go through university in a city will be likely to join the relevant skill cluster for their career (if one exists) because of complementarities among skills. This is consistent with the evidence (above) that graduates have a relatively high probability of remaining in the city in which they graduated. As noted earlier, it is also likely that at least younger graduates will have formed a significant part of their contemporary social network at university. Social networks play an extremely important role in the early decades of graduate careers, providing support of all sorts and discussion of employment opportunities and directions, and, critically, including the likelihood of meeting future friends and in particular future partners. This also means that graduate social networks are likely to be open and inclusive, rather than exclusive. Because membership of such networks is so valuable, there is a tendency to remain living in the same very broad area as members of one's network. This puts a premium on living in cities with many different career opportunities for high value-added employment and many skill clusters. This then reinforces the beneficial effect for a city of having a wide range of higher value-added occupations in the first place (the early 1990s), rather than being a city dedicated to manufacturing; variegated cities make them attractive to wide social networks and hence open to agglomeration bias.

Finally, assortative mating is a development of recent decades, and for several reasons it reinforces agglomeration effects. One is that the proportion of graduates has greatly increased, increasing the pool of choice; a second is that the return to higher education has increased by a large amount in the last quarter century; we suggest that a third reason is the importance of graduate social networks. This last point can take different forms; but at the most basic level, since socializing in a network is likely to be with one's partner, one's own attraction to the network will depend in part on one's partner's attraction to the network; and that will depend on intelligence, ability to engage in discussions, and also on the partner's career—all likely to be positively correlated with education.

As we explained above, assortative mating increases cross-household inequality. Because college graduates are at the higher end of the distribution it has the effect of increasing the demand for family residences in a city with a large graduate population, raising house prices, initially in "better" areas of big cities. As prices rise there, demand shifts to inner-city areas, often with attractive but rundown housing stock (gentrification). It is likely that these processes are self-reinforcing, because they encourage further assortative mating, leading to additional upwards pressure on house prices. In the next section in this chapter we look at increasing educational and geographical segregation; we will see that one element in this is the movement of less-skilled (nongraduates) out of big cities into peripheral areas as a result of rising house prices.

B. Variety, FDI, and Globalization across the Advanced World. As we explained earlier, the effect of the ICT revolution and the great expansion of new and related technologies has been to create a map of knowledge concentrations across the agglomerations of the advanced economies. The huge motivating force behind globalization across the advanced world has been the patterns of specialization in each of these agglomerations of knowledge. A lot of work will be needed to understand exactly why these patterns have taken the form that they do: they represent partly the difference between the nature of innovation in LMEs and CMEs, with more radical technological developments in LMEs (and especially in the United States) being diffused, adapted, and customized in CMEs. And within and across CMEs, where specialized networks had long been in existence with highly skilled workforces, the location of those networks has played a large part in subsequent locational specialization.

Within these skill clusters the effect of combining ICT and the newly expanding technologies with more established products and services has been to produce an explosion of competition in new and more sophisticated product varieties across the advanced world. This has touched almost all areas of economic activity, especially in the agglomerations of knowledge. It has certainly affected sheltered sectors in the agglomerations, given both their access to these goods and services and the rapidly growing educational levels within the agglomerations. This is true both of the private sector in areas from culture to entertainment and retail, as well as sheltered high value-added services, and also public-private services, most notably in health and education.

Given these knowledge specializations and their associated skill clusters, knowledge-based multinationals have themselves developed as networks of companies across the advanced world, though typically in one of the triad regions (Rugman 2012). There are two important motives for this: first, companies need access to new developments in technologies complementary to their core technologies, thus acquiring or allying with companies (often small) in the relevant agglomeration (Cantwell and Mudambi 2005; Kuemmerle 1997, 1999). For this reason a critical concern of advanced knowledge-based companies has been the ability to make foreign (or perhaps domestic) direct investments in other parts of the advanced world. At the same time it has been associated with highly educated individuals moving to the relevant part of the knowledge-competency atlas, again in the advanced world. These movements have been the responses to the generally very limited ability of advanced companies to buy and move whole companies from one agglomeration to another (even more to a low-cost environment which would be unlikely to provide the infrastructure for the maintenance of their social existence). Second, most of the sophisticated products and services of these advanced companies are sold to sophisticated consumers or companies who want these products customized. Insofar as there are patterns of customization across the advanced world, this again leads to knowledge-based multinationals creating networks of subsidiaries or alliances to respond directly to these customization needs.

Summarizing the above forces, the agglomeration process results from the combination of incoming FDI, reinforcing and reinforced by technological change, together with the development of high value-added demand, creating and sustaining the demand for highly educated workers and, thus, university participation. It is further reinforced by employment multipliers increasing the demand for (usually) skilled labor in the sheltered sectors of the agglomeration (Moretti and Thulin 2013), from medical services to the arts to public administration. There are arguably, therefore, many winners from the development of the knowledge economy, with a large proportion in the successful big city agglomerations.

While much work has been done on the various components of the argument of the last few pages, much detailed work will be needed to see how these mechanisms work themselves out in a wide range of real world cases. As an aide-mèmoire we summarize the argument in figure 4.9.

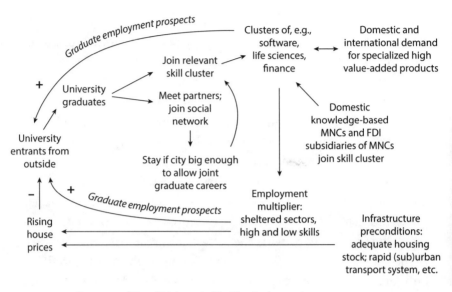

FIGURE 4.9. Summary of Causal Linkages in Big-City Agglomerations.

4.6. Creating Educational and Geographic Segregation: Centripetal and Centrifugal Forces

There are also losers. Anne Power (2016) has suggested a nice model of (in very broad terms and in relation to the UK) who the losers are and where they are located. In the Fordist postwar period, major industrial metropolitan areas were centered on major core industrial cities, such as (in the North of England) Manchester, Leeds, Liverpool, Newcastle, and Sheffield. These cities were surrounded by a group of smaller peripheral industrial municipal areas—in the case, for example, of Manchester, towns such as Burnley, Bolton, Oldham, Rochdale, Bury, and Accrington. The more sophisticated the manufacturing, the more likely the major company headquarters would be located in Manchester (when not in London), and high-value-added service sectors (finance, insurance, accountancy, and so on) and the main universities and research institutes in the region were also centered in Manchester. Thus Manchester provided the more complex services for industry in the periphery.

The peripheral towns (again in very broad terms) concentrated on less sophisticated manufacturing, acting partially as component suppliers to the core industrial city. But for a long period of time, going back to the last century, these peripheral towns had been prosperous areas, mainly in cotton manufacturing (mill towns) and engineering. They were and are endowed with good housing stocks; but their road and rail transport systems (between each other and to Manchester) were built for industrial transport, which was not high-speed, and not for rapid transport commuting.

A second, slightly different model of core-periphery is provided by London as core city, and the seaside towns around the southern and southeastern coasts of England, such as Margate, Ramsgate, Folkestone, Hastings, and Clacton. Parallel with Fordism, these towns provided a good housing stock for annual holidays for large numbers of working-class and lower-middle-class holiday-makers, many from London. Equally, there was little need for rapid train services to London, since the commuter need from the seaside towns was limited, apart from Brighton. The collapse of Fordism very broadly (though not causally) coincided with the collapse of sea-side holidays in Britain, as cheap and, weather-wise, vastly more reliable holidays and seaside retirement became available on the continent, notably in Spain.

A number of factors have reinforced the separation, which exist to different degrees in different countries:

A. Transport systems. Had there been effective rapid transport systems, parts of the peripheral towns might have become commuter communities for those who worked in the agglomerative cities in response to rising house prices. And had there not been residential segregation as well as work segregation, it is quite possible to imagine that graduate commuter communities might have developed into fully fledged appendages to the margins of the successful cities. Indeed, a number of smaller cities around London—including Reading, Swindon, and Slough—have developed into dynamic knowledge-based cities; moreover, based on patent statistics, a whole area including these smaller cities, from Cambridge, Milton Keynes, and Oxford to Bristol and back along the M4 motorway to London represents the most knowledge-intensive region of the UK. Not only does it have six or seven of the top British universities, it also has unparalleled access abroad via Heathrow (as well as Gatwick, Stansted, and City airport) and the Channel Tunnel and Eurostar.

But it is interesting that such development of commuter communities did not happen in general. The reasons are twofold: first, if the areas in question were not originally commuter belts to the big cities or major universities, then there would have been few reasons for mass individual transport to have been in place. Second, if (reasonably rapid) mass transport systems were not already in place in the 1980s and early 1990s as the knowledge economy was initially developing in the big cities, then there was typically a major collective action problem involved in creating one. Absent a preexisting graduate residential community in a peripheral town, an individual graduate would have had little desire to live in a nongraduate community outside the big city. Thus there was no private market for developing rapid mass transport systems. For the private sector, therefore, rate of return calculations would have shown a very low rate of return on such projects.

Public actors could have stepped in to push for rapid mass transport systems to link agglomerative cities to peripheral areas, but this only happened to a limited extent, although there is considerable cross-national variation. In general, young professionals and public authorities have strong reasons for promoting gentrification, because it typically involves many young graduates simultaneously, and thus presents much less of a collective action problem than might be remotely involved in developing a commuter community in a peripheral area without mass transport. And, from the perspective of public authorities, it is both a cheaper option than commuter communities and much less risky. A similar logic appears to cause locational segregation in the United States and in France.

When better transit systems to peripheral areas have often been built in parts of northern Europe it is because the political system affords greater political influence to peripheral areas, either through bargained federalist systems or through left and center political parties in centralized proportional representation systems (increasingly, right populist parties, with large constituencies in small towns, are the purveyors of these interests). Peripheral areas have benefited from better infrastructure and public transportation as a result, but apart from efforts to locate central government agencies outside the city centers, the effect has not generally been to move knowledge clusters away from the cities. The self-reinforcing agglomeration dynamics in the urban centers are simply too strong.

Yet, there are exceptions. Horsens is a typical provincial seaside town of about sixty thousand inhabitants on the eastern coast of Jutland, Denmark. It was once a proud industrial town manufacturing turbines, TVs, telephones, and various metalworking goods, but it was hit hard by the crisis and accelerating deindustrialization of the 1970s and later by the drain of young people to the capital and especially Aarhus, a large university town further up the coast, with a thriving service economy. Still, Horsens made a highly implausible comeback through a concerted effort to reinvent itself as a mini-mecca for culture and entertainment. Riding the vision and the deep art-world connections of local businessman Frank Panduro, a progress-minded city government upgraded its museums, opened a new theatre, developed a vibrant music scene that brought a "who's who" of the biggest names in rock and roll to give concerts, and turned its main street into an attractive pedestrian area for shopping and dining. With frequent train service to Aarhus and next to an expressway, commuting to Aarhus takes about half an hour by car or train. This combination of easy transit and a lively cultural scene, as well as affordable, family-friendly housing, convinced many young professionals with families working in Aarhus to reside in Horsens. There are still many older middle-class residents with roots in the industrial economy who feel they have lost out, but by investing heavily in culture Horsens has attracted a commuter network of well-educated professionals who are integrated in a regional knowledge cluster (which increasingly includes the town itself), pointing to a brighter future. Being a small forgotten industrial town is not destiny.

B. Private services. Horsens is very unusual by essentially complementing cultural offerings normally reserved for much bigger cities. But it highlights the importance of another factor that in most instances widens the "lifestyle" cost for any graduate contemplating moving from the agglomerative city and the peripheral town (or left-behind community)—namely, the difference between the degree of sophistication in services supplied by the private sector.

The private services sector either consists of companies with many branches, as in banking or insurance or real estate; in chain stores, as with the retail supermarket giants, department stores, or restaurant chains; or of a multitude of individual companies, from legal services and accountant partnerships to all sorts of specialist concerns or individual corner shops. The level of sophistication of the goods and services they provide, and the level of sophistication of their personnel in terms of their education and training, differ greatly between successful cities and peripheral, left-behind communities. It is perhaps an obvious point to make that private sector undertakings gear their offerings to the relevant market. But it hugely reinforces the lifestyle cost for the graduate, were he or she to move locations.

C. Quality of education and health. This lifestyle cost of moving to peripheral communities is also reinforced by differences in the level of provision of public services. The level of provision of public services depends in part on the governmental level at which decisions are taken.

In principle, in countries where services are provided at the national level as (in principle) in England, the level of provision is (in principle) the same in different locations. Yet, as is widely known, NHS provision is less good in less-well-off communities. There are a number of different reasons for this. But an important reason is the quality of medical professionals. Doctors cannot be assigned to different locations, and able, young, recently trained doctors will be keen to both live and work in big cities, where they have access to leading-edge practice, research, and colleagues, as well as to their social networks. There are of course many young professionals in the public sector with altruistic concerns; but also, in teaching, the lifestyle attraction of social networks in big cities is a powerful one, and the likelihood of being in relationships with partners in high value-added occupations based in big cities may make it very costly for many teachers (especially the best-educated ones and hence most likely partnered with those equally well-educated and in the high-paying private sector in big cities) to teach in peripheral areas.

Hence, the knowledge economy has itself raised the lifestyle cost for graduates of breaking the residential segregation.

D. Social networks and cultural choices. Finally, it is important to return to an earlier discussion of culture and social networks. There appears to be a significant difference between the social networks in peripheral areas and graduate social networks in agglomerative cities. As Mike Savage (2013) has underlined, cultural values and discourses are embedded in social networks. Our approach is based on the idea that cultural values and discourses ultimately reflect the personal characteristics and preferences which enable people to be successful in the economic world they find themselves in. So, as we see it, the differences in the nature of social networks and discourses between these very differentiated and deeply segregated environments reflect "material" responses to the differences in the nature of work and of the associated relationships which facilitate successful careers in the two environments. (In the next chapter, on the politics of populism, we discuss how these networks are used to reinforce and further construct these discourses.)

Put most simply: in the agglomerative city, the successful and horizontal low-hierarchical risk-taking innovative environment requires those who are open to highly educated smart people from diverse backgrounds, and where neither sexual nor ethnic diversity matter. For these are "open" characteristics important for successful careers in the big-city environment. Thus, graduate social networks in big, successful cities are (as is known empirically) both large and open or inclusive—though the inclusiveness relates to other well-educated interesting people, perhaps people who themselves open the doors to other valuable social networks. It is exemplary of the "strength of weak ties (Granovetter 1973). While commentators who think in "cultural" terms may see the above description as reflective of cultural values, pure and simple, we see it as reflecting the material base of the successful big-city culture.

By contrast, in peripheral communities, social networks are small, long-lasting, high-trust, and closed. They reflect the need of community members to be able to rely on each other in difficult times. They are suspicious of outsiders. And it is not difficult to understand how their discourses and ideas about, say, recent immigrant groups—whom they are unlikely to meet, since recent immigrants tend to be drawn to large cities where jobs are available—may be at odds with reality. (Refugees are often located outside big cities by governments because of housing and other costs; here the problem is that they are less likely to be able to communicate because of language difficulties, as well as being difficult to integrate economically.) In any case, the respective social networks of successful big cities and peripheral communities attract and push away the incomers implied by our earlier discussion.

4.7. The Financial Crisis

In this book we have emphasized the symbiotic relationship between advanced capitalism and democracy, which raises the question of how to explain major economic crises. The financial crisis, or Great Recession, is particularly salient, because it occurred as governments were implementing the broad set of reforms that we have argued created the foundation for the knowledge economy. If the reforms were intended to produce prosperity, how did the crisis happen?

It is tempting, and indeed common, to interpret the crisis as an outcome of irreconcilable contradictions in capitalism, as does Streeck, and to see it as a major example of how the state has lost control over a globalized economy. We instead argue that the crisis illuminates the relationship between modern capitalism and the advanced nation-state as we have set it out in this book. Advanced nation-states are deeply concerned—in a world in which they can no longer count on protection, direct intervention, or subsidies—with promoting the interests of their high value-added sectors, which are central to their innovation and human capital investment systems, as well as the source of well-paid employment and tax revenue. The reforms discussed in this chapter were designed to accomplish precisely this. In relation to the crisis, comparative institutional advantages led the US and UK governments to be concerned with regulatory environments that promoted, among other things, their innovative and high-risk financial sectors; they also led Germany and Japan to fashion or maintain regulatory environments that promoted high value-added export sectors.

Two central regulatory systems were key to the crisis. The first was the system of financial regulation, and in particular the set of rules governing the leverage of so-called highly leveraged financial institutions (HLFIs) and the systemic monitoring of these institutions. The second was the system governing macroeconomic regulation, including the operation of fiscal and monetary policy. The financial regulatory system failed to prevent major HLFIs from developing exceptionally high-leverage multiples in financial systems in which major HLFIs were systemically interdependent. And the macro regime failed—indeed was not designed—to prevent the development of global imbalances.

That these two regulatory systems, however, should have proved dysfunctional would have been surprising to many commentators through the two decades before the crisis during which the systems took shape. The systems imposed something like international uniformity on macroeconomic management and national financial regulation for the first time since Bretton Woods. In the system of inflation targeting, independent central banks were given responsibility for macroeconomic management and used interest rates to return deviations of inflation and unemployment to their target or equilibrium values. They did so in the common New Keynesian macroeconomic framework that we discussed above. Many policy-oriented macroeconomists agreed with Ben Bernanke's assessment that this system was responsible for the Great Moderation in inflation and unemployment since the early 1990s. In addition, that inflation targeting should be carried out without international coordination was not disputed. Indeed, inflation targeting within the New Keynesian framework and without international coordination is still generally accepted.

As we have discussed, the broad regulatory system of financial liberalization and international mobility of financial assets and financial institutions also became widely agreed upon over the last two decades, and, as with the macroeconomic system, the regulators were primarily national. Again, this was widely endorsed by professional economists, at least in relation to the advanced economies. In hindsight, one can be critical of some of these arrangements, but many analysts see, and still see, financial liberalization as a positive development for at least three reasons. First, it generated competition for domestic banks and led to reductions over time in borrowing costs. This reflected the oligopolistic structure of much domestic commercial and retail banking that had developed since the 1930s. Second, the great rise in international competition in goods and services associated with the development of the global knowledge economy led large companies to use financial markets to pressure employees, including management, to become more flexible. Third, and as a consequence of this, risk, openness, and the complexity of business investment increased, generating the need for complex financial derivatives to hedge these risks.

In broad terms, then, these two key regulatory systems were accepted and approved by the governments of the advanced countries, as well as by their business communities. But what is critical for understanding the crisis is that these systems were not internationally administered, nor were there detailed international agreements on their rules. For example, as far as banking regulation was concerned, the attempts to do this via the Bank for International Settlements (BIS) and Basel II were unsuccessful; and the story, though unending, of the International Accounting Standards Board (IASB) and common accounting standards is similar. The broad principles were accepted internationally, but both the detailed rulemaking and regulatory authorities were at the national level. Interpretation of rules in specific cases, monitoring of financial institutions, sanctions, and assessment of systemic risk, as well as interest-rate setting and fiscal policy choices that affected external imbalance, all took place at the national level.

National control of these systems was not accidental but instead reflects the political incentives of democratic governments to promote the high value-added sectors of their economies, in which they enjoy comparative institutional advantage. Because these sectors vary across countries, governments want to control the detailed operations of regulatory systems in their own environments. There is now little dispute that the UK and US governments allowed a lax interpretation of the financial regulations governing leverage, both in the valuation of the risky assets that HLFIs owned and in the assessment of bank capital. They did so because they saw it as beneficial to one of the most important economic sectors in which the United States and the UK had comparative institutional advantage. It was certainly true that the large banks were politically powerful in the United States, but this was far less so in the UK, with its centralized and disciplined political system—yet Thatcher had made the first move to the liberalization of the City with the Big Bang in 1985 and Blair had enthusiastically supported light-touch financial regulation.

Analogously, in terms of external surpluses, the governments of Germany, Japan, China, and other nations whose leading high value-added sectors are export oriented were not—and are still not—prepared to accept constraints on external surpluses. Such constraints would imply expansionary fiscal or monetary policies generating real exchange rate appreciation, thus damaging the interests of the sectors in which they have comparative institutional advantage.

The origins of the crisis are by now quite well understood, and we have discussed them in detail elsewhere (Iversen and Soskice 2012; Carlin and Soskice 2014). One key trigger was the difficulty of HFLI to cover their losses once prices on risky assets they owned by borrowing against equity started to fall. Greatly complicating the situation was the expansion of two financial instruments which had radically reduced the riskiness of individual assets: one was collateral debt obligation (CDOs) that bundled loans such as mortgages, credit card debt, student loans, and bank loans, and thus minimized individual default risk, and cut the securitized packages into different risk tranches. The other was credit default swaps (CDSs) that "insured" assets against a wide range of defaults. These instruments were not new—in some form or other they had always existed—but they had expanded in a massive and increasingly complex way over the previous two decades. In turn, both CDSs and CDOs were or could be rated by the rating agencies. As long as individual risks were idiosyncratic, at least not hugely positively correlated, these instruments acted effectively to reduce aggregate risk.

The two major problems with the development of this system were both based on the weight of a limited number of very large HLFIs, all of which invested in similar classes of risky assets, including CDOs and CDSs, and the relatively shallow market for these assets outside the HLFIs. This meant that if the price of a class of assets fell exogenously, even without provoking a bankruptcy, it required all the HLFIs to sell risky assets to restore their desired leverage ratios, causing significant price falls across their asset classes. This in turn generated a multiplier process of further asset sales, further price falls, and so on, to restore a leverage at which short-term borrowers would be prepared to lend. Second, if a large HLPI did get forced into bankruptcy, the system as a whole came under risk. This was directly because each major HLFI was engaged in the hugely profitable CDS business, so that a HLPI bankruptcy (think Lehmann Brothers) set to zero the value of all the CDSs it had issued and were held through the system. Next, it put under pressure the issuers (counterparties) of CDSs contingent on the bankruptcy of that HLFI (Lehmann's collapse was the major hit on AIG (American International Group)). In addition, the market was flooded with its erstwhile risky assets, leading to further price falls in the relevant asset classes. Finally, it necessarily defaulted on some portion of its liabilities, of which a proportion came from other HLFIs, with knock-on effects on the assets of the other HLFIs.

All of this was in principle consistent with agreed values of the risky assets. But a further and massive complication was the uncertainty of their value, which was a consequence of the absence of monitoring and detailed surveillance of the relevant markets. Ratings agencies were too close to the HLFIs to offer reliable ratings of their assets. As a result it became unclear whether other HLFIs might go bankrupt. And this led to an effective freezing of the market for short-term borrowing, as no financial institution was prepared to lend overnight without exceptionally high interest. This situation was unsustainable without the government support then forthcoming. In this sense, all the major HLFIs were probably too big to fail.

Key to understand, however, is that global imbalances hugely magnified this process. The external surpluses of the net exporters played a dual role. On the one hand, they allowed U.S. consumers to spend above U.S. GDP, and U.S. consumers had to dissave to finance this deficit. On the other hand, the external surpluses provided short-term loans to the HLFIs to cover the acquisition of a large proportion of the risky assets—that is, securitized loans—that financed the consumption.

We have argued above, and in detail in past work, that the institutions of the export-oriented advanced economies generated restraint in the use of domestic resources and promoted the supply side of exports. This is not true in liberal economies where wage-setting and training policies do not favor the export sector, and where macroeconomic policies are geared toward maintaining demand. In Iversen and Soskice (2014) we show how, in equilibrium, export-oriented economies not only exhibit high exports but also tend to run a surplus on the external balance, and that the opposite is true for liberal countries. This produces capital exports to the liberal countries, which fueled the high leverage in those countries. This is an inherent feature of the current international economic regime, because there is no reason to think that it would be feasible to reach an agreement to promote a balanced trade constraint.

Leaving aside China, a key question is, why we do not see sustained attempts to reform the current system toward a balanced trade regime? Trump talks a lot about trade deficits, but his administration has not put forward a single proposal that is likely to address it. Such a shift would involve export-oriented economies adopting a much more accommodating macroeconomic regime, and liberal countries adopting a much more restrictive regime. The reason this does not happen is that it is inconsistent with the domestic political coalitions that sustain the current policies in the two types of economies.

Consider first the export-oriented economies. Because the most productive and skill-intensive firms are concentrated in the export sector—as implied by the now universally accepted Melitz model of trade—a large export sector goes together with high investment in public training so that the supply of skilled workers will meet the demand. This in turn requires that unions in the export sector hold down their wages to allow for newly trained workers to be priced into jobs, and a key mechanism in ensuring this, as we have argued, is a nonaccommodating macroeconomic regime.

Assume now that policies become more accommodating in order to eliminate the trade surplus. This leads to a decline in the demand for skilled workers, so if the government continues to train at the previous level, there will be redundancies among skilled workers. The government would not want that, of course, but the alternative of reducing training intensity runs up against the interests of two very different constituencies. First, and most obvious, export-oriented firms will be opposed because they would face an increase in labor costs and will have to scale back their operations. Second, the relative supply of low-skilled workers will rise, which will cause a corresponding decline in their relative wages. Although this will be somewhat compensated for by a higher real exchange rate and cheaper imports, the compensation is less than one hundred percent, and much less in large countries. From this it follows that low-skilled workers will block lower funding for training if they are represented by a party in government. Insofar as PR electoral systems—which all export-oriented countries in Europe adopted in the early twentieth century—produce more center-left governments, it would be hard for such governments to agree to a balanced trade international rule. But this would even be true of center-right governments in these export-oriented countries, since the interests of export sectors dominate business and employer organizations.

Now consider the situation from the perspective of liberal countries. Because wage-setting is decentralized, governments in liberal countries cannot induce restraint through nonaccommodating macroeconomic policies. Such policies can instead affect demand only by reducing government spending and, if the economy is large, by raising interest rates. This will lead to lower wages, which in turn boosts exports and reduces the real exchange rate, cutting domestic demand. Both skilled and semiskilled workers would both be worse off under these policies, except if the government substantially boosted subsidies for training and thereby reduced the supply of low-skilled workers. But in majoritarian political systems, which are linked historically to liberal economic systems, the median voter is likely to be a skilled worker and would not support such a policy. Hence, governments in liberal countries will also not see it in their interest to back a balanced trade international regime.

The conclusion of this analysis is that national governments, even though they control policy instruments that could effectively reduce global imbalances, have no domestic political incentives to adopt such policies. The only threat that could potentially bring governments across the advanced democracies together would be another financial crisis. But given the domestic costs of adopting policies that would be effective, politicians in the liberal bloc will be prone to believe that the likelihood of a future crisis can be tackled by changing the financial rules of the game in relatively small ways, most notably by more careful monitoring of the effective leverage ratios of HLFIs, and in particular those who pose a systemic risk. And the dominant political coalitions in the export-oriented economies also believe that changing the financial rules is preferable to adopting a more relaxed attitude to fiscal policy; indeed, the latter is close to anathema for them. Note that there is no sense here that the root of the problem is loss of policy control; nation-states have powerful instruments at their disposal to regulate the economy. The real question is whether the political incentives to promote the advanced sectors of the economy—that, as we have argued governments are principally concerned with—are compatible with an international regulatory and macroeconomic regime that will ensure stability. We doubt it.

So it is not the case that ACDs are inevitably macroeconomically stable, as many economists had come to believe at the end of the 1990s. The interaction of different varieties of capitalism in an integrated international system caused a buildup of global imbalances that fueled the financial crisis, which was the unintended consequence of financial liberalization. Such crises are eventually resolved by governments injecting liquidity, restoring demand, tightening regulations, and reestablishing the solvency of major banks and insurers, but their underlying political causes are never resolved, and when they happen they threaten the welfare of a large number of middle-income groups and call into question the capacity of the system to generate upward mobility. The result is that the audience for populist appeals—especially among what we might call "disappointed aspirational voters"—grows. It is not an accident, therefore, that the spread of populism, which we discuss in the next chapter, was particularly rapid in the aftermath of the Great Recession (or, in a more dramatic form, in the aftermath of the Great Depression).

4.8. Conclusion

This chapter has covered a wide terrain, fitting the extraordinary changes brought about by the great shift of technological regime. Never before in human history could it have been imagined that around half of young people in the advanced world would be going through higher education in the early twenty-first century, and that a slight majority would be female. As late as the 1950s (apart from the US North) the large majority of young people had left school by the age of fifteen, and the small university-educated elite was overwhelmingly male.

If we think loosely of the ICT revolution as the "shock" to the advanced societies, it required a major corresponding reconfiguration of the political economic framework, as we explained, from the relatively organized national and international rules within which Fordism worked to what we have called the embedded knowledge-based liberal framework that enabled the knowledge economy to develop. In fact, as shown in 4.4, the result is that the core parts of the advanced societies have indeed transformed themselves into knowledge economies; but the centripetal forces of the attraction and agglomeration of knowledge competences in big, successful cities has sharply segregated them from the less educated, who have stayed in or seen themselves as forced to move to peripheral (neglected) communities. So where does that leave us in our analysis of the resilience of advanced capitalist democracies in the face of external shocks?

In the next chapter we discuss the development of populist opposition—typically in peripheral communities—and the political responses to it. But we note at this point, and will elaborate in the next chapter, that it has not been the case that the populist reaction has been against systems of advanced capitalism; it has not been a socialist reaction. The reaction has rather been against what has been seen as the political establishment, particularly in the United States, which controls the government: Trump portraying himself as the antiestablishment outsider to Washington, even if he is a wealthy businessman. Populists see themselves as "neglected" by successive governments. Populism, evidently, isn't a reaction against the nation-state, or against democracy in any obvious sense; it is more an expression of the desire to recapture government, perhaps from foreigners—to "take back control of the frontiers."

Apart from the seriously disadvantaged, there is no evidence that most voters are against advanced capitalism. Populism reflects the understandable belief that they—and, equally worryingly for them, their children—have been excluded from the slow-moving upward escalator of progress; and from this they draw the conclusion that immigrants (or, under Obama in United States, African Americans) have taken their place. It is no surprise that such sentiments are particularly strong in the aftermath of major economic crises, which ACDs are not immune to.

5

The Politics of the Knowledge Economy and the Rise of Populism

In this chapter we consider what we (paraphrasing Hall) in chapter 3 called "second-order" effects of the transition to the knowledge economy. By this we mean the set of preferences, beliefs, and party allegiances that are crystallizing as a consequence of the political-economic realities brought about by the knowledge economy. In chapter 3 we considered "first-order" effects—immediate policy responses reflecting existing political coalitions—and we saw that these responses were relatively limited and in most countries failed to offer much compensation for those who lost out in the collapse of the Fordist economy. This failure, we argue in this chapter, has created the political conditions for the rise of populism. By populism we have in mind a set of preferences and beliefs that rejects established parties and elites, that sees established politicians as gaming the system to their own advantage, and that at the same time sees the poor as undeserving of government support. Above all it opposes immigrants, who are always counted among the undeserving (getting the benefits of immigration without paying the costs), and it rejects the cosmopolitan outlook associated with the rising cities in favor of the traditional family, conforming sexual orientations, and nationalism. In Lipset and Rokkan's (1967) terminology it is a new social cleavage.[1]

As we saw in chapter 3, populism has in fact gained a foothold in all advanced democracies at the expense of established parties, especially those on the center-left. Yet the conditions that are conducive to populism vary a great deal by existing political and economic institutions—in particular, the extent to which these address, or fail to address, the adverse effects of the transition to the knowledge economy. Very briefly, our claim is that skill and education systems that are conducive to a more equal distribution of income and that facilitate inter- and intragenerational mobility limit the spread of populist parties and values. In addition, when the skill system relies heavily on industrial workers with company-specific skills, companies have an incentive to upgrade these skills instead of laying off workers. This reduces the number of mostly male workers who are susceptible to populist appeals because they find it so hard to compete for jobs in services. We also suggest that populist values are much less prevalent in the major cities because these are hubs for the new knowledge economy, with the attendant concentration of location cospecific assets and social networks. Indeed, we find in the cities—broadly characterized by tolerance of diversity and cosmopolitan values, from acceptance of immigrants to tolerance of nonconforming lifestyles—the antithesis of populism, even after controlling for education and income. Contrary to the common view in the literature, that such values are orthogonal to materialist preferences, we see them as a complement to the decentralized urban economy, which places a premium on open-ended interaction with others regardless of their national origins, sexual orientation, or lifestyle choices. Intolerance and conformism is not conducive to economic success in the knowledge economy.

It is important to note that populist values do not necessarily translate into populist parties, because of barriers to party entry built into the electoral system, and because of preemptive moves by existing parties. In PR systems even relatively small groups can be mobilized by political entrepreneurs, but in majoritarian systems they typically have to change the policy position of a major party to gain political clout. Some established parties have also been more effective in capturing the changing sentiments of voters even as we would not label them populist. Japan is a case in point. Historically immigration policies have been very restrictive, traditional family policies are relatively entrenched, and same-sex marriage is not allowed. The LDP has benefitted from this, and responding to the growth of populist sentiments, a nationalist emphasis in policies has been reinforced by Shinzō Abe more recently, as LDP leader. In part this reflects the overrepresentation of rural districts in the electoral system, but the main point is simply that populist sentiments are less likely to spill over into new party formation when policies—and, in the case of Japan, the LDP—are already reflective of such sentiments. For this reason we cannot simply measure the extent of populism by the vote shares of populist parties. Neither major party in the United States, for example, would have counted as populist in the past, but Donald Trump is now seen as a primary example of large-scale populism (even, as we will argue, the Republican Party still cannot be counted as a populist party). The contemporary Conservative party in England is another example, if in a more muted way. Still, we will consider the dynamic effects of economic change on the support for populist parties within countries.

The rise of populism is a significant shock to the political system, but it is unlikely to put the new knowledge economy at risk. In part this is because populism is not primarily an attack on policies that promote the advanced economy, nor on advanced capitalist companies, but a reaction by those who have not benefited from actual growth and opportunities. Most obviously, populism is quite opposite to socialism; while a left-socialist (or, in the 1930s, communist) reaction to the Depression and perceived failure of capitalism was to dismantle the capitalist system, that is not the populist reaction. Part of the populist reaction is a call to be included in the wealth stream of the new economy, and the key demand of reducing low-skill immigration is largely irrelevant to the knowledge economy. Other policies associated with populism—especially trade protection, state restrictions on product market competition, and serious interference with lifestyle choices—are clearly antithetical to the knowledge economy, but they are unlikely to garner sustained majorities. This is because there is a much more attractive path for the middle classes: namely, inclusion in the stream of wealth created by the new economy and associated support for policies that will produce more of the same. We count here not only those with higher education who are already benefiting from the new economy, but also aspirational voters who see their children benefiting from the expansion of higher education and new opportunities in the rising cities. For families in which upward intergenerational mobility is a reality, populist appeals typically fall on barren soil. In addition, many nongraduate service sector workers in large cities whose livelihood depends on the knowledge economy are typically supportive of it. We would argue that neither Trump nor the British Conservative Party are concerned to weaken the knowledge economy, since for both it would be a dangerous result politically. As Thelen (2004) shows, even Hitler, once he had understood the consequences of Nazi control of the advanced companies in Germany, desisted from doing so (and his "big lie" was the international Jewish conspiracy).

For large minorities in the old middle classes, however, the fading Fordist economy can no longer sustain well-paying jobs, creating a "hollowing-out" effect that shows up as declining demand and wages (Autor and Dorn 2009; Goos and Manning 2007). If this reflects predominantly the collapse of industry, it is also mirrored in the decline in status and loss of many lower-level management, clerical, and service sector occupations as a result of computerization. When coupled with poor educational opportunities for children, a profound sense of malaise and status decline sets in (Gidron and Hall 2017). These are the groups who find the siren songs of populism hard to resist. Even if populist policies are unlikely to notably improve their lives, making outgroups the cause and established politicians responsible has proved an effective political platform.

5.1. Theory: A New Cleavage

Fordism, as we argued in chapter 3, was a system that produced strong interdependencies across skill groups, neighborhoods, and regions, which in turn fostered relatively low levels of economic inequality. The new knowledge economy, by contrast, has undermined these complementarities and favors those with high skills, especially those in the cities. Several puzzling facts accompany this shift that either contradict standard political economy models, or find no explanation there. The most frequently noted is the lack of redistribution in response to higher inequality (what Lindert has dubbed the "Robin Hood Paradox"). Another is the decline of the Left at a time when more people than ever feel that governments are not doing enough for them (De Waele 2014). Alongside the decline of the Left has been the rise of populism, which defies classification on a left-right scale even though incomes, presumably the source of left-right politics, are becoming more polarized. Finally, cross-class solidarity seems to have collapsed; this is not only reflected in a lack of appetite for redistribution from high-income earners, but in a striking lack of concern among the middle classes for the plight of the poor (Georgiadis and Manning 2012; Cavaille and Trump 2015; see also chapter 3).

All these phenomena are linked to an empirical regularity that has recently attracted much attention in economics (Corak 2013a, b; Durlauf and Seshadri 2017): a strong negative relationship between inequality and social mobility across generations—what Krueger (2012) has dubbed the Great Gatsby curve (GGC). It is illustrated in figure 5.1. It appears that this relationship is very general, at least among advanced democracies. It holds up in a cross section of advanced democracies, across American states, and across time in the United States (Durlauf and Seshadri 2017). (Time series data for other countries have yet to be parsed in this manner.)

Mobility is important for the simple reason that it ties together the interests of different income classes. Those at the lower end have some expectation that they, or their children, will move up in the distribution, while those at the higher end have some fear that they, or their children, will move down. This induces a commonality of interests, which is partly captured by standard insurance models as a concern for downward movement, and hence concern for the people below (Baldwin 1990; Moene and Wallerstein 2001; Iversen and Soskice 2001; Rehm 2009, 2016); and partly captured by social mobility models as an expectation of upward movement,

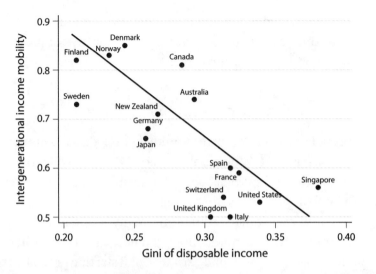

FIGURE 5.1. The Great Gatsby curve. *Notes*: Intergenerational income mobility is one minus Corak's (2013b) estimates of the elasticity between paternal earnings and a son's adult earnings, using data on a cohort of children born during the early to mid-1960s and measuring their adult outcomes in the mid-to late 1990s. Income inequality is the Gini of disposable household income for about 1985. *Sources*: Intergenerational mobility is from Corak (2013b); disposable income inequality is from OECD Income Distribution Database (IDD): Gini, poverty, income. Data extracted on December 31, 2017, 13:11 UTC (GMT) from OECD.Stat. Data for Singapore is from 2000 and comes from Ministry of Finance (2015), "Income Growth, Inequality, and Mobility Trends in Singapore." Ministry of Finance Occasional Paper.

and hence appreciation for the people above and their concerns, notably the costs of taxation (Okun 1975; Bénabou and Ok 1998). This dual logic of mobility creates a simple one-dimensional division of preferences—support for more or less taxation and spending—where conflict of interests follows class lines but without the intensity expected in pure redistributive models. In this kind of high-mobility world, social democracy with a universalist message of "we are all in the same boat" naturally appeals to a large number of people. So do Christian democratic appeals to class cooperation. Indeed, the Fordist economy was one that attracted many tags in politics, culture, and academia which had unity as a common theme: social pacts, one-nation projects, class compromise, and so on. Scheve and Stasavage (2016) talk of an implicit social contract, which they attribute to the joint sacrifices in major wars. But such a social contract can be understood to have survived into the postwar period in large part because of propitious economic conditions for inclusiveness.

5.1.1. THE OLD MIDDLE CLASS AND POPULISM

The end of Fordism may correspondingly be seen as an unraveling of the social contract. When mobility slows down, so does the sense of common cause, especially when inequality is high. Those at the bottom will support redistribution, and those at the top will oppose it, in a typical class-polarized pattern. Many in the middle classes will see themselves as more closely aligned with the top because they either have good jobs and earnings, or if starting graduates they expect to move up the job ladder, or because they can still reasonably expect to see their children do well by acquiring the education needed in the new economy. We will refer to these groups as the *new middle classes* because they have made the leap into the new economy, at least from an intergenerational perspective. The *old middle classes*, by contrast, are those who have experienced stagnating wages because of skill-biased technological change, outsourcing, or import competition from the ECE countries or East Asia—the "hollowing out" of the middle—and who have low expectations that the educational system will allow their children to make the leap into the new economy. The old middle classes are stuck, and they will not simply split the difference between low and high redistribution and taxes by adopting middle positions.

As we argue below, the extent of such segmentation of opportunity depends on the national education and skill system. But with limited mobility we expect the old middle class to display a new combination of preference that has no parallel in the Fordist economy. One the one hand, they demand redistribution from the educated middle classes, whom they cannot hope to join; on the other hand, they see no commonality in interests with those at the very bottom. The poor are lazy or "undeserving," while the rich are gaming the system. Furthermore, since upward mobility is seen as impossible, jobs and income become perceived as a zero-sum game where immigrants are viewed as unwelcome competitors. Sometimes this competition is real. While the share of immigrants is not a strong predictor of wages—in large part because most immigrants settle in the cities—the balance of the evidence suggests that there are some substitution effects among those with lower skills (Ottaviano and Peri 2012). High-educated immigrants, on the other hand, are generally complements to resident workers with high education, allowing skill clusters to expand and thrive (Borjas 2013). New data from the United States also show that in localities where there have been significant increases in low-skill immigration and imports from China, wages have fallen (Autor, Dorn, and Hanson, 2013). Competition in labor markets may also spill over into perceived competition for scarce resources like schools and welfare benefits (Feeman 1986; Cavaille and Ferwerda 2017); and regardless of the true magnitude, it is a potent populist political message during a decade of austerity. Even where there is no direct competition, among those who received their education and entered the labor market in the Fordist economy (mostly men fifty years and older) there is a sense that immigration is a threat to the implicit social contract of the Fordist economy. This implicit contract was a national program of inclusion for those who acquired basic training and worked hard, and it did not extend to foreigners.

Note the two-dimensional nature of old middle-class preferences. They want jobs and benefits targeted to themselves, just like those at the top and at the bottom, but their preferences are incompatible with either traditional center-left or center-right platforms. And because the shift to the knowledge economy has resulted in lower wages and mobility for these groups, it also implies less support for traditional welfare policies, less support for the Left, and less cross-class solidarity. From this perspective, the GGC captures the puzzles identified with the rise of the new knowledge economy because, once again, the transition to this new economy has indeed been linked to higher inequality and, at least for the old middle classes, less mobility. As argued by Hochschild (2016), declining mobility breeds a sense of status loss as the old middle class fails to keep up with others.

5.1.2. THE REBIRTH OF THE CITIES
AND THE NEW MIDDLE CLASS

In addition to education, a major fault line in the new economy, which also marks the split between the new and old middle classes, is between large cities and smaller towns and rural areas. Cities and their feeder towns declined in tandem with the end of Fordism as well-paying manufacturing jobs for middle-skilled workers collapsed everywhere. Inner-city neighborhoods decayed as plants closed, causing a significant uptick in crime, with the fortunes of surrounding towns that supplied the industrial centers declining in tandem. The term "rust belt" is a fitting metaphor for the areas most affected by deindustrialization. In response to urban decay, better-educated and higher-income families migrated to the new suburban enclaves that promised safety, better schools, and better infrastructure.

Urban malaise and the associated process of suburbanization is described in a large literature in economic geography and sociology. But for all the gloomy predictions at the time, the trend was reversed (Power 2016). As we saw in the previous chapter, the rise of the new knowledge economy presaged the revival of the cities. Knowledge-based production embodies the logic of agglomeration and increasing returns, which lead to strong complementarities among highly educated workers and between these and knowledge-intensive firms—complementarities that require physical proximity and interaction. Cities provide the spatial and social proximity, as well as the public infrastructure, that are required for these complementarities to work themselves out (Glaeser 2010, Storper 2013). As a consequence cities began to grow again, in a process economic geographers (following Ehrenhalt 2012) call the Great Inversion.

But the Great Inversion is not simply a revival of cities; it is also a reconfiguration of the underlying class structure. Many well-educated, high-income professionals who fled the cities in the 1970s and 1980s have moved back, and the young college-educated now congregate in the cities where they form the new middle classes. These are the winners of the transition to the knowledge economy, and they see their interests bound up with its expansion. Unlike the old middle classes, the preferences of these groups tend to incorporate urban working-class preferences for public goods like safety, public transportation, education, housing, and a clean and green environment, although they are naturally wary of redistribution and excessive taxes.

On noneconomic matters the new middle classes tend to take progressive stances. A major reason is that it is very difficult to have traditionalist views on gender, race, and sexuality and still thrive in a decentralized and fluid urban economy where teamwork and creative invention are paramount, unlike the hierarchically organized production systems associated with Fordism. The main assets of the knowledge economy are embedded in its skilled labor forces, and boundaries between firms tend to be blurred by the fluidity of production teams and by the social networks that complement this fluidity. Workers have to get along with others, and this is hard for those who harbor strong racist, misogynist, or homophobic views. Higher education, a critical prerequisite for working in the knowledge economy, reinforces this logic because education militates against fact-distorting beliefs, which bigoted attitudes typically necessitate. Of course, part of this effect may be due to self-selection into cities, but the key point is that there is a complementarity between participation in the urban economy and "left-libertarian" political values, in the broadest sense of embracing policies of economic integration and cultural diversity.

Outside the urban knowledge corridors, however, the class structure is increasingly petrified. Workers with the equivalent of high school degrees can no longer afford to live in the cities, and as they move to smaller towns and less attractive suburbs they form old middle-class enclaves that no longer feel there are good opportunities for jobs and advancement. These are middle-aged people who, in the Fordist economy, once acquired what was seen as a solid education, and who once had well-paying jobs with good benefits. If one can talk about a social contract in the democratic capitalist system, these people saw themselves as part of this contract. Correspondingly, as they experience marginalization in the new economy they see a broken social contract. In their perceptions, immigrants in the cities take up jobs that would potentially be within reach for the old middle class—in retail, cleaning, and low-end social services—but for many reasons (housing, transport and status) they do not take them. Direct competition with immigrants for these jobs may be limited, but their employment symbolizes how people who were never part of the original social contract have seemingly cut in line.

It is useful here to recall Hochschild's (2016) striking metaphor of the escalator to the American Dream, on which the old middle classes, especially male manual workers over fifty, feel the escalator slowing down just as they see immigrants and African Americans being helped by the (Democrat) political establishment to cut to the front of the line. And with their disassociation from the successful cities also comes resentment of the educated urban classes and the values they represent. It is common in the literature to describe this as cultural backlash, but in our view it has deep material roots in the breakdown of cross-class and cross-space interdependencies. It is hard to imagine populism in the absence of major economic upheaval. Lipset and Rokkan (1967) saw economic cleavages and values as intimately related, and so do we.

Of course, these resentments have to be politically activated, and this is where populist politicians and parties enter. Populism gives voice to grievances, and it is not necessarily the case that this voice conforms to what political economy models would predict to be in the best economic interests of the intended audience. The key is to present a clear alternative to established parties in a manner that is anti-elite/anti-intellectual and captures a nativist version of the old social contract, which is based on notions of working hard, especially in industry, obeying the rules, observing traditional family values, and attachment to the nation. If the status of the old middle classes was bound up with this construction, it is the decline of manual labor, the decline in the traditional family, and the blurring of national boundaries that are causes of status anxiety. All populist parties appeal to these sentiments by promising to restore the social contract, even if there is no path back to the old economy.

The old middle classes are not necessarily antigrowth, nor anti–new technology ("Luddites"); they were, after all, part of

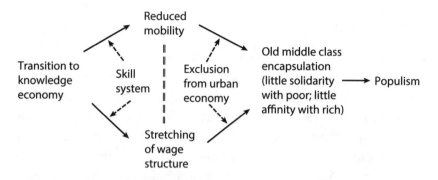

FIGURE 5.2. The link between the transition to the knowledge economy and populism. *Notes:* Solid arrows indicate direct causal effects; dashed arrows indicate conditioning effects. The double-dashed line implies the Great Gatsby curve.

the industrial machine that once propelled the economy forward. Rather, they want the government to work for *them* and to restore their sense of place and pride. The poor and immigrants are undeserving in this understanding because these groups were never part of the social contract to begin with. The old middle classes are not against the capitalist system per se, but they want to resume a more central position in the political system. Of course, this is not easy to accomplish under democratic rules in the new economy, and appeals to nationalism and the need for a strong leader may be seen as a response to this reality.

In figure 5.2 we have labeled the processes that adversely affect those in the old middle classes *encapsulation*; and we see this as a main source of support for populist values and political parties. Encapsulation occurs as a result of the simultaneous reduction in mobility and a stretching of the wage distribution—the intertemporal Great Gatsby curve—which is caused by the transition to the knowledge economy. Such encapsulation is associated with lower education and particularly pronounced outside the urban centers, while those who remain in the cities all benefit in some measure from the success of the new economy. The new middle classes and high-flying professionals, in particular, see themselves as the engine of the new economy and see the government as, broadly speaking, working for them.

5.2. National Variation

The cleavages we have outlined are present in all advanced democracies, but this is true to different degrees. Inequality and mobility are negatively correlated, but countries are in different locations on the Great Gatsby curve. This matters for the extent to which the new versus old middle-class split has materialized. When inequality is high and mobility is low, the constituencies for populism in the middle grow. When inequality is low and mobility is high, these constituencies tend to shrink—even though some groups in the middle will still resemble the old middle class as defined above.

Because the new knowledge economy is based on highly skilled, increasingly college-educated workers, a critical factor in explaining the degree of inequality and mobility is the distribution and acquisition of skills—in other words, the national system of training, education, and upskilling. Precisely because of the weak complementarities between lower- and higher-skilled workers in the knowledge economy, the distribution of skills becomes a key determinant of the distribution of income and intergenerational mobility (Nickell 2004), in addition to geographical mobility. In this section, we discuss several dimensions of the educational system that have been identified in the literature as important to securing equal educational opportunity and upward intergenerational mobility. We summarize these dimensions in a single index of educational equality of opportunity, which we will use in the subsequent empirical analysis to explain cross-national differences in populist values.

The distinctions we identify are closely related to the varieties of capitalism and democracy that we already encountered in chapter 2 and the two paths to democracy. In the protocorporatist cases that morphed into coordinated market economies, vocational education has always been highly institutionalized with broad support from both employers and unions, as well as all major political parties. This stands in contrast to the protoliberal cases that developed into liberal market economies, which never acquired effective vocational training systems. As we have explained, this distinction is highly correlated with electoral systems, and the latter have produced distinct coalitional dynamics (see chapter 3), conditioned by the strength of Christian democratic parties.

Following Iversen and Stephens (2008), one can broadly distinguish three "worlds" of human capital formation, which match the institutional distinctions we made in chapter 3. The Scandinavian PR countries, with frequent center-left governments, are characterized by "inclusionary" policies with high levels of spending on daycare and preschool, primary and secondary education, higher education, active labor market policies, and vocational education (with late tracking of students to minimize class inheritance). The continental European countries with frequent Christian democratic government participation are characterized by high levels of vocational education (and late tracking), but only medium levels of public spending on primary, secondary, and tertiary education, and low levels of spending on daycare and preschool and active labor market policies. The liberal countries are characterized by low levels of spending on daycare and preschool, active labor market policy, and vocational education, low level of employment protection, and moderate levels of spending on primary, secondary, and tertiary education. Private spending on higher education and, in some countries, daycare is substantial in this group. The east Asian cases are unique, perhaps a fourth type, by combining firm-based vocation training system with largely liberal features of the other parts of the educational system (notably very high private spending).

The specific differences across countries in training and educational systems, which make up the components of our index of equality of opportunity, can be summarized in slightly greater detain as follows:

The first distinction is (again) between countries where most education and training is through the formal educational system only and countries that combine academic schooling with strong vocational training tracks (Estevez-Abe et al. 2001; Busemeyer and Trampusch 2012). A strong vocational training system offers those in the lower half of the academic-ability distribution the opportunity to acquire valuable skills, and it is closely related to more coordinated wage-setting and a more compressed wage distribution. In addition, since these systems offer institutionalized school-to-work transitions, workers at the lower end of the ability distribution have strong incentives to work hard in school to get into the best vocational schools or apprenticeships. By contrast, in general skills systems, such as that in the United States, there tends to be a bifurcation of the high school population between those students who expect to go on to college and, therefore, have strong incentives to work hard to make it into the best schools, and those who do not and expect to leave the formal educational system during or right after high school.

A second distinction is between early and late tracking of students. Tracking comes in two variants. In some countries with strong vocational training systems, notably Germany and Austria, students are divided into vocational and academic tracks in primary school, at ages ten through twelve, while in others, notably the Nordic countries but also the Netherlands, tracking does not begin until secondary school. In general-skills systems, vocational tracks and therefore tracking is missing, but it is common to divide students by academic ability—what OECD (2012a) calls "ability grouping"—or to have academic admission standards for better schools (the two can substitute for each other). In all LMEs, including Ireland, more than ninety percent of schools differentiate by ability, although the age at which this occurs varies (see OECD 2012, 57). Academic admissions standards are less common, but not exceptional.

Tracking and ability grouping are consequential for intergenerational mobility. A large literature in sociology and labor economics shows that when students are divided into separate tracks at an early age, family class background becomes a strong determinant of the track that is chosen (Gamoran 2010; Ammermüller 2005). The explanation is that children from nonacademic backgrounds tend to start out academically weaker, and they are also typically expected to follow in the footsteps of their parents (by both parents and teachers). There is also evidence that early tracking by ability magnifies academic achievement gaps later in life (Hanushek and Woessmann 2006). Tracking, especially when it occurs early, is thus heavily class biased, undermining intergenerational mobility.

Third, the sorting of students starts even before primary schooling. Heckman (2011) shows that preprimary investment in skills—including cognitive, noncognitive and socioemotional skills—improves the acquisition of skills and academic performance later in life. Like primary education, parents from working-class backgrounds depend almost entirely on public provision of preprimary education, and for this reason, spending on preprimary education can help break class inheritance in academic achievement later in life (Restuccia and Urratia 2004; Blau and Currie 2006; Schuetz, Ursprung, and Woessmann 2008). Unlike primary education, there is a great deal of variation in how much governments spend on preprimary education.

Fourth, class differentiation in educational attainment is affected by differences in the quality of schools, which has multiple institutional sources. In centralized educational systems, where most decisions about funding, curriculum, academic standards, teacher salaries, and so on, are set at the national level, there is less scope for school quality to diverge, fostering greater equality across socioeconomic boundaries. Conversely, when there is considerable scope for local differentiation in funding, teacher salaries, and curriculum, variation in school quality rises. Such variation is strongly reinforced by neighborhood segregation with high-income, high-educated families moving to the best school districts and bidding up housing prices (Gingrich and Ansell 2014). Such sorting not only expands the local tax base for schools in good districts; it also raises quality in these districts through higher involvement of parents in their children's education (Durlauf 1996a, b).

There is no straightforward way to capture class differentiation in school quality, but the OECD has created a useful measure of "social inclusion," which is calculated as the *between* secondary-school variance in the PISA index of the social, economic, and cultural status of students (basically a measure of parents' class background), divided by the sum of the between-school and the within-school variance in students' socioeconomic status (OECD, 2013). The greater the between-school portion of the variance, the greater the sorting of schools.

We do not have a similar measure of socioeconomic differentiation at the tertiary level, but we can use private spending (mostly individual) on higher education as a rough proxy. A higher share of private schools and private funding matters because it creates financial barriers for low- and middle-income families to reach the best schools. Measured by the private share of tertiary educational spending, in LMEs it varies between forty percent (UK) and sixty-two percent (United States), whereas most spending in CMEs is public, with Germany and the Netherlands being mild outliers, at around twenty-six percent (OECD 2010, 233). Japan and Korea resemble the liberal group in this respect, and in fact have the highest shares in the whole sample, with sixty-six and seventy-three percent private spending, respectively.

Finally, we consider the role of adult education and retraining. This is clearly a factor that is more important for intra- than intergenerational mobility, but it has become more important over time as the rate of technological change has accelerated, rendering many skills obsolete within a lifetime and placing a premium on workers' adaptability. For those with high resources and strong initial skills, such adaptation is often feasible by using savings or borrowing to go back to school or enroll in adult training programs. At the lower end of the distribution, however, there are great financial barriers to this type of upskilling. Just like preprimary education, it depends critically on government subsidies. We try to capture this by the average share of participation in adult training and education programs among those with low initial skills, using OECD data (see table 5.1 for specifics).

The multiple distinctions we have made in skill systems are summarized in table 5.1. The indicators measure different dimensions of educational systems at different levels of education, corresponding to each of the logics outlined above. We use the data from the original sources without modification, and while a case can be made for giving more or less weight to particular indicators, the index of equal educational opportunity in the last column is a simple mean (after 0-1 standardization) of the seven indicators (to reduce concerns about curve-fitting). The index is meant to capture the ease by which people can acquire new skills and, crucially, the ability of younger generations to escape their class background and

TABLE 5.1. key indicators of skill systems

	Vocational training share[1]	Age of tracking[2]	Lower secondary schools with ability grouping[3]	Social inclusion of secondary schools[4]	Private share of tertiary spending[5]	Adult training opportunity[6]	Preprimary public spending[7]	Index of equal opportunity[8]
Australia	62	16	70	77	50	27	0.10	0.45
Austria	72	10	59	71	6	26	0.52	0.44
Belgium	69	12	37	72	10	31	0.93	0.59
Canada	5	16	65	83	43	42	n.a.	0.55
Denmark	48	16	33	82	3	38	1.08	0.77
Finland	65	16	31	91	3	25	1.11	0.83
France	43	16	41	n.a.	17	n.a.	0.70	0.71
Germany	59	10	57	74	13	26	0.65	0.43
Ireland	2	15	62	80	22	32	0.14	0.43
Italy	25	14	61	76	26	14	0.45	0.37
Japan	24	15	81	78	65	20	0.11	0.27
Korea	28	14	79	78	73	21	0.40	0.28
Netherlands	68	12	89	82	26	42	0.37	0.49
New Zealand	4	16	79	78	41	n.a.	0.73	0.39
Norway	60	16	40	91	4	50	1.82	0.95
Spain	43	16	32	75	25	26	0.62	0.58
Sweden	54	16	42	87	9	42	1.84	0.86
Switzerland	64	12	74	83	n.a.	n.a.	0.20	0.42
UK	42	16	64	79	40	35	0.33	0.52
US	0	16	64	74	62	37	0.42	0.36

Source: OECD. 2008. Education at a Glance: Indicators, Table C1.1. New Zealand, where data are missing, is based in data in Estevez-Abe et al. (2001) after adjusting for difference in averages. [2] Notes: Share of total upper secondary enrollment who are in vocational training programs. [1] Source: OECD. 2012. Equity and Quality in Education: Supporting Disadvantaged Students and Schools, OECD Publishing, Table 2.2. [3] This is the mean on the share of students in schools using ability grouping and the share of schools having ability criteria for admission (France is missing data on the first indicator and is based on the second only). Sources: OECD. 2012. *Equity and Quality in Education: Supporting Disadvantaged Students and Schools,* OECD Publishing, Table 2.2., and OECD, PISA 2012 Database, Table 2.11. [4] OECD's index of social inclusion calculated as 100*(1-rho), where rho stands for the intra-class correlation of socio-economic status, i.e. the between-school variance in the PISA index of social, economic and cultural status of students, divided by the sum of the between-school variance in students' socio-economic status and the within-school variance in students' socio-economic status. *Source:* PISA, OECD. 2013. *Results: Excellence Through Equity: Giving Every Student the Chance to Succeed (volume II).* OECD Publishing, Annex B1, Chapter 2, Table II.2.13a. Data are missing for France. [5] Average of private share of spending on tertiary education, 1995–2013. Source: OECD, Education at a Glance 2014; 2016. [6] The average share of participation in adult training and education programs among those with adult literacy scores below level 3 in the OECD Adult Literacy Survey. Source: OECD. 2012. Survey of Adult Skills (PIAAC), Table A5.7 (L); [7] OECD. 2016. Education at a Glance 2016 OECD Indicators, Table C2.3.

be successful in the new knowledge economy. We see these differences, summarized by the three worlds of human capital formation, as rooted in distinct political and economic institutions, which we have traced back to conditions and political developments in the early 20th century (chapter 2).

5.3. New Materialism or Postmaterialism?

Our argument owes much to Kitschelt's influential work on "right authoritarianism," which is conceptualized as a political-cultural response to the rise of "left libertarianism"—itself a response to the postwar expansion of education, prosperity, and the welfare state (1994, 1995). Kitschelt's account, when compiled from multiple writings, is in fact a subtle interpretation of socioeconomic change that acknowledges the role of occupational experiences (including his distinction between "object processing" and "people processing") and economic organization (notably the extent of hierarchy), which indirectly point to the importance of the nature of capitalist production and technology (see Kitschelt 1994, 1995; Kitschelt and McGann 1995; Kitschelt and Rehm 2014). Daily work experiences are part of a process of identity formation whereby, in the words of Oesch (2012, 3), "voters generalize from one important sphere of life (work) to another (politics)." In addition to Kitschelt and Oesch, Kriesi and Pappas (2015) and Häusermann (2010) have made important contributions to this line of research.

Yet, we do not view the "sociocultural" dimension identified in this literature as orthogonal to distributive politics (also see Häusermann and Kriesi 2015). Although distinct, it is itself rooted in materialist interests, even if it is clearly separate from the old left-right dimension of social spending and redistribution. The new middle classes are broadly satisfied with policies that promote the advanced sectors—investment in education, in particular—and they naturally see cosmopolitan and tolerant attitudes, often combined with a concern for a clean environment, as complements to successful careers in the decentralized urban economy organized around social and economic networks with fluid boundaries. The old middle classes, by contrast, have been locked out of the new economy, and they increasingly find that their children are as well. They blame globalization, immigrants, and the breakdown of the traditional family, which are reminders of their own loss of status, and they see elites as politically beholden to the new urban and educated classes. This division is orthogonal to the midcentury social, economic, and political integration of the middle and lower middle classes, held together by strong complementarities in production, but it is not in our view "post-materialist" (Inglehart 1971, 1990).

What we reject is thus the notion that the "new politics" of populism is a purely cultural phenomenon, as a "cultural backlash" against the rise of "postmaterialism"—a view expounded by Inglehart and Norris (2017). They show that those voters who have populist predispositions on "cultural" issues like law and order, immigration, and multiculturalism also tend to vote for populist parties that are themselves identified by the same general set of issues (see also Bornschier 2010; Bustikova 2014). This is not surprising, nor is it contrary to our political economy interpretation.[2] "Postmaterialists" and "populists" are rooted in different parts of the modern economy, and it is impossible to detach their values from this underlying economic reality.

Cultural backlash as a phenomenon removed from the reality of the material world also cannot explain, as we will see, why populist values vary systematically across countries in close correspondence to the structure of skill systems. Educational institutions matter because they are critical to the economic opportunities of the middle class and their children.

5.4. Evidence

We offer several pieces of evidence for our argument. First, we explore the relationship between values and various indicators for education and economic position using survey data from the World Values Survey (WVS). WVS contains several useful variables for measuring values and covers a broad range of advanced countries in Europe, North America, and East Asia. Four of the six waves, carried out in the period 1995–2012, include a substantial number of advanced democracies, and we pool all four waves when possible. Not all countries are included in all waves, but the following sixteen are in at least one wave: Australia, Canada, Finland, France, Germany, Italy, Japan, South Korea, the Netherlands, New Zealand, Norway, Spain, Sweden, Switzerland, Great Britain, and the United States. For the full sample, we have nearly fifty thousand observations.

Second, we explore the macrorelationship between the prevalence of populist values in national electorates and the equality of educational opportunity as measured by the index developed in the previous section. We do this in a multilevel regression setup with all individual-level controls included. While we recognize the correlational nature of the data, this is the most direct comparative test of the argument that institutionalized access to educational opportunity determines the share of the electorate who are susceptible to populist appeals. We are aware of no other evidence of this nature.

Third, we repeat the individual-level analysis, but using populist vote choice as the dependent variable. Of the sixteen advanced democracies included in the World Values Surveys, half had significant populist parties at the time of at least one of the waves. Unfortunately, vote intention was not recorded in France or Italy, so we are left with six countries: Finland, Germany, the Netherlands, Norway, Sweden, and Switzerland. Still, this gives us about 9,600 observations and enough populist voters to allow multivariate analysis.

5.4.1. Identifying the New Cleavage

A limitation of virtually all comparative opinion surveys is that they do not conceptualize distributive politics as a multidimensional concept. Instead, respondents are asked to express more or less support for redistribution or for government spending, as opposed to asking which groups should benefit from, or pay to, government policies. This is also true for WVS, which asks whether incomes should be made more or less equal, whether governments should have primary responsibility to provide for people, and whether competition is good or harmful. These questions reflect, to some degree at least, the traditional left-right dimension as crystallized in the Fordist era, and we will use them to identify that "old politics" dimension.

A fourth question about distribution is different. It asks whether poverty is the result of laziness or social injustice. We have argued that the old middle classes (in line with Cavaille and Trump, 2015) will be in favor of redistribution from the rich (as are the poor), but against redistribution toward the poor (as are the rich). Since the poor will presumably always be inclined to say that poverty is a problem of social justice and higher-up groups will not, the item will be correlated with a traditional left-right dimension. But insofar as the old middle classes take distinct positions on populist, noneconomic attitude variables, views on the poor will be correlated with this dimension as well. The old middle is in favor of redistribution, but not toward the poor.

To measure other attitudes relevant to the new cleavage, the WVS offers a range of potential questions. Three of these are used across our four waves and in all our countries: one asks whether the environment should be prioritized over growth; another whether homosexuality is justifiable; and a third whether natives should be favored over immigrants in allocating scarce jobs. We use factor analysis (technically, principal component with varimax rotation) to determine whether these items belong to a distinct dimension when the four "old" economic policy items are also included. The results are shown in table A5.1 in the appendix.

We find that there are only two salient dimensions where three items are highly correlated with a traditional left-right economic dimension, and three with a libertarian-populist dimension. The poverty item exhibits an exceptional pattern, because it is correlated moderately with *both* dimensions. This reflects, we believe, the two-dimensional nature of distributive politics, as argued above, and the willingness of the old middle classes to support both antipoor and antilibertarian positions.

Next, we use the results of the factor analysis to create indices for the two dimensions, and economic left-right dimensions and an orthogonal "value dimension"; the latter will serve as dependent variable in the following analysis. Higher values signify more populist values, although we prefer to treat this as a measure of the distinctiveness of old middle-class values rather than a measure of any universally accepted concept of populism. Populist values are hypothesized to be a reflection of the underlying materialist cleavage, whereas populist politics take distinct forms in different countries.

On the independent variable side, we seek to capture the division between the old and new middle classes using several indicators. The first is income, measured in deciles. The old middle classes are not poor, but they have experienced a relative decline that typically puts them at the lower end of the distribution (i.e., the hollowing-out effect in the task-specific SBTC thesis). The same is true of education, where the old middle classes typically have acquired some secondary education, but they lack the college degrees that would give them a foothold in the new economy. Gender is also important, because male breadwinner households dominated the Fordist economy: a pattern that became hard to sustain as industrial employment dropped. Moving to two-earner households, or poor one-earner households, adversely affected the status of men in these families while making women more economically and politically independent (Iversen and Rosenbluth 2010).

We also try to capture location in the old economy by occupation. Manual workers with routine jobs have been particularly pressured by new technology and by the shift of demand upwards in the product chain to goods and services requiring higher education—those provided by professionals, in particular. We distinguish between skilled and semiskilled manual workers to see if the former might be less vulnerable on account of their higher skills. We also compare both groups to white-collar workers in lower-level nonmanual occupations, mostly in low-skill personal and social services, where lack of routinization makes codification difficult. The last group consists of higher-educated professionals who are the main beneficiaries of the ICT revolution, with technology strongly complementing complex nonroutine tasks.[3]

Finally, we consider the importance of the city-country divide by separating those living in rural areas and smaller towns from those living in the bigger cities. The measure is the size of the resident town of the respondent. Unfortunately, this variable is not available for France, Japan, or South Korea, and we therefore run our regressions both with and without the urbanization variable.

In addition to these microlevel variables, we consider the effects of factors that promote educational opportunity and mobility, as recorded in table 5.1. In egalitarian skill systems, workers are assisted in upgrading their skills, and children from working-class backgrounds have better opportunities of acquiring an education that exceeds that of their parents. Higher mobility, as we have argued, is, in turn, expected to reduce the audience for populist appeals. We test this in a multilevel model that includes the equality of educational opportunity index as a macrolevel regressor. This also allows us to explore the relationship between the index and the estimated country fixed effects, which make the cross-national patterns easy to visualize.

5.4.2. Values

Table A5.2 in appendix shows the detailed results of the individual-level regressions. We find effects mostly as expected: older male manual workers with lower education—the main losers from the transition to the knowledge economy—are far more likely to express populist values than younger female nonmanual workers with higher education. The difference between professionals and semiskilled manual workers alone, keeping everything else constant, is about 0.2 on the value scale, which corresponds to nearly one-quarter of a standard deviation on that scale. Living in a small town, especially when compared to living in a large city, significantly increases this difference, as does having lower income. The self-employed are, perhaps surprisingly, *less* likely to express populist values. These are individual-level results and are estimated with dummies for each country ("fixed country effects"), but they are largely identical when we substitute in the educational opportunity index for the dummies.

Figure 5.3 illustrates the differences in populist values between what we might think of as a typical representative of the old middle classes and a typical representative of the new middle classes. We define the former as an employed male semiskilled manual worker

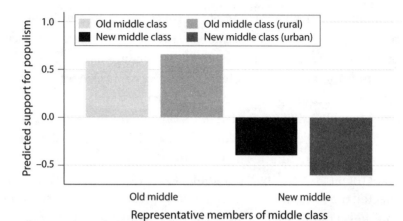

FIGURE 5.3. The difference in populist values between the old and new middle class. *Notes*: Estimates are based on regression results in table A5.2, column 1. The old middle class is "represented" by an employed male semiskilled manual worker with low education and an income in the fourth decile; the new middle class is defined as an employed female professional with high education and an income in the sixth decile. The second column for old middle adds rural residency, while the second column for new middle adds urban residence.

with low education and an income in the fourth decile; we define the latter as an employed female professional with high education and an income in the sixth decile. We separate out city versus small-town residence, because the distinction between large cities and small towns captures an aspect of the cleavage between the old and new economy.

Conceptualized this way, we see a large gulf in the propensity to express libertarian versus populist values. The predicted populism value for the old middle class representative is .6, while for the new middle class representative is –.4. The scale varies from –2 to +2, and the difference of 1 is equivalent to one standard deviation. This gap in preferences is notably greater than on the economic left-right dimension identified in the factor analysis. Here, the difference between the two groups is equivalent to one-third of a standard deviation on the dependent variable. So, while the left-right division that defined the Fordist economy only elicits modest disagreement, the new libertarian-populist division distinctive of the post-Fordist economic is quite sharp. Still, it is notable that, on matters of redistribution and spending, the new middle classes are to the *right* of the old. They may be social progressives, but they are not keen on promoting equality. Given that they are well positioned in the new economy, with better incomes and skills in higher demand, they have no reason to be.

The result underlines that the division between old and new middle classes is closely related to economic position: a conclusion that is reinforced by considering the effect of urbanization. Distinguishing between people living in small towns versus large cities raises the gap by about forty percent (although this estimate is based on a smaller sample). As we argued above, the urban-rural split is a major new cleavage brought about by strong agglomeration effects and the decline in the importance of smaller towns as "feeders" for the urban economy.

5.4.3. CROSS-NATIONAL VARIANCE

It is important to note that the individual-level estimates are average within-country differences. However, *more than half* the total explained variance is *between* countries, and we have argued that this variance is related to the educational system—in particular, to how conducive the system is to intra- and intergenerational mobility. Cross-national differences are in fact closely correlated to our educational opportunity index, as illustrated in figure 5.4, which shows the relationship between the index and predicted values of populism controlling for all individual-level differences. We see that the Nordic countries are in the bottom-right, with good educational opportunities across the academic ability distribution, low class barriers to higher education, good adult retraining options, and, correspondingly, low levels of populist values (Finland is a bit of an outlier, conceivably due to the lingering effects of the huge drop in manufacturing caused by the collapse of the Soviet Union). At the other end we find Japan and South Korea, with the United States and other liberal market economies not far behind. Especially in the East Asian cases, this may seem surprising, but only because we usually measure populism by the strength of populist parties, not

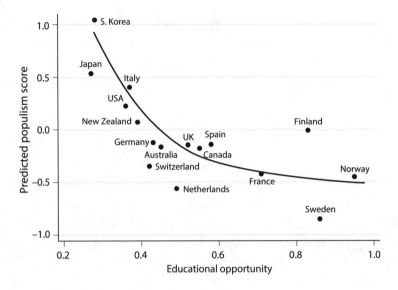

FIGURE 5.4. Educational opportunity and populist values.

populist values. The latter are quite pervasive in these countries, precisely as we should expect. A country like Norway, by contrast, with a significant populist party, has in fact significantly lower levels of populist attitudes.

There are a few cases where the educational opportunity scores may raise concerns. Britain, for example, show a proportion of upper secondary students in vocational training that is probably too high if "vocational" is to have the same meaning across countries. France also gets a suspiciously high opportunity score. Here, the likely reason is that information is missing on two indicators, social inclusion and adult education, where France most surely scores at the lower end (but again, we have no comparative data). Still, the overall pattern is strongly supportive of our argument that equality of opportunity in the educational system, by fostering both intra- and intergenerational mobility, undermines the spread of populist values and expands the size of the electorate supporting the knowledge economy.

Of course, there are many potential confounders, but it is hard to think of any with a more clearly specified micrologic (consistent with our other evidence). The most obvious candidate would be GDP per capita, but while it has a borderline statistically significant negative effect (not shown), it has no effect on the finding for educational opportunity. Other potentially confounding variables such as occupational structure are already controlled for at the individual level, and we can confirm this by including industrial employment shares as a macrovariable: it has no effect. No other argument we are aware of explains the cross-national pattern observed in the data.

In concluding this section, we would like to draw attention to the remarkable fact that countries with relatively weak populist sentiments are often noted for having strong populist parties, and vice versa. The most obvious explanation for this is that countries with the most permissive electoral rules, and hence low barriers to new party formation, also tend to have the most open and publicly funded educational systems, while the opposite is true for liberal market economies with majoritarian institutions (Iversen and Stephens 2008; Iversen and Soskice 2010). In the East Asian cases, the reasons differ. These are countries with strict controls on immigration, public censure of homosexuality, weak equal-treatment statutes, punitive criminal law systems, and lax environmental standards. There is simply little room for new parties to challenge established parties on these issues; it is populism without (overtly) populist parties. Even so, there may still be a lot of unrealized discontent among the old middle classes, because cultural closure does not provide real solutions to their economic grievances. As some observers of the Trump presidency suspect, populist policies do not necessarily help populist constituencies: an intriguing fact.

More generally, we think the close connection between educational institutions and populism is robust evidence that populism is not simply a cultural reaction to the rise of "sociocultural elites." It reflects a socioeconomic encapsulation of the old middle classes that makes them susceptible to the messages of populist politicians attacking the symbols of the new economy, an economy they and their children feel they have been left out of.[4] A real solution would be a broadening of opportunity—from public preprimary schools, vocational training, integrated school districts, centralized allocation of school funding, subsidized university education, and more resources for adult training and retraining. These are, of course, policies that could also help advance the knowledge economy, and that is precisely the point. If elites on the Left and the Right want to effectively confront the rise of populism, it would be by opening the educational system to the middle and lower middle classes. The old middle classes may switch their support in response, or populist parties may moderate their messages. They are not against progress, but they are cynical, often rightly so, about whom this progress will benefit.

5.4.4. POPULIST VOTING

For populist values in the electorate to matter politically they have to be organized and aggregated into political representation. Political parties play the key role in this translation. As we have insisted above, support for populist parties is not equivalent to support for populist values. In a case like the United States, with its majoritarian electoral institutions, no populist party has been successful, at least since the Progressive Party, but this did not prevent Trump from winning the Republican Party nomination while campaigning on a populist platform. In a case like Japan, populist values are pervasive, but so too relatively is the status quo, and there is consequently little demand for populist parties—at least as commonly classified. Yet where populist parties *do* form, we expect those individuals with strong populist values to be attracted to them, and we expect such voting to be closely associated with the old middle classes. This hypothesis is explored below.

Figure 5.5 shows the average vote share for populist parties—defined to include new right and "protest" parties—in advanced democracies over time. The solid line is the average for a broad sample of twenty countries, while the dashed line restricts the sample to countries with significant populist parties. Measured either way we see a pronounced increase in populist voting from less than 2.5 percent of the vote in the early 1980s to between ten percent (large sample) and fifteen percent (restricted sample) in 2015. This is a remarkable four-to-six-fold increase in support, and it occurs precisely during the transition from the old industrial economy to the new knowledge economy. Yet it should be kept in mind that populist

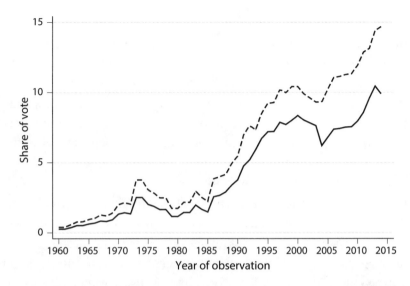

FIGURE 5.5. The rise of populist voting. *Notes*: Vote shares are calculated by country-year and then averaged. Populist parties are those coded as "right-populist" or "protest" in Amingeon et al. (2016). The solid line is the average for a broad sample of 20 advanced democracies while the dashed line restricts the sample to 12 countries with significant populist parties (Austria, Belgium, Denmark, Finland, France, Germany, Italy, the Netherlands, Norway, Sweden, Switzerland, and the UK). *Source*: Amingeon et al. (2016).

party support started from a very low base and has not come close to a majority anywhere—not even in the US presidential election, where a large portion of Trump voters were traditional Republican supporters rather than populists, or in the Brexit vote, where a significant portion of people voting Leave did so for reasons other than opposition to immigration or globalization or hostility to the European Union, indeed where Euroscepticism was historically more established than elsewhere in the EU.

As we noted above, half of the sixteen advanced democracies included in the World Values Surveys had significant populist parties, but missing vote intention in France and Italy means that we are left with six countries and about 9,600 observations. An argument can be made for including Canada by treating the Canadian Alliance party, which contested an election in one of the Canadian waves, as a populist party. We tried to include it, and show the results separately below (it makes almost no difference to the findings).

In our small sample of countries and years, the recorded incidence of populist voting is modest at 5.25 percent, but we have enough observations to identify significant correlates. Table A5.3 in appendix A shows the results of a logit regression using populist voting as the dependent variable. Not surprisingly, populist values is a strong predictor of populist voting: going from the lowest to the highest populism score increases the probability of voting for a populist party from 1.4 percent to 13.3 percent. Yet this effect of values clearly does not imply that populist voting is primarily a story about "cultural backlash"—the interpretation offered by Inglehart and Norris (2017)—since we know that values are themselves strongly affected by economic position. In fact, what is surprising in these results is how much of an independent impact economic variables have on voting even after controlling for values. Thus, workers with lower education and income—unskilled manual workers, in particular—are more likely to vote populist, even after controlling for their populist value system. A plausible interpretation is that the populism index does not fully capture distributive demands, which are correlated with values but not perfectly so. This is perhaps most clear in the case of the self-employed. Although they are less likely to express populist values, they are more likely to vote for populist parties. Presumably this is because they have distinct concerns related to the economic conditions of small business owners, who tend to find that regulations are cumbersome and favor large firms. Age also offers a small surprise: older people are less likely to vote populist, controlling for populist values. A generational interpretation is that while older generations tend to be adversely affected by technological change, they are also more anchored in political-social networks that predate the rise of populism. A life-cycle interpretation may be that people grow more risk-averse as they age, shunning new, nonmainstream parties.

Summarizing the evidence on populist voting, if we define old and new middle classes as before, the former is about eight times more likely to vote populist, taking into account both direct (through economic position) and indirect (through populist values) effects. Among the new middle classes, populist voting is negligible, at less than two percent. (See figure 5.6.)

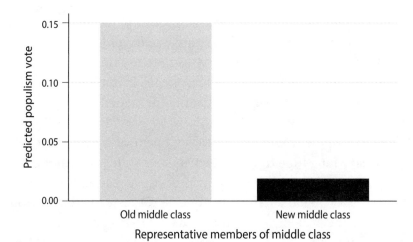

FIGURE 5.6. The difference in populist vote between the old and new middle class. *Notes*: The effects are the sum of the direct effects of economic variables on populist vote (from table A5.3, column 1) and indirect effects through populism (results not shown but analogous to table A5.2, column 1, only smaller sample).

5.4.5. CRISIS AND THE IMPORTANCE OF ECONOMIC PROGRESS

Advanced capitalist democracies are politically constructed around the idea of progress. When we refer in this book to the continuous reinvention of capitalism, it is to draw attention to the incentives of political parties to appeal to the desire of middle voters to continuously improve their own lives and those of their children. Mobility—both in the sense of being able to create a better life if you play by the rules, acquire a suitable education, and work hard, and in the sense of younger generations enjoying better opportunities than their parents—is a central feature of ACDs and ensures broad political majorities for their reproduction. This is why economic crises, such as the Great Depression or the Great Recession, are politically problematic. The same is true of the general slowdown in economic productivity and growth, in part because it magnifies the pain of recessions.

A simple way to think about the effect of economic crises is as a downward shift of the Great Gatsby curve, which reduces mobility and expands the audience for populist politics. Combined with economic hardship in the middle and lower middle classes, deep and long-lasting recessions pose a threat to the political legitimacy of ACDs. Again, it is the capacity of these democracies to reinvent themselves in the face of such threats, including the decline of Fordism in the 1970s and 1980s, that have made the system so resilient.

Yet one of the troubling features of financial crises is that they take a very long time to work themselves out: a problem that has been magnified in Europe by the institutional constraints on expansionary fiscal policies in the Eurozone (as discussed in the previous chapter). The prolonged downturn has without a doubt added fuel to the populist fire. Although our individual-level data do not have enough cross-time variation to pin down this effect—Brexit, Trump's election, and the rise of the Five Star Movement are all too recent—they do show that lower income and unemployment predict populist values, and it is hardly an accident that the countries with the sharpest rise in unemployment and low growth rates in the aftermath of the financial crisis (Italy, Spain, and France, in that order) have all seen a surge in populist politics.

The nature of populism in these cases take very different forms—left populism in Spain and right populism in France (with Five-Star mixing elements of both), and with distinct support bases (much younger and educated in Spain and Italy than in France)—but it is precisely what unites these movements that illustrates the importance of economic stagnation and austerity: all are supported by groups who have encountered major barriers to sharing in prosperity because not enough high-quality jobs have been created in the advanced sectors. They blame politicians for this failure, and in that sense they also illustrate the role of democracy in putting pressure on political elites to reform the economy. This is not happening in France, and while Italy is undergoing serious political upheaval with uncertain results, the contradictions in the platforms of Lega and the Five Stars governing alliance give reason to be skeptical that there is an alternative to growth-promoting policies, which would certainly benefit the constituencies of both parties.

5.5. Conclusion

THE CONTINUATION OF THE SYMBIOTIC RELATIONSHIP WITH DIFFERENT DISTRIBUTIVE OUTCOMES

Populism marks the most important shift in politics since the first four decades after the Second World War. In the Fordist economy, interests across skill and income groups were linked by complementarities in production, correlated risks of unemployment, and considerable scope for both up- and downward mobility. There was distributive conflict, but it was muted by cross-class interdependencies. The ICT revolution unraveled these interdependencies, and created a disjuncture between an old middle class that was increasingly marginalized by technological change and a new educated middle class that thrived. The consequence of what we have called middle-class encapsulation was to create a greater preference gap between both the old middle class and those above, and between the old middle class and those below. This was manifested as populism, which is a set of beliefs and values that seeks to exclude the poor and immigrants form the welfare state while rejecting the diversity and libertarian values associated with the rising cities.

Since populism is a reaction to the rise of the knowledge economy, is it also a threat to it? Is this a fundamental realignment that will undermine what we have called the symbiotic relationship between democracy, advanced capitalism and the nation state? We think not.

There are three main reasons for this. First, policy demands associated with populism are on the whole compatible with a prospering knowledge economy. The resentment among the old middle classes are directed at the poor and at low-skill immigrants, who do not play a large role in this economy. They are also directed at the cities and cosmopolitan elites, but policy demands are mostly diffuse and symbolic. We do believe that the homophobic, sexist, and generally intolerant views associated with populism are incompatible with the way modern cities work. But rarely are such policies adopted and implemented in a manner that seriously interfere with the live-and-let-live ethos of modern urban life. The same is generally true of more radical proposals to restrict international trade. Trade liberalization has been revisited politically, but, on the whole, open world trade has not been seriously threatened. It is true that Brexit was a blow to the principle of a Europe without borders, but few seriously think that the UK will shut its borders to trade and investment with the EU, or vice versa.

This brings us to the second reason: populists are unlikely to make up a sustained majority. Over time, support for populist parties has risen, but rarely do these parties made up more than a third of the vote, and the mean performance is no better than ten to fifteen percent (depending on the sample). The limit to the support of populism is the broad inclusion of large numbers of people in the knowledge economy and the opportunities it offers, especially among younger generations. According to the latest numbers from OECD more than sixty percent of young adults (in the relevant cohort) entered tertiary education in 2015 (OECD 2017), and the share of the population with university degrees has risen steadily with over forty percent of twenty-five- to thirty-five-year-olds compared to twenty-six percent among fifty-five to sixty-four-year-olds. For most of these people, and for a substantial proportion of older generations with secondary degrees and often children acquiring university degrees, supporting policies that promote the knowledge economy make sense. Advanced economies are based on highly skilled workers, and these economies consequently tend to produce their own constituencies. Economic decline shrinks these constituencies because support for the institutions of ACDs is based on the expectation of material advancement, but the Great Recession has not fundamentally undermined either democracy or capitalism, at least over the medium to long run.

Finally, and importantly, populism can be readily undermined by public policies designed to open educational opportunities for more people. We see this very clearly in the data. Where barriers to good education and upskilling are low—starting all the way back in preschool and continuing right through college and adult education—populist values are decidedly less prevalent. Access to good education and opportunity for upskilling later in life are of course themselves policies that depend on political majority coalitions. But where such majorities are threatened by populist backlash, elites, who are invariably dependent on the knowledge economy, have a strong incentive to broaden the coalition to ensure that it survives and thrives. In this sense we see the rise of populism as a signal to elites that they must widen access to education—a healthy democratic mechanism. We may perhaps think of such opening up as a third-order policy change (following Hall 1993) in response to populism, designed to sustain advanced democratic capitalism. Nothing in the workings of the capitalist economy would prevent this.

So, what is at stake is not survival of the system, as some have suggested. Governments both have the power and the incentives to respond to the challenges of economic change. Rather, what is at stake is its degree of inclusiveness, and that is ultimately a matter of democratic choice. These choices, however, are embedded in cross-national institutional differences. We draw attention to three such institutions in particular. First is the electoral system. PR, as we have argued, is more likely than majoritarian systems to produce policies that are inclusive of lower and lower middle classes, and Busemeyer and Iversen (2014) show that PR is strongly associated with a higher public share of educational spending, and that much of this effect is through a historically higher incidence of left-leaning governments (less so in counties with strong Christian democratic parties).

Second is the vocational training system, which has deep historical roots, as discussed in chapter 2. An effective vocational training system requires coordination between employers, unions, and governments, and, because it depends on consensual policies, it is facilitated by PR and collusion on regulatory policies through parliamentary committees (although PR is as much a consequence as a cause of strong vocational skill systems). The reason that vocational training is important is that it gives especially children of working-class parents an opportunity to acquire valuable skills that can be upgraded through firm upskilling (where individual firms have made a significant initial investment in the skills) or through adult retraining (where the government, in cooperation with their social partners, has made the investment).

Finally is what we might call the degree of centralization in the educational system. This largely captures the extent of school district differentiation in school quality and the share of academically committed students. This is facilitated by high local autonomy in school funding and setting the school curriculum, but it is also affected by city planning and zoning regulations that affect the class composition of school districts. The more differentiated school districts are, the greater the incentive of those families from higher educational backgrounds and with higher income to locate in good school districts, which bids up house prices and creates barriers to entry for families from lower educational backgrounds and with lower income.

As the last example suggests, the consequences of these institutional differences are strongly magnified by self-reinforcing strategic complementarities. Class differentiation by the quality of school districts is an example of Tiebout's (1956) sorting mechanism, and it is reinforced when the income distribution responds to a more unequal skill distribution, strengthening incentives to sort, driving up house prices further, etc. In the case of vocational training, an effective system depends on a large number of young people choosing such training and providing firms with an incentive to orient their product market strategies to depend more on specific-skill workers, which raises demand and gives a stronger incentive to acquire such skills, etc. In the case of public investment in education, especially higher education, there are also strong network effects. This is because when spending is largely public it is difficult to opt out of the public system, and the high-educated instead tend become strong supporters of public spending to improve the quality of the system. In educational systems where a large proportion of the cost is private, by contrast, those with high income who pay most of their expenses themselves will tend to oppose more public spending to protect the returns to their investment (both for themselves and their children). Correspondingly, the relationship between income and support for public spending is positive in countries where there public spending share is high, and negative in countries where it is low. Again, we see a self-reinforcing logic.

The key point of this discussion is not to imply that governments have no discretion, but that the constraints on this discretion are largely due to the workings of domestic institutions. So are the sometimes stark differences in distributive outcomes, and indeed the scope for populist politics. This has nothing to do with the operation of the dark forces of capitalism, footloose capital, or even the influence of the rich. It is all about how we have organized our democratic institutions. These institutions are, therefore, also the real targets of reform.

Appendix to Chapter 5

FACTOR ANALYSIS AND REGRESSION RESULTS

TABLE A5.1. Factor analysis with varimax rotation (numbers are Eigenvalues)

Including Views on the Poor

Variable	Factor 1 Populism dimension	Factor 2 Economic dimension	Uniqueness
Support Equality	−0.0465	0.6447	0.5821
Government Responsibility	0.2069	0.704	0.4616
Competition Is Good	0.0033	−0.4172	0.8259
Homosexuality	−0.7476	0.0463	0.4389
Immigration View	0.6987	0.1076	0.5003
Protecting Environment	−0.3908	−0.1228	0.8322
View: Poor Is Lazy	0.428	−0.5565	0.5071
Observations	12,211	12,211	12,211

Excluding Views on the Poor

Variable	Factor 1 Populism dimension	Factor 2 Economic dimension	Uniqueness
Support Equality	0.1439	0.7287	0.4483
Government Responsibility	−0.1464	0.7493	0.4172
Competition Is Good	−0.0601	−0.4615	0.7834
Homosexuality	0.7149	0.0424	0.4871
Immigration View	−0.7202	0.0471	0.479
Protecting Environment	0.5343	0.0157	0.7143
View: Poor Is Lazy			
Observations	49,783	49,783	49,783

Note that because attitudes toward the poor were only gauged in one wave (Wave 3, 1995–98), including this item reduces the number of observations from approximately 50,000 to approximately 12,000. We, therefore, did the factor analysis both with and without this question and show the results separately in table A5.1. Since each index created from the left and right panels in table 5.1 are almost perfectly correlated (r=.954), we use the one identified in the right panel in the main analysis in order to maximize the number of observations.

TABLE A5.2. Individual level regression results

Explanatory variables	Dependent variable			
	Populist values			
	(1)	(2)	(3)	(4)
Age	0.007***	0.008***	0.005***	0.005***
	(0.001)	(0.001)	(0.000)	(0.000)
Gender (male)	0.184***	0.166***	0.200***	0.204***
	(0.016)	(0.013)	(0.012)	(0.009)
Income	−0.026***	−0.024***	−0.024***	−0.037***
	(0.005)	(0.004)	(0.002)	(0.002)
City/town size	−0.040***		−0.044***	
	(0.004)		(0.002)	
Low-level education	0.540***	0.475***	0.581***	0.424***
	(0.029)	(0.034)	(0.017)	(0.014)
Middle-level education	0.338***	0.311***	0.349***	0.191***
	(0.024)	(0.024)	(0.013)	(0.010)
Unemployment (binary)	0.055	0.059*	0.067***	0.058***
	(0.046)	(0.033)	(0.025)	(0.020)
(i) Managers and supervisors	0.036	0.025	0.082***	0.111***
	(0.028)	(0.022)	(0.019)	(0.016)
(ii) Professionals	−0.082	−0.093**	0.015	−0.040*
	(0.052)	(0.040)	(0.028)	(0.024)
(iii) Lower-level white collar	−0.027	−0.037	0.013	0.117***
	(0.047)	(0.032)	(0.030)	(0.024)
(iv) Skilled manual workers	0.087**	0.101***	0.174***	0.210***
	(0.035)	(0.026)	(0.021)	(0.018)
(v) Unskilled manual workers	0.095**	0.105***	0.196***	0.266***
	(0.040)	(0.038)	(0.044)	(0.037)
Self-employed	−0.078***	−0.037*	−0.050**	0.128***
	(0.027)	(0.021)	(0.025)	(0.018)
Educational opportunity			−1.304***	−1.766***
			(0.032)	(0.024)
Country-year fixed effects	✓	✓		
Constant	−0.225***	−0.518***	0.260***	0.522***
	(0.060)	(0.044)	(0.033)	(0.022)
Observations	25550	42800	25550	42800

Standard errors in parentheses

*p<0.10, **p<0.05, ***p<0.01

Notes: The reference group for the educational classes is higher (tertiary) education; reference group for the occupational classes is respondents who do not have or declare and occupation.

TABLE A5.3. The determinants of populist voting in six countries with significant populist parties

Explanatory variables	Dependent variable	
	Populism vote	
	(1)	(2)
Populism	0.594***	0.540***
	(0.078)	(0.079)
Age	−0.012***	−0.009*
	(0.004)	(0.005)
Gender (male)	0.260***	0.276***
	(0.085)	(0.064)
Income	−0.043**	−0.018
	(0.018)	(0.022)
Low-level education	0.636**	0.386
	(0.276)	(0.335)
Middle-level education	0.745***	0.428
	(0.134)	(0.288)
Unemployment (binary)	−0.073	−0.466
	(0.262)	(0.348)
(i) Managers and supervisors	0.035	0.167
	(0.127)	(0.170)
(ii) Professionals	−0.060	−0.078
	(0.091)	(0.088)
(iii) Lower-level white collar	0.186	0.277
	(0.402)	(0.184)
(iv) Skilled manual workers	−0.383	−0.284
	(0.366)	(0.225)
(v) Unskilled manual workers	0.281***	0.035
	(0.080)	(0.201)
Self-employed	0.514***	0.444***
	(0.097)	(0.112)
Country-year fixed effects	✓	✓
Constant	−2.438***	−2.579***
	(0.216)	(0.221)
Observations	9,551	10,769

Standard errors in parentheses
*p<0.10, **p<0.05, ***p<0.01
Notes: The reference group for the educational classes is higher (tertiary) education; reference group for the occupational classes is respondents who do not have or declare and occupation. Model (2) includes Canada (Canadian Alliance Party).

Conclusion: The Future of Advanced Capitalist Democracies

6.1. Brief Recap

In this book we have argued that advanced capitalism and democracy coevolved over long periods of time in a manner that entrenched support for policies and institutions, especially public investment in education and vocational training systems, as well as more generally the acceptance that effective government has meant responsibility for management of economic change and international competitiveness in periods of uncertainty, which promoted the advanced sectors and produced a large number of well-paying jobs for the middle classes and their progeny. Advanced capitalism has not subverted democracy, as is often suggested in the intellectual media and parts of the academic literature. There are two very straightforward reasons for this. First, business is too competitive to begin to solve the associated collective action problems to begin to present a common front, and competition is politically imposed by democratic governments through a range of policies that prevent collusion and keep product markets open. If firms had the necessary political clout, they would seek shelter from competition, as in Latin America, and economic performance would suffer as a consequence. Democracy *makes* markets, contrary to the notion that democracy replaces markets.

Second, advanced capital cannot put pressure on governments by threatening to move to foreign shores, because it depends on networks of highly skilled workers who are deeply anchored in the national economy and local social networks. This is *increasingly* true as production becomes more knowledge-intensive and specialized, and as rising trade and foreign direct investment augment both the knowledge content and the degree of specialization of production. Contradicting much of the literature on globalization, advanced capital is not footloose, because it is deeply embedded in existing networks of skilled labor in specialized national markets.

Because democratic governments have an intertemporal electoral incentive to create and recreate the basis of a knowledge-based and high value-added economy, they largely shun the calls from business for protection and rents. Paradoxically, advanced capitalism thrives under democracy precisely because it cannot subvert it, and democracy thrives under capitalism because the middle classes are rewarded with education, good jobs, and upward mobility (if not for themselves, then for their children). This symbiosis explains why advanced democratic capitalism has been so resilient to subversive change from its inception in the early twentieth century.

We have summarized the argument in figure 6.1. Governments in the developed world pursue policies to expand the advanced capitalist sectors (ACS), including tough competition policies, which force capitalists to compete and take risks rather than guaranteeing them safe and high returns on their capital. The resulting national frameworks (in different forms) both supply the public goods required for innovation, and impose the competitive incentives to generate innovation. The political basis for these policies are educated workers and aspirational constituencies who vote for parties with a reputation for expanding the ACS while acquiring skills needed for these sectors to succeed. This generates what we have labelled a symbiosis between advanced democracy and advanced capitalism. There is thus a fundamental difference between advanced capitalist democracies and many less developed states.

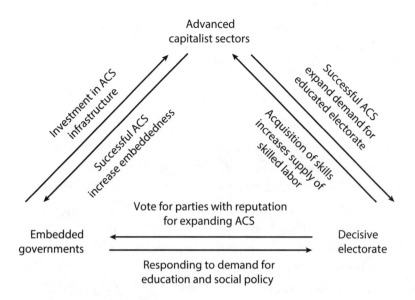

FIGURE 6.1. The symbiotic relationship.

What makes advanced democratic capitalism so resilient to change also gives rise to notable institutional and policy variation across countries and over time. Precisely because advanced capital is tied down by its high-skill employees—what we have called location cospecific assets—governments have considerable freedom to redistribute and design institutions as they see fit in response to democratic demands. We have traced this variation across countries in the form of democratic rules, economic institutions, and public policies, and we traced it back through time to the breakthrough of democracy in the early twentieth century. In this concluding chapter, we try to gaze into the future and outline likely scenarios through the lens of the ACD analytical framework presented in this book.

Most debates about the future are about new technology and its likely evolution and consequences over time. Less attention is paid to economic or political institutions, which are treated (if considered at all) as consequences of technology. This book takes a different approach, in which technological change is codetermined with government policies and directed onto distinct paths. In the next section (6.2) we review the great debate over technological change in light of our framework and then consider in the following section (6.3) the role of politics in mediating the effects of new technology.

6.2. The Great Technology Debate

To paraphrase Niels Bohr, it is hard to predict, especially about the future. This is particularly true for our purposes, since the future we are trying to predict is profoundly shaped by new technology and inventions, which by their very nature cannot be known. In addition, predictions about the future will cause voters, firms, and governments to change their behavior in ways that are likely to counteract the predictions. But it is precisely the potential for human agency to shape the future that is the reason for engaging in predictions in the first place. Prediction and human agency go hand in hand.

The point of departure for our exploration is an emerging two-by-two table with "techno-optimists" and "techno-pessimists" on the one dimension, and socio-optimists and socio-pessimists on the other. This divides thinkers in fields as diverse as economics, business, and evolutionary biology. Techno-optimists are futurists such as Ford (2015), Frey and Osborne (2017), and Susskind and Susskind (2016), who expect that AI and robots will one day replace even high-education occupations. Socio-pessimists fear this scenario because it will produce massive labor market displacements and even render humans obsolete. Techno-optimists, are paradoxically, also often socio-pessimists. Less gloomy accounts such as Brynjolfsson and McAfee (2012) point out that while technological progress tends to eliminate some jobs, it will not be the end of work itself (cf. Autor 2015). It may even encourage the creation of better and more fulfilling jobs. Yet socio-pessimism is never far behind in the techno-optimist world, because automation is feared to bring "not less work but more worse jobs," resulting in a "huge, casual, insecure, low paid workforce" (Wajcman 2017, 124).

At the most socio-optimistic end is the major new book by Robert Gordon (2016), a techno-pessimist, who sees new IC technologies as merely modest additional layers in a history of economic change marked by more profound inventions such as electricity, telephony, and the internal combustion engine. Gordon argues that productivity growth has declined and that more, not less, work will be needed to sustain an aging population. Perhaps new technology in the past few decades has not been conducive to equality and demand for semiskilled labor, but the future looks bright in that regard. The problem is rather that ICT technology is not sufficiently transformative to lead to rapid productivity growth, and hence to major improvements in living standards. If the state is constrained, it is because of a crunch on public finances.

We count Piketty (2014) as the ultimate pessimist. Like Gordon, he believes that the capacity of technology to produce high rates of GDP growth is low. Specifically, he argues that "global growth is likely to be [only] around 1.5 percent a year between 2050 and 2100" (355). At the same time, he believes that capital is becoming more mobile and that "fiscal competition will gradually lead to total disappearance of taxes on capital in the twenty-first century." Combined with a relatively constant rate of return on capital of about four percent, the result is $r > g$ and a massive rise in inequality. There may be work for all, but the fruits of this labor will be increasingly captured by the rich.

How does our framework cast light on these debates? We return here to the core idea of location cospecific assets and their embeddedness in social networks. This is the foundation, we have argued, for the nation-state and for all politics in advanced democracies, including the welfare state and redistribution. If everything could be done equally well anywhere on earth it would undermine the need for *colocation*, and the world would gradually become as flat as Friedman's metaphor implies. Alternatively, if AI and robots can replicate the cospecificity of skill clusters by essentially generating de novo the knowledge that otherwise emerges from human interaction and exchange of ideas, then educated workers and technology would no longer be necessary complements to technology. Without *colocation* and *cospecificity* we would clearly be in a different world with wide-ranging implications for advanced capitalism, the state, and democracy. We discuss each challenge in turn before turning to the role of politics.

6.2.1. WILL AI REPLACE COSPECIFICITY?

The threat here is that AI and robots will eventually be able to mimic everything humans are currently capable of, regardless of educational level. This is already happening to an extent unimaginable a decade ago. Alphabet (Google's parent company) has recently created a new research unit, called Verily Life Sciences, to use AI approaches to medical data analysis that can assist in diagnosing and devising treatment plans, and Microsoft's Healthcare NeXT is focused on collecting huge amounts of individual data from a variety of sources to cloud-based systems, including a virtual assistant that takes notes from patient-doctor meetings using speech recognition technologies (Singer 2017). In principle, doctors are not even required to arrive at an accurate diagnosis; all these systems need are individuals who can ask patients for the right information, a task computers could easily take over if not for the unease people might feel about revealing private information to a machine. The work of accountants and paralegals is already being increasingly assumed by computers, and there is no reason that lawyers who rely on interpretation of written rules, precedent, and accumulated experience (read: data) could not be replaced for many legal services as well. Robots can even design better robots. Once you allow your imagination to project the capabilities of AI, there are seemingly no limits to the extent of substitutions effects. No job is safe. If so, cospecificity between humans and technology ends. Instead of SBTC we get MBTC (machine-biased technological change).

Yet there are reasons to think this is, at best, a quite distant prospect. First, a key function of decentralized production networks is to develop new solutions to complex problems in uncertain environments. The objective of innovation is to develop new algorithms, as opposed to merely optimizing old ones, and computers are currently best at implementing algorithms rather than creating new ones. For the immediate future AI is therefore likely to augment the ability of high-skill networks to innovate, or to focus on more team-centered, nonroutine tasks. To return to the previous example, doctors may increasingly be eclipsed by AI-assisted diagnostics, but that will simultaneously free up time for interactive and personalized treatments devised by teams of doctors with different specialties and in close interaction with patients. Complex interaction with humans is not something computers currently do well), and many high-end services depend on such interaction. Even a fairly mundane task of waiting a table at an upscale restaurant requires anticipation of the needs of customers, which are sometimes unspoken or poorly articulated. And in the kitchen chefs use their tacit knowledge of the complex interaction of ingredients—spices, herbs, vegetables, meats, etc.—to produce surprises for the inscrutable human palate. The AI chef is not about to win any Michelin stars.

Perhaps a more consequential limitation of AI, at least in business, is the need to solve intricate coordination games within production networks. All complex organizations, such as modern firms and regulatory agencies, involve multilayered coordination games that have many different solutions or equilibria. It is hard to see how computers can solve these coordination games without the involvement of humans. It takes leadership, bargaining, persuasion, and coalition-building to arrive at particular solutions, and because these solutions have distributive as well as efficiency effects, they are merely temporary understandings that require constant negotiation and renegotiation in response to changes in prices, preferences, technology, and power. Computers may enhance the ability of humans to map out possible courses of actions and their consequences contingent on the actions of others, but in a very broad range of economic interactions they cannot choose the actions or outcomes for us.

Even when delegation to computers is feasible there are many legal and political constraints. For example, in adjudicating civil conflicts—say, between a firm and a supplier—showing bad faith and intent to cause harm is essential, yet computers rely on probability and association that require neither intention nor causality. For this reason people who empowered computers to make decisions will be held accountable, and they will be asked to provide an explanation for how these decisions were made. This need for explanation is not confined to the courtroom. For decisions to be persuasive and acceptable to people they ordinarily have to be justified by appealing to causal logic, good intentions, or higher principles, unless brute force is involved. In AI research this is known as the black box problem.

The black box problem is that while powerful computers will yield solutions to pretty much any problem they are given, or at least they have the potential to do so, people, whether they are judges or managers or partners in a firm, have to accept these solutions for them to be binding. This in turn requires that they can be justified, and justification fundamentally requires that they make sense to people. Meaning is humanly constructed, and plays no role in computers. In turn, meaning is closely tied to providing a causal interpretation of how a particular solution is arrived at—whether it is a particular medical treatment plan, a management decision, or investing in a particular startup—and causality requires more than association (as most post–Humean philosophers of science would agree). The black box must be opened up and infused with human meaning.

In computer science and AI research this search for meaning is called "explainable AI," or XAI, and it involves a parallel search for human explanation of the associations and predictions generated by machines. In this very fundamental sense computers and humans are likely to remain complements unless computers could literally be taught think like humans. In the very long run the latter is thinkable—or, perhaps more likely, humans and machines would merge into a new species using bioengineering, resulting in what Kurzweil (2005) calls "the singularity." It hardly makes sense to speculate how the economy would work in this science fiction world, but even here there can be no a priori reason that "individuals"—AI-augmented humans or humanized machines—would not continue to invent and produce through interactive networks, implying cospecificity.

Certainly, before we reach anything like Kurzweil's singularity, AI and robots are destined to form strong complements to highly educated workers for the reasons discussed above—especially among the most intelligent and creative of those workers. A critical question, then, is where in the ability distribution complementarity effects dominate substitution effects. In the past decade substitution effects have probably expanded in terms of number of workers affected, displacing not only routine manual jobs but also a range of nonroutine low- and increasingly high-skill jobs. Among the professions, accountants and money managers are performing tasks that, while nonroutine because of their complexity, have gradually been codified and translated into algorithms that are performed with much greater efficiency by computers. Even in risky environments, as long as the risk–expected reward trade-off can be defined, computers are exceptionally good at everything from picking stocks to translating insurance risks into actuarial tables. Correspondingly, money managers and actuaries are also dying occupations. As noted, some tasks performed by doctors, such as diagnostics based on detailed data on individuals, may also be replaced, and in higher education online introductory courses may be taught effectively using a combination of webcasts and computer-based interactive learning. AI has even been used to create art and music that many people find compelling and hard to distinguish from human creations.[1]

Substitution effects may also increasingly invade lower-level nonroutine tasks, which were thought possible until recently (as assumed in the SBTC polarization hypothesis). In Autor and Murmane's seminal piece from 2003, long-haul truck driving was used as an example of nonroutine low-skill jobs that would be very unlikely to be replaced by robots. But even as the ink was drying, inventors in Silicon Valley plotted to do just that, and today Google (through subsidiary Waymo), Über, and Apple are all testing self-driven cars on public roads, and spin-offs are developing self-driving trucks. Tesla recently unveiled electric long-haul trucks with self-driving capabilities, and few analysts doubt that such trucks will be a regular sight on public roads within a decade or two.

Nonroutine manual tasks involving human interaction, such as nursing, are also not immune from the AI/robotic invasion. Robots are already being tested in hospitals and nursing homes to provide patients and residents with a range of services—monitoring, dispensing medicine, bringing food and drinks, etc.—and when connected to an app or voice-controlled device such as Amazon's Echo, the robots are easy to fetch and command. When armed with detailed individual data in patient databases, they could provide a truly personalized experience, and in early experiments, people seem to take to these robots rather well. Unlike humans they are always polite and respectful, and children seem particularly happy to accept them. Human interaction will undoubtedly remain indispensable for a range of nursing functions, and robots will never replace relatives and friends, but many jobs in social and personal services will be.

At the high end, ICT technologies will continue to offer strong complementarities to the most talented, well-educated, and creative individuals, and market rewards will likely become increasingly concentrated among these workers. This "winner-takes-all" logic is, of course, just an extrapolation of a trend that is identified with the task-specific SBTC hypothesis, which is a process that has been unfolding for decades. What is new is the acceleration of this trend and the increasing vulnerability of many high-skill occupations and nonroutine low-skill jobs. Clearly this has yet to massively affect the high-educated, since investment in education still commands high returns, but dispersion in wages and job opportunities is increasing among the well-educated, and it is certainly not inconceivable that substitution effects will in the future come to dominate complementarity effects for a majority. This points to a less radical, but nevertheless transformative, techo-optimist scenario.

Yet in assessing the consequences of such a shift we cannot extrapolate from what has happened to the minority of low-skilled workers in the past. Losers in the labor market are not automatically protected by democracy, but it makes a huge difference if they are in a majority or in a minority. Techo-optimists/socio-pessimists do not have a conception of democratic politics that allows them to understand the political consequences of this shift, and their dire predictions should therefore be taken with a grain of salt. The last section will consider the political dynamics in a future world where a majority is negatively affected by SBTC.

6.2.2. IS AI REPLACING THE NEED FOR COLOCATION?

The previous analysis suggests that AI and robots cannot in the foreseeable future replace economic networks based on cospecificity. But can they replace the need for colocation and therefore undercut the power of democratic governments to tax and spend, and thereby also undermine their incentives to invest in institutional infrastructure? We think not. Since all advanced production depends on co-located skilled workers who are in locally embedded and immobile social and economic networks—including spouses, children, parents, siblings, and friends—it is hard to upend the location specificity of production. This is reinforced by the fact that colocation is over time. This reflects both the individual payoffs from colocation, but also the need to build reputations for working responsibly and reliably with a particular group or groups of employees. The greater the knowledge and complexity and specialization of such production, the harder it will be to replace or transplant the network.

Can new technology lead to cross-border specialization, making production less location-specific? We think it is unlikely that this will be a common pattern or that it will seriously undermine the power of the nation-state to the extent it does happen. To the contrary, what instead is happening is that globalization is taking not only the form of increased *trade* in goods and services in the advanced world, but also and predominantly since the start of the 1990s a huge growth of multinational companies (MNCs). These MNCs—in many cases, the contemporary descendants of large Chandlerian/Fordist companies—have specialized increasingly on a core range of inter-related products. In the knowledge economy, as we have argued, specialized innovations and the embedded knowledge from which they derive is distributed around the advanced world. Instead of producing these goods and services from scratch, these MNCs have relied on tapping into these knowledge sources. To be more accurate, this activity has taken place within the individual triads (North America, Western Europe, and East Asia) into which the advanced world is divided (Rugman 2004, 2012). Thus specialization and tria-dization are complementary to each other. Far from reducing the power and autonomy of the advanced nation-state, the nation-state is enhanced by MNCs since the transfer of embedded knowledge takes place through the networks of subsidiaries of MNCs. The key role of the advanced state is therefore both to promote the growth of its specialized embedded knowledge and to allow access to it. As a consequence, knowledge production remains embedded while its use with other complementary sources of knowledge embedded in other geographically different areas can be transferred through the networks of relevant MNCs. How such knowledge-based MNCs will evolve is of course of great interest, but the most important point to make here is that they *increase* the comparative advantage of embedded knowledge production, and with it the autonomy of the nation-state.

This points to an optimistic conjecture: even as new technology replaces more jobs, the advanced sectors are location-specific and can support policies that ensure broad sharing of the benefits of a more productive economy based on broad, although never all-encompassing, electoral coalitions. Such coalitions do not depend on a particular structure of labor markets in the sense that even if skill-technology complementarities are concentrated in, say, the top third of the skill distribution, governments can still tax the advanced sectors because they remain location-specific. So, quite independent of the wage effect of new technology, income inequality will be a function of democratic politics in the immediate future.

But what about the longer term? Our book is not futuristic, and its arguments rest on the *empirical* assumptions that advanced sectors require large educated workforces, and that those workforces are to an important extent embedded. Our empirically grounded conclusions therefore relate to understanding the present and the next decade or so. But it is difficult to resist the temptation to think further ahead, and we see continued support for our position even if we do.

In a longer time horizon, there may be reasons that AI and neurobiology might enable the formation of production networks across countries that could undermine location specificity and perhaps allow firms to shift production in response to taxation and costs. Scientists are already relying on international networks, and for many tasks involved in the scientific process, being in the same location is simply not important. Ideas, research protocols, and data can be shared in seconds over the internet, so what prevents economic and social networks across other high-skill professions from locating without regard to national borders?

As we argued in chapter 4, incomplete contracting is part of the answer, because direct network monitoring is hard if people are dispersed and simply "log in" to the network when needed. Yet monitoring technologies and software are improving fast, and they will gradually make possible more cross-country networking. People may even be able to *choose* to be monitored by cameras and software that is accessible—probably preanalyzed by computers—to others in their network (perhaps with the possibility of credibly sharing their stored information with businesses and potential employers outside their network).

Another answer is the difficulty of picking up cues about sincerity and commitment at a distance. This is easy in physically proximate networks because humans are evolutionarily coded to display (unconscious) body language and emotions that we are equally good at decoding. It is true, however, that AI computers are getting much better at interpreting physical cues, sometimes with surprisingly accurate results. For example, machines can use Facebook photos to predict sexual orientation with much greater precision than humans: for males the AI accuracy is ninety-one percent versus sixty percent for humans.[2] The limitation is that information can be manipulated. As soon as we know how computers process particular information—in this case, photos—we can game the system by manipulating our appearance. This is already what people do when they present themselves on Facebook, LinkedIn, and other online networks, in a particularly flattering light. Such manipulation is not a problem that is likely go away in long-distance production networks. Virtual reality, for example, has great potential to offer realistic 3-D replacements for on-location interaction, but they rely on avatars that can be manipulated.

For techno-optimists, the answers are, of course, always just around the corner. Neuroscience is making advances in the ability to peek into the brains of people through MRI and CT scans, and to decipher whether brain activity has the markers of someone who is sincere and truthful rather than manipulative and deceptive. Such "truth machines" may only require inexpensive electrodes placed around our skull, perhaps embedded in a "truth hat" that is linked to the computer and the internet. These distant descendants of clunky lie detectors are quickly becoming cheaper and simpler, and they may one day come in the form of tiny permanent implants under our skin.

Whatever the real potential of such technologies, assume we can imagine a future where it is easier to form knowledge clusters beyond national borders and where specialization is less spatially confined. Even then, we believe there are powerful arguments why the effects on location specificity will be modest. The reasons are related to the continued importance of social networks. First, it is costly to develop economic networks that crosscut social networks. We have argued in this book that the boundaries between economic and social networks are increasingly coterminous because social and economic networks reinforce each other, especially in an advanced world of assortative mating. Information about job opportunities and new ideas and business opportunities percolate through social networks, and economic networks make use of social connections to recruit new employees and cultivate large pools of qualified workers within close proximity. Moreover, the overlap between economic and social networks produce homophily, often enhanced by recruitment from a small number of complementary educational programs, and such homophily is conducive to friendship, assortative mating, and community.

This symbiosis of economic and social networks makes it costly to configure production networks that crosscut national borders insofar as social networks remain locally confined. Coupled with the difficulties of creating effective long-distance production networks that we noted above, there consequently have to be very weighty reasons to divide specialized production across borders. It could happen when two technologies and knowledge clusters have developed independently in different countries but subsequently persist in both because of self-reinforcing network effects with strong complementarities. However, given that most new technologies are spun off from existing production networks, such instances will be rare.

But if production networks are embedded in social networks, would it not be possible to reconstitute social networks across borders to coincide with any reconfiguration of the economic network, or perhaps causing such a reconfiguration? We think this is even more unlikely. Friendships, marriages, and social gatherings require colocation, and it is hard to see how such proximity could be achieved across national borders without quantum-leap innovations in transportation. Furthermore, social networks are built up through real time and therefore require continuous presence. So, high-skill workers and the firms that depend on these will continue to have their social networks in a local area, and while they can become part of cross-national knowledge clusters, they are not becoming more mobile for that reason. Indeed, if specialized cross-country production networks do become more feasible to some extent, there is *less* pressure for an individual to join a knowledge cluster in another country if that person happens to have skills that are strong complements to the foreign cluster. Consequently, consumption and income taxes can be assessed as before. Firms can also continue to be taxed on the revenues or profits generated in a particular country. "Network arbitrage" (i.e., shifting production from one network to the other) may be possible in some measure, but it is limited by the difficulty of quickly expanding a network and by the small size of cross-country clusters. For the reasons spelled out above, there are reasons to believe they will not be widespread.[3]

The upshot of this discussion is that while new technology may make cross-national production networks more feasible, we are inclined to think that knowledge-based MNCs increase the likelihood of a future like the present, in which highly specialized knowledge remains embedded and in which networks connecting many different locations of embedded knowledge become more and more efficient ways of putting complementary specialized knowledge together. There are, in any case, steep costs to organizing production networks that do not coincide with social networks, and even when it happens it will not much affect the capacity of the state to tax income and consumption (the only constraint being possibilities for network arbitrage). Nor will it undermine the incentive of governments to invest in education and institutions that support knowledge-based production so long as other countries do the same. This complementarity between government policies and knowledge clusters is also likely to continue to spur successful cities, and these are themselves attractive sites for educated workers to live, adding a further guarantee of the continuation of colocation.

6.3. The Politics of the Future

In this book we have argued that the ACD has proved resilient because it produces its own electoral constituency of high-skilled workers who want to see the advanced sectors expand and prosper. We have attached great importance also to aspirational voters, those who look to expansion of good employment in the advanced sectors of the economy both for their own betterment and for that of their children. This combination of the direct beneficiaries of the advanced economy and aspirational voters has been we believe—with inevitable ups and downs—in the majority throughout most of the history of ACDs in the last century. Because the state is strong and democratic, governments have responded to this composite constituency by investing in the institutional infrastructure of the advanced sectors. But can we expect this symbiosis to continue if new technology increasingly concentrates the benefits of the new economy in the top end of the distribution while substituting for workers in perhaps a majority of occupations? While still a hypothetical question, what would happen if the substitution effects of new technology affected a *majority*? This, and not whether globalization will undermine the power of the nation-state or suborn democracy, strikes us as the more salient political question to ask about the future.

We first note that even if winner-take-all markets become more pervasive, this does not eliminate the need for a large-scale higher education system. As long as the productivity of workers in their thirties cannot be confidently predicted from observable traits when they are in their teens, the economy will continue to depend on educating large numbers of young people. The critical question is whether such a system will produce democratic majorities for policies and institutions that sustain the system.

We think this is likely for two reasons. First, acquiring a higher education may be a ticket to living a fulfilling life, even if it does not lead to high-powered careers. Artistic expression and consumption, for example, are likely to depend on higher education, or at least be enhanced by it. But, secondly, living a fulfilling life requires resources, and those in the majority who are not in high-paying occupations will surely demand a share of output through public transfers. Paradoxically, perhaps, when a majority no longer benefits directly from employment in the advanced sectors, the redistributive welfare state is likely to experience a renaissance. We saw in chapter 3 that the majority of voters currently benefiting from advanced capitalism pay little attention to the minority of voters who does not. But this does not prevent a majority of the high-educated in lower-paying activities to demand redistribution from the top to the middle as a way of subsidizing the pursuit of lower-paid (by the market), yet highly meaningful, careers. Because so many tasks might be performed by robots and AI, we may well see a blurring of the distinction between work and leisure. The key is that nothing prevents a majority from putting a value on these activities that is not equal to their value in the market. The "social wage" is politically determined, and it is not equal to the "market wage." Indeed, we have expressed this logic in what we called the fundamental equality of ACDs: the capacity of middle-class voters to guarantee a net income that is a constant share of average net income. This fundamental equality is not likely upended by a dictatorship of AI and robots. The evidence by Piketty and others that inequality is rising is not inconsistent with the fact that the middle classes have maintained their share of output.

Here it is natural to bring in the debate about a guaranteed minimum income, which has been forcefully advocated by Van Parijs and Vanderborght (2017) and others. When a majority can no longer count on the labor market to generate high-paying jobs, it makes sense to think that this majority would support a state that offers a basic income, independent of work. The more education and income is delinked, the greater attraction this idea might command among the middle classes.

Yet it strikes us as more likely that the level of such guaranteed income will be linked to education for two reasons. The first is that the economy will still be dependent on a large number of young people going through higher education, since intellectual and creative potential are not fully developed until people are well into their twenties. If only a relatively small number end up in highly paid jobs, it may not be sufficient to motivate enough young people to acquire high education, unless education itself is rewarded through the transfer system. Educational stipends may be required as a top-up to any guaranteed income.

Secondly, while the "second-tier" university-educated will surely demand income redistribution to themselves, they have little interest in sharing with others. Given a dearth of well-paying jobs, the plight of the low-educated will increasingly depend on their capacity for collective action as well as their usefulness for the educated middle classes in forming majority coalitions. This political dynamic is, of course, not a sharp discontinuity from the past, but rather a continuation of a trend that started with the breakdown of Fordism. Democracy, both inside and outside of representative institutions, will decide distributive outcomes. This repeats a refrain that we have used throughout this book: democracy, not capitalism, is what should be the focus of efforts to counter rising inequality. We think this will be more, not less, true in the future.

But what makes us confident that the educated will continue to be pivotal in this hypothetical economy? Apart from the superstars, if their income is now politically determined there is no way to ex ante order people from left to right by market income. Here we think that the role of social networks is again critical. The fluidity of the demarcation between social networks and firms in the new economy has raised the role of the social network as a force of political organization. What is politically needed is worked out in the social network rather than through the union or the party organization. This is consequential, since some will be in much stronger networks than others, and some networks are likely to be much better informed than others.

Again, social networks are geographically based, and homophily rules social network membership: The social networks of the well educated in big cities are more "open," receptive, and tolerant to others like themselves: namely, educated and working in a wide range of "acceptable" occupations from culture, the media, and education to law and finance. Given these characteristics, diversity, nationality, and ethnicity is no obstacle—even the reverse. The discursive politics of such networks reflect both the values placed on education and universities, as well as the promotion of the public goods needed for life in dense urban environments, such as inner-city rapid transport, housing, health care, a green and clean environment, and openness to diversity and immigration. Those in left-behind communities are equally "organized" in social networks: while there are important common political preferences, as with health and schools, their positions are more likely otherwise to be populist, and these social networks are more closed and hostile to those from different backgrounds. In particular, these networks have no place for the poor and for immigrants (as discussed in the previous chapter). And the poor, the precariat, is marginalized politically.

If this analysis is accurate, it is both good and bad news for ACDs. On the one hand, there is no need to worry about the ability of the well-educated to organize politically and defend their interests, which includes strong support for education and the knowledge economy; from this perspective, it is possible to be both a techno-optimist and a socio-optimist. On the other hand, so too are populists capable of articulating a political agenda, albeit not necessarily (or at all) in their interests: they live in their own social networks, and political entrepreneurs have proved highly capable of using them. In chapter 5 we argued that populism has its roots in the barriers to inclusion in the knowledge economy, but also that populism wanes when such barriers are lowered.

In this view, populism seems not such a problem in coordinated systems where education, training, and retraining systems are effectively organized. In addition, negotiated political systems make the effect of populism less potent, and unlikely to be a serious problem for the development of the knowledge economy. The Great Gatsby curve underlines the problem for the United States, and is reinforced by a decentralized political system. How to ensure intergenerational mobility in and out of the higher educational system is one of the most vexing issues for the future of democratic capitalism.

But just how sure can we be that populists may not constitute a political majority, and advocate policies of closure which would hold back advanced capitalism? It seems not accidental that Trump, Brexit, and now the Italian success of the Lega and the Five Star Movement are so bunched in time, nor that the share of populist votes has continued to rise quite sharply since the late 2010s, as is shown in figure 5.5. As we noted in chapter 5, it seems clear that an important factor is the prolonged recession (the "Great Recession") which is the drawn-out legacy of the financial crisis. This fits very well with our analysis of populism, since it is not difficult to see it as the cause of the dramatic slowdown in the growth of graduate jobs. In turn, such a slowdown directly reduces intergenerational mobility into a graduate world, at the same time as likely dampening aspirational voting. The Great Gatsby curve gets pushed down.

Thus we have an explanation in terms of our Great Gatsby hypothesis, of the continued rise in populist support across the advanced world. But we also have a reason for believing that if and when the prolonged recession comes to an end and economic growth begins to pick up in a sustained way, the growth of populism is likely to be correspondingly damped. Italy in particular will benefit from an end to slow growth, which is a joint concern of both the Lega and Five Stars. But the Italian situation is more complicated and arguably not a harbinger of populist majorities elsewhere. This is because the underlying interests of the Lega, which wants to reduce transfers to the South, and Five Stars, which wants to increase transfers to the South, are incompatible.

A final, and potentially important, theme is the consequences of a much more decentralized economic system. The ICT revolution empowered educated and skilled workers by giving them access to personal computers and to the internet, and by allowing them to take the necessarily decentralized decisions. Across-the-board decentralization of decision-making in terms of both corporate strategy and employee autonomy facilitated the opening up of product markets across the advanced world and led to a radical geographical specialization of goods and services. Compared to the highly centralized, vertically integrated, and hierarchically organized companies of the Fordist era, the organization of companies in the knowledge economy are rooted in clusters of high-skilled workers working with complementary and often very specialized technologies in geographically confined spaces—above all the major cities that have experienced a remarkable revival since the collapse of Fordism.

The United States is an important case in point because not only has the US knowledge economy been driven by the major cities and great conurbations, as well as by certain states (such as California, New York, and Massachusetts), but also by increasing political autonomy. Additionally, they all strongly support—indeed, they depend on—the flourishing of the knowledge economy. A similar major constitutional push is taking place in England, where the government has created six city regions (based on Manchester, Liverpool, Birmingham, Bristol, and the urban regions of the Tees Valley and Cambridgeshire/Peterborough) with directly elected mayors with decision-making powers over a wide area of policies. The government explained this in terms of the agglomerative capabilities of large cities inherent in the knowledge economy.

Both in the American cases and in the UK city regions, education and training are seen as a key policy area. It may be more generally true that cities in the advanced economies will become politically more powerful, in line with the development of the knowledge economy and reinforcing its development politically. Geospatial divisions, in other words, may complement the continued expansion of the knowledge economy. The major urban corridors have become hubs for new technology, higher education, and progress, and in contrast to the declining periphery they tie together people in ways that reach beyond class and ethnicity. Whether it is possible to be both a techno-optimist and a social-optimist will depend more and more on where you look.

NOTES

Preface

1. Among major theorists of advanced capitalism, only Lindblom saw it as consistent with democracy. But he saw (as we don't) advanced capitalism imposing its interests on the political system and the electorate.

Chapter 1: Introduction

1. The centrality of clusters for the location decisions of knowledge-based companies was underlined by Porter's seminal *The Economic Advantage of Nations* (1990; also 2000). At a similar time, Cantwell's synoptic *Technological Innovations and Multinational Corporations* (1989) set out the changing geographical and locational roles played by MNEs, on which we draw. Other leading contributors and relevant citations are Acs (2002), Audretsch (1998), Feldmann (2000), Iammarino (Cantwell and Iammarino 2003, Iammarino and McCann 2013), McCann (Iammarino and McCann 2013), and Overman (Overman and Puga, 2010). Two main contributors are Glaeser's *Triumph of the City* (2013) and Storper's *Keys to the City* (2013). An important related literature emphasizing the advanced Triads of the modern "global" economy is developed by Rugman (2000, 2005).

2. We see the primary driver of authoritarian regimes in the 1930s in Germany and Japan as private militias and the military (in Austria under Dollfuss and Schussnigg, it was a concern to keep out a Nazi incursion); this is discussed in chapter 2.

3. And even then the primary driver was China, not Hong Kong.

4. In fact, surprisingly, there are rather few "common" models linking up advanced capitalist systems to democratic advanced nation-states. Outside of Marxist works on capitalism and the state (Poulantzas 1973, 1978; Miliband 1969; Jessop 1985; Glyn 2007; Lapavitsas 2014; Piketty 2014; Streeck 2014), there are a limited number of well-known approaches, most notably Hayek (1944), Lindblom (1977), and Schumpeter (1942); in public choice theory, a somewhat different approach (Buchanan and Tullock 1962; Brennan and Buchanan 1980; Peltzman 1976; Stigler 1971; Krueger1974; Olson 1982); and, in a quite different take, Przeworski and Wallerstein (Przeworski and Wallerstein 1982).

5. In the Przeworski and Wallerstein model, capital and labor can reach a compromise where workers restrain wages and capitalists invest the higher profits to raise the welfare of all as long as time horizons are sufficiently long.

6. The list of literature that has heavily influenced our thinking is long: from Shonfield (1968), Johnson (1982), Wade (1990), Berger and Dore (1996) and Zysman (1983),to neo-corporatism and the study of labor market institutions (Schmitter 1974; Streeck 1987; Crouch 1993; Lehmbruch 1993; Pontusson 2005), varieties of capitalism (Hall and Soskice 2001; Amable 2003; Iversen 1999), skill cospecificity and electoral systems (Iversen and Soskice (Iversen and Soskice 2001; Iversen and Soskice 2006) and Katzenstein's seminal work on "small states" (Katzenstein 1985), as well as the Regulation School (Boyer 1990), power resources theory and the welfare state (Rueschemeyer, Stephens, and Stephens 1992), the developmental state (Weiss 1998; Block 2010; Mazzucato 2015), to the historical evolution of institutions (Hall 1986; Thelen 2004; Martin and Swank 2008).

7. There is a strong emphasis in our discipline on causal identification, and some readers will find our focus on multidirectional causality challenging. While each causal claim we make can in principle be identified, we do not limit our argument to those claims that can be easily identified, and often we resort to historical interpretation and examples. We thus engage with evidence at multiple levels, from natural experiments to statistical analysis and historical narrative— all tied together by the theoretical framework outlined here. See Hall (2003) for an insightful discussion of these methodological issues.

8. For other work in the structural Marxist tradition see Block (1977), Wright (1979), and Jessop (1982), and in the more instrumentalist version of Miliband (1969), where senior judges, civil servants, and politicians share schools, universities, gender, ethnicity, and therefore interests with capital.

9. Lindblom agrees with the Marxists in their emphasis on the structural power of business, but unlike them he recognized that politicians are ultimately motivated to win democratic elections by building up a reputation for good governance. To do so required public policies to be well-aligned with the interests of capital so as to create conditions that would incentivize business to invest and grow the economy. We take from Lindblom his emphasis on electoral incentives, but we do not agree that these necessarily lead to policies that capital would want.

10. There is, however, a great deal of variance in the extent to which this is true, which is tied to the structure of the training and educational system. This helps explain variance in the strength of populist sentiments across countries.

11. Piketty hedges his bet by saying that "things are more complicated in practice," but he clearly believes that capital mobility will put great fiscal pressure on governments.

12. Indeed, it has long been the position of social democratic parties that it is not the returns of capital that should be taxed, but only the portion of those profits that is consumed rather than reinvested (for illustrations and an analysis of a postwar policies in Europe, see Eichengreen 1997).

13. The rich can in some measure reduce their tax burden by recording some of their profits in offshore tax shelters, as uncovered in the leaked Panama and Paradise Papers. Of course, this has always been true (think Switzerland), and tax authorities are in a never-ending cat-and-mouse game with corporations and wealthy individuals to try to close loopholes and clamp down on outright tax

evasion. The OECD estimates that the use of tax havens cost governments world-wide about 240 billion in 2015 ("After a Tax Crackdown, Apple found a New Shelter for Its Profits," *New York Times*, November 6, 2017). That is a considerable number, but it must be kept in perspective: it amounts to less than 0.05 percent of the OECD GDP (and about 0.03 percent of worldwide GDP).

14. The requirement is in fact slightly weaker—namely, that net transfers to the middle class are a constant share of the net incomes of the rich (see Elkjær and Iversen 2018, who show that this condition is easily satisfied for a larger country sample over a longer period of time).

15. The other major international grantor of patents is the European Patent Office, but data are only available from 1980. After adding European patents to USPTO, the numbers make no difference to the overall pattern in comparing 2015 to 1980, and we would not expect that to change for 1976.

16. This approach sees politics in capitalist democracies as a function of relative class power and class alliances and sometimes class compromises, which together determine cross-country variation in distributive politics (see Stephens 1979; Huber and Stephens 2001; Korpi 1983, 1989, 2006; Esping-Andersen 1990).

17. According to Streeck, "More than ever, economic power seems today to have become political power, while citizens appear to be almost entirely stripped of their democratic defenses and their capacity to impress upon the political economy interests and demands that are incommensurable with those of capital owners" (2011, 29).

18. We will argue below that if, counterfactually, innovation-oriented capitalism had not been intensive in human capital, but required a small educated workforce, and, say, large uneducated workforces, then society might very well have been quite differently organized, with military dictatorships and so on. Advanced capitalism has labor requirements quite different, for example, from resource-based capitalism.

19. This is also true in macroeconomics, where there is little empirical support for the notion that governments in advanced countries engage in massive and frequent manipulation. In past literature, the absence of political business cycles in the real economy has been explained by the limited capacity of governments to affect real economic outcomes. But today most leading economists believe that monetary and fiscal policies can have large short- and medium-term effects; yet governments do not appear to take advantage of this power for short-sighted electoral purposes.

20. A confusing factor is that there has been as a great increase in regulatory systems over the same period, covering the growth of complexity, uncertainty, environmental and safety issues. We discuss these developments in chapter 4.

21. It is true that before investing in an economy advanced companies have to have some guarantees that they will not be expropriated or taxed at rates that will make the investment unprofitable. But that guarantee is built into the incentives democratic governments have in promoting the advanced sectors and therefore not taxing them at rate where forward investments do not pay. Because access to knowledge clusters and the associated specialization (see next section) come

with attractive pricing power, there is considerable scope for governments to share in the "rents" of the knowledge economy.

22. This includes Piketty and Streeck, discussed above, but also writers from a wider left tradition: Hacker and Pierson (2011) do so in relation to the extraordinary inequalities of the United States and the stagnant incomes of middle-class America. For Simon Johnson the great investment banks, with close links to successive administrations, caused the financial crash. Glyn's *Capitalism Unleashed* (2007) offers a tour de force of the political economic history of the last four decades, and argues that advanced capitalism—with the continuing support of the state—has had adverse economic consequences on distributional outcomes (the share of profits, income inequality, the welfare state) as well as unemployment and financial stability. Central to all these arguments is the claim that advanced capitalism has neutered, bought out, taken over, or suborned democratic politics to act in the interests of advanced capitalism.

23. Individual Income Tax Rates and Tax Shares, Internal Revenue Service Statistics of Income, http://www.irs.gov/uac/SOI-Tax-Stats-Individual-Income-Tax-Rates-and-Tax-Shares.

24. The consequences of the Republican tax reform of 2017 are not clear at the time of writing, but it is unlikely to change much in the analysis. For individual filers with incomes between 200,000 and 425,000, the tax rate will rise from 33 to 35 percent, while most joint filers with incomes between 400,000 and 480,000 will see little or no change. Filers above this level will see their rates cut from 39.6 to 37 percent. Joint filers below 300,000 (200,000 for single filers) will see rates decline by between 1 and 3 percent. Of course, the net effect is complicated by changes to deductions, but nothing suggests significant burden shifts except among the top one percent (the very rich will pay less; other rich more).

25. The increase in inequality and labor market dualism have been subject of a rich literature in recent years, most notably Rueda (2005; 2008), Thelen (2012), Rehm (2009; 2011), Rehm, Hacker, and Schlesinger (2012); Hacker et al. (2013); Margalit (2013); Emmenegger et al. (2012); and Wren (2013). Our own work builds on and contributes to this literature.

Chapter 2: Two Paths to Democracy

1. Ziblatt provides a nice and analytically sharp survey of both Acemoglu and Robinson and Collier (Ziblatt 2006).

2. We do not study Ireland, Italy, and Japan in this chapter.

3. The first is Switzerland: the working class is classified as not involved by Collier, and we agree, but since "democracy" in effect included a veto to the right against redistribution, we do not count it as a full democratic episode; thus it is analogous to Acemoglu and Robinson's treatment of Singapore. In Norway, from 1898 to 1915, the Social Democrats and unions were involved in pressuring the liberals to accept working-class candidates before developing an independent party (Luebbert 1991), and were involved in the final push for democracy (Rueschmeyer et al. 1992), so we classify Norway as a case of working class pressure.

4. In fact, our explanations generate novel views of the reticence over female and black enfranchisement, as we discuss below.

5. The evidence for this is presented in Cusack et al. (2007); for Sweden, Magnusson (2000).

6. In the subsequent decade these laws were extended across much of the continent, but, apart from the west bank of the Rhine, they had limited long-term effect.

7. By bourgeoisie we follow Rueschemeyer et al (1992) as meaning the industrial elite.

8. In the Australian colonies and New Zealand, the politically induced development of national arbitration systems at the turn of the century implied a greater centralization of unions, but this was long after democratization (Castles 1984).

9. Working-class consciousness is not at issue. Revisionist labor historiography of the United States in the nineteenth century demonstrates its existence there as much as in Australia, Britain, and France. But it is not of relevance to the argument here.

10. The term public goods is used somewhat loosely.

11. But democracy is not always necessary and educational success in predemocratic Germany is explained by Lindert by decentralization, not out of line with the explanation for literacy in protocorporatist systems which we develop here.

12. Scotland is a separate case as far as education and literacy are concerned (yes, they were better educated than the English in the mid-nineteenth century), on which we need to do more work.

13. It would be interesting also to speculate on the role that views about black education played in the way black communities in the big Northern cities in the first half of the twentieth century were cut out of effective participation in the City Hall system: their votes were welcome, but not in return inter alia for serious expenditure on their education (Katznelson 1981). The assumption of blacks into the large Northern towns politically on different and less advantageous terms to the earlier waves of white immigrants, well-described in Katznelson's *City Trenches*, may fundamentally reflect a lower return to educational investment *precisely because* the lack of democracy in the South under Jim Crow and before had led to their being an undereducated community in the South.

14. In fact, demonstrating against the Commons defeat of the Liberal government's Reform Bill of 1866.

15. Upper Canada literacy and primary education: high from the mid-nineteenth century on but lower than US before then (Lindert 2004, 122n64). This suggests that enrollment started to rise around the time of constitutional change, but more work is needed here.

16. This section is based on our detailed analyses with Thomas Cusack (Cusack et al., 2007; 2010, including an online historical appendix).

Chapter 3: The Rise and Fall of Fordism

1. This section builds on Torben Iversen and David Soskice, "Politics for Markets." *Journal of European Social Policy* 25 (1), 2015, Section 3.2.2., pp. 141–148. DOI: https://doi.org/10.1177/0958928714556971

2. OECD *Social Expenditure Statistics*. Online Database Edition. http://www
.oecd.org/social/expenditure.htm.

3. Since Switzerland has a collective executive that is not the result of coalition bargaining, we exclude it from the analysis. It has no effect on the substantive results.

Chapter 3: Appendix

1. These controls are only relevant for total spending because unemployment and ALMPs only apply to the working-age population.

2. Automatic unemployment disbursement is defined as the first difference in unemployment as a percent of the working-age population times the net replacement rate in the previous year, which is the ratio of net unemployment insurance benefits to net income for an unmarried single person earning the average production worker's wage.

Chapter 4: Knowledge Economies and Their Political Construction

1. Intel's first microprocessor, the 4004, was conceived by Ted Hoff and Stanley Mazor. Assisted by Masatoshi Shima, Federico Faggin used his experience in Silicon-Gate MOS technology (1968 Milestone) to squeeze the 2300 transistors of the 4-bit MPU into a 16-pin package in 1971.

2. This is, of course, a major simplification; for example, education had been on an upward trajectory before the 1970s and 1980s, even if the dramatic expansion of higher education in most advanced economies took place in the 1980s onwards.

3. Note that this implies a different approach to FDI and trade than the now dominant Helpman-Melitz model (Helpman et al. 2004). In that model only the most productive firms engage in FDI as a substitute for trade because they can produce at a scale that bring the additional fixed costs of FDI below the variable unit costs of trading. Our knowledge cluster argument instead implies that FDI and trade go hand in hand, both over time and in the sense that firms engage in both, and it provides a more plausible explanation, we submit, for why the stock of FDI has been rising exponentially in the past three decades (we provide numbers below). Our story also makes sense of why governments across the advanced world liberalized inward FDI and trade as a way to take advantage of complementarities between FDI technology and domestic knowledge clusters. In the HM model, by contrast, FDI is a threat to domestic firms and only benefit the consumer insofar as FDI reduces labor cost. This would put FDI into conflict with producer interests—employers as well as unions. This does not seem to happen in ACDs.

4. The private versus public shares of this rising investment in education vary across countries. In continental Europe almost all spending is public, whereas in the Anglo-Saxon countries and in Japan and Korea a substantial share is private. Generally speaking, the higher the private share the greater the barriers to entry into tertiary education for low- and lower-middle-income families. In chapter 5

we show that this is an important determinant of the extent to which populist values have taken hold in the transition to a knowledge economy.

5. The economy-wide regulation index is based on more than 700 questions that are asked member governments in 18 regulatory domains, which are aggregated into three broad regulatory areas: (1) state control, (2) barriers to entrepreneurship, and (3) barriers to trade and investment. The 18 domains covered by these areas are: (1) scope of state-owned enterprises (SOEs); (2) government involvement in six network sectors (electricity, gas, rail transport, air transport, postal services, and telecommunication); (3) direct control over business enterprises; (4) governance of state-owned enterprises; (5) price controls; (6) command and control regulation; (7) licenses and permits systems; (8) communication and simplification of government rules and procedures; (9) administrative burdens for corporations; (10) administrative burdens on creating an individual enterprise; (11) entry barriers in services sectors; (12) legal barriers to entry: (13) antitrust exemptions; (14) barriers to entry in network sectors; (15) barriers to FDI; (16) tariff barriers; (17) differential treatment of foreign suppliers; and (18) barriers to trade facilitation (see Koske et al. 2015 for more detail). The summary measure is a weighted average across the three areas and varies between 0 and 6, where 0 is the most procompetition regulatory framework and 6 is the most anticompetition framework. We inversed this scale so that higher number means more pro-competition regulatory frameworks.

6. We do not want to imply that patents and standard-setting technologies that limit competition cannot sometimes be welfare-improving, and therefore justified. The point is that public regulation must ensure that successful companies are constantly under pressure to innovate in order to retain their hard-fought market positions and serve the interests of consumers and governments eager to show economic progress.

7. George Shultz's noted remark to the Soviet leaders in the early 1980s.

8. The distinction between egotropic and sociotropic voting is sometimes taken to mean that individuals either optimize their own welfare or that of the nation. But as Lewis-Beck and Stegmaier (2014) point out, no such inference can be made. It is difficult for rational, selfish individuals to identify the effect of government policies on their own experiences with unemployment, income-growth, etc.—there are simply too many idiosyncratic factors that affect personal fortunes—and it can therefore make sense to focus on the performance of the macroeconomy under the assumption that it is likely to also have some effect on their own welfare. This is essentially a signal extraction problem (of course, this does not rule out that altruism also matters).

9. The political business cycle literature is something of an evil twin to the economic voting literature because it conjectures that governments will try to "fake" good performance around elections by engaging in policies that will only create short-term benefits (see Adolph 2013 for a review and test). But this argument does not work for policies that only have beneficial effects in the future, and long-term economic performance is based on investments in the institutions supporting the advanced sectors. Spending on education, for example, only

translates into economic outcomes several years down the line, and the same is true for R&D, opening of trade and FDI, and competition policies. It is true that spending in some of these areas may have immediate and concentrated benefits, such as the hiring of teachers, but it is not plausible that the massive expansion in higher education over the past four decades is due to short-term business cycles (and no one, to our knowledge, argues that). The one area where politicians may create short-term boosts to growth and employment is macroeconomic policies. But in our reading of the evidence, governments in ACDs do the opposite: they tend to pursue far-sighted macroeconomic policies (Iversen and Soskice 2006). The shift to low-inflation targeting is an example of this, and so is the Stability and Growth Pact in the Eurozone and the general shift toward strong ministries of finance that we discussed above.

10. This is an issue in interpreting results that suggests that economic voting in small open economies is less prevalent (Hellwig 2001). This could be because governments have less effect on the economy (and therefore more constrained), but it could also be that they have a stronger incentive to behave in a responsible manner, since loss of competitiveness and trade deficits will quickly signal problems.

11. This is broadly consistent with the argument and evidence in Mau (2015) that the middle class endorsed neoliberal reforms and bought into the key institutions of the new economy, including higher education, a more credit-based financial system, and opportunities for home ownership (although we disagree that this was caused by a cultural shift towards individualization, or that the middle class ultimately lost out from these changes—to the contrary).

12. For example, imagine that those with low education and income have a naïve, "household-budget" understanding of fiscal policy, while those with high education and income have a sophisticated "Keynesian" understanding of fiscal policy. Also assume that fluctuations in spending and deficits as a share of GDP around some politically determined equilibrium level is a function of the business cycle (via automatic stabilizers implied by entitlement spending). In that case, the correlation between preferences for changing in spending and actual spending will be negative among those with poor education and income (since a household budget approach to spending is procyclical), and positive among those with high education and income (since a Keynesian approach is countercyclical). Yet this this *does not* mean that equilibrium spending levels are more responsive to the preferences of the highly educated and affluent.

13. This is a cross-nationally comparable test of respondent skills in prose, document handling and interpretation, and mathematics. It was administered to a random sample of the adult population in OECD countries.

14. See also Uterwedde (1998, chap. 7).

15. This can work in somewhat different ways: for instance, a consultant may be brought in for an assignment, but if the assignment is important, either the consultant brought an existing reputation with him or her, or worked for a partnership which would suffer if it became known that the consultant had not fulfilled his or her brief; but, ultimately, reputations are built in historical time.

Chapter 5: The Politics of the Knowledge Economy and the Rise of Populism

1. Lipset and Rokkan associated social cleavages with major socioeconomic transformations, and they identified three elements of a cleavage: (i) a deep structural division in society; (ii) shared collective identities; and (iii) political organization. In our story the transformation is the ICT revolution, the structural division is along educational and geographical lines, the collective identity is a set of shared values and beliefs, and the political organization is populist parties.

2. For example, dependence on the welfare state is found to be negatively related, and rural residency positively related, to populism. Both are precisely as we would expect, but Inglehart and Norris take this as evidence *against* the economic perspective. They also treat education, gender, and age as "demographic controls," whereas we see them as critical in any definition of the old middle classes (which overall have less education, are older, and grew out of male-headed households). Also, while Inglehart and Norris interpret the robust effects of the cultural attitude variables (even after economic controls) as evidence in favor of the cultural interpretation, these variables are in our view *mechanisms* linking economic conditions to populist voting.

3. Nonworking married or cohabiting respondents were coded according to the occupation of their spouse.

4. We agree with some of the party-centered literature that elites help to "activate" latent grievances: a process we do not capture in this paper. At the same time, we note that strong populist values flourish even where strong populist parties are absent. Much of the story is a demand story, even if it is not the whole story.

Chapter 6: Conclusion

1. Still, researchers who work in this area, such as Google's Magenta project on "creative machines," consider these capabilities more likely used as creative extensions of ourselves than replacements (interview in the Danish newspaper *Politiken*, October, 14, 2017).

2. See *New York Times Magazine*, "Can AI Be Taught to Explain Itself?" November 21, 2017.

3. Note also that although firms have an interest in cross-country knowledge clusters, all else equal, individual firms do not create clusters. They instead depend on the broader institutional infrastructure set up by the state, which has no interest in investing in infrastructure that can be used by firms abroad.

BIBLIOGRAPHY

Abney, Ronni, James Adams, Michael Clark, Malcolm Easton, Lawrence Ezrow, Spyros Kosmidis, and Anja Neundorf. 2013. "When does valence matter? Heightened valence effects for governing parties during election campaigns." *Party Politics* 19 (1): 61–82.

Acemoglu, Daron, and Joshua Angrist. 2000. "How Large Are Human-Capital Externalities? Evidence from Compulsory Schooling Laws." *NBER Macroeconomics Annual* 15: 9–59.

Acemoglu, Daron, and James Robinson. 2005. *The Economic Origins of Dictatorship and Democracy*. Cambridge, UK: Cambridge University Press.

Acs, Zoltan. 2002. *Innovation and Growth of Cities*. Cheltenham, UK: Edward Elgar.

Adolph, Christopher. 2013. *Bankers, Bureaucrats, and Central Bank Politics: The Myth of Neutrality*. Cambridge, UK: Cambridge University Press.

Aldrich, John. 1995. *Why Parties? The Origins and Transformation of Party Politics in America*. Chicago: University of Chicago Press.

Amable, Bruno. 2003. *The Diversity of Modern Capitalism*. Oxford: Oxford University Press.

Ammermüller, Andreas. 2005. "Educational Opportunities and the Role of Institutions." ZEW Centre for European Economic Research Discussion Paper 05–044.

Angrist, Joshua, and Alan B. Krueger. 1991. "Does Compulsory School Attendance Affect Schooling and Earnings?" *The Quarterly Journal of Economics* 106 (4): 979–1014.

Ansell, Ben W. 2008. "University Challenges: Explaining Institutional Change in Higher Education." *World Politics* 60 (4): 189–230.

Armingeon, Klaus, Christian Isler, Laura Knöpfel, David Weisstanner, and Sarah Engler. 2016. Comparative Political Data Set, 1960–2014. Bern: Institute of Political Science, University of Berne.

Atkinson, Anthony B. 2003. "Income Inequality in OECD Countries: Data and Explanations." *CESifo Economic Studies* 49 (4): 479–513.

Atkinson, Anthony B., Thomas Piketty, and Emmanuel Saez. 2011. "Top Incomes in the Long Run of History." *Journal of Economic Literature* 49 (1): 3 –71.

Audretsch, David. 1998. "Agglomeration and the Location of Innovative Activity." *Oxford Review of Economic Policy* 14 (2): 18–29.

Aukrust, Odd. 1977. "Inflation in the Open Economy: A Norwegian Model." In *Worldwide Inflation: Theory and Recent Experience*, eds. Lawrence B. Krause and Walter S. Salant, 107–53. Washington, DC: Brookings Institute.

Autor, David H. 2015. "Why Are There Still So Many Jobs? The History and Future of Workplace Automation." *Journal of Economic Perspectives* 29 (3): 3–30.

Autor, David H., and David Dorn. 2009. "Inequality and Specialization: The Growth of Low-Skill Service Jobs in the United States." NBER Working Paper Series.

Autor, David, David Dorn, and Gordon H. Hanson. 2013. "The China Syndrome: Local Labor Market Effects of Import Competition in the United States." *American Economic Review* 103 (6): 2121–68.

Autor, David H., Lawrence F. Katz, and Melissa S. Kearney. 2006. "The Polarization of the U.S. Labor Market." *American Economic Review* 96 (2): 189–94.

———. 2008. "Trends in U.S. Wage Inequality: Revising the Revisionists." *The Review of Economics and Statistics* 90 (2): 300–23.

Autor, David H., Frank Levy, and Richard J. Murnane. 2003. "The Skill Content of Recent Technological Change: An Empirical Exploration." *Quarterly Journal of Economics* 118 (4): 1279–1333.

Baethge, Martin, and Andrä Wolter. 2015. "The German Skill Formation Model in Transition: From Dual System of VET to Higher Education?" *Journal for Labour Market Research* 48 (2): 97–112.

Baldwin, Peter. 1990. *The Politics of Social Solidarity: Class Bases of the European Welfare State, 1875–1975*. Cambridge, UK: Cambridge University Press.

Barkow, Jerome H., Leda Cosmides, and John Tooby, eds. 1995. *The Adapted Mind: Evolutionary Psychology and the Generation of Culture*. New York: Oxford University Press.

Baron, David P., and John A. Ferejohn. 1989. "Bargaining in Legislatures." *American Political Science Review* 83 (4): 1181–1206.

Bartels, Larry M. 2005. "Homer Gets a Tax Cut: Inequality and Public Policy in the American Mind." *Perspectives on Politics* 3 (1): 15–31.

———. 2008. *Unequal Democracy: The Political Economy of the New Gilded Age*. Princeton, NJ: Princeton University Press.

Beck, Nathaniel, and Jonathan N. Katz. 1995. "What to Do (And Not to Do) with Time-Series Cross-Section Data." *The American Political Science Review* 89 (3): 634–47.

Bénabou, Roland, and Efe A. Ok. 1998. "Social Mobility and the Demand for Redistribution: The POUM Hypothesis." National Bureau of Economic Research, No. w6795.

Berger, Suzanne, and Ronald Dore. 1996. *National Diversity and Global Capitalism*. Ithaca, NY: Cornell University Press.

Betz, Hans-Georg. 1994. *Radical Right-Wing Populism in Western Europe*. New York: St. Martin's.

Blackbourn, David. 1980. *Class, Religion, and Local Politics in Wilhelmine Germany: The Centre Party in Württemberg Before 1914*. New Haven: Yale University Press.

Blackbourn, David, and Geoff Eley. 1984. *The Peculiarities Of German History: Bourgeois Society and Politics in Nineteenth-Century Germany*. Oxford: Oxford University Press.

Blais, André, Agnieszka Dobrzynska, and Indridi H. Indridason. 2015. "To Adopt or Not to Adopt Proportional Representation: The Politics of Institutional Choice." *British Journal of Political Science* 35 (1): 182–90.

Blanchard, Olivier, and Justin Wolfers. 2000. "The Role of Shocks and Institutions in the Rise of European Unemployment: The Aggregate Evidence." *Economic Journal* 110 (462): 1–33.

Blau, David M., and Janet Currie. 2006. "Preschool, Day Care, and After-School Care: Who's Minding the Kids?" In *Handbook of the Economics of Education*, eds. Eric A. Hanushek and Finis Welch, 1163–1278. Amsterdam: North-Holland.

Block, Fred. 1977. "The Ruling Class Does Not Rule: Notes on the Marxist Theory of the State." *Socialist Revolution* 33 (7): 6–28.

Boix, Carles, and Susan Stokes. 2003. "Endogenous Democratization." *World Politics* 55 (4): 517–49.

Boix, Carles. 1998. *Political Parties, Growth, and Equality*. New York: Cambridge University Press.

———. 1999. "Setting the Rules of the Game: The Choice of Electoral Systems in Advanced Democracies." *American Political Science Review* 93 (September): 609–24.

———. 2003. *Democracy and Redistribution*. Cambridge, UK: Cambridge University Press.

Bonnet, Odran, Pierre-Henri Bono, Guillaume Chapelle, and Etienne Wasmer. 2014. "Does Housing Capital Contribute to Inequality? A Comment on Thomas Piketty's *Capital in the Twenty-First Century*." Sciences Po Economics Discussion Paper, 7: 1–12.

Borjas, George J. 2013. "Immigration and the American Worker: Review of the Academic Literature." Center for Immigration Studies, Washington, DC. https://sites.hks.harvard.edu/fs/gborjas/publications/popular/CIS2013.pdf.

Bork, Robert. 1978. *The Antitrust Paradox: A Policy at War with Itself*. New York: Basic Books.

Bornschier, Simon. 2010. *Cleavage Politics and the Populist Right: The New Cultural Conflict in Western Europe*. Philadelphia: Temple University Press.

Bourlès, R., G. Cette, J. Lopez, J. Mairesse, and G. Nicoletti. 2013. "Do Product Market Regulations in Upstream Sectors Curb Productivity Growth? Panel Data Evidence for OECD Countries." *Review of Economics and Statistics* 95 (5): 1750–68.

Boustan, Leah Platt. 2009. "Competition in the promised land: Black migration and racial wage convergence in the North, 1940–1970." *The Journal of Economic History* 69 (3): 755–82.

Brady, David, Evelyne Huber, and John D. Stephens. 2014. Comparative Welfare States Data Set, University of North Carolina and WZB Berlin Social Science Center.

Braverman, H. 1998. *Labor and Monopoly Capital: The Degradation of Work in the Twentieth Century*. New York: New York University Press.

Brennan, Geoffrey, and James Buchanan. 1980. *The Power to Tax: Analytical Foundations of a Fiscal Constitution*. Cambridge, UK: Cambridge University Press.

Breznitz, Dan. 2007. *Innovation and the State: Political Choice and Strategies for Growth in Israel, Taiwan, and Ireland*. New Haven: Yale University Press.

Brynjolfsson, E., and A. McAfee. 2013. *Race Against the Machine: How the Digital Revolution is Accelerating Innovation, Driving Productivity, and Irreversibly Transforming Employment and the Economy*. New York: W. W. Norton.

Bryson, Alex, Bernhard Ebbinghaus, and Jelle Visser. 2011. "Introduction: Causes, Consequences, and Cures of Union Decline." *European Journal of Industrial Relations* 17 (2): 97–105.

Buchanan, James M., and Gordon Tullock. 1962. *The Calculus of Consent: Logical Foundations of Constitutional Democracy*. Ann Arbor: University of Michigan Press.

Busemeyer, Marius. 2007. "Determinants of Public Education Spending in 21 OECD Democracies, 1980–2001." *Journal of European Public Policy* 14 (4): 582–610.

———. 2009. "Reformbaustelle oder Vorzeigemodell?: Die deutsche Berufsbildung im Wandel." In *MPIfG Jahrbuch 2009–2010*, 39–45. Köln: Max-Planck-Institut für Gesellschaftsforschung.

———. 2014. *Skills and Inequality: Partisan Politics and the Political Economy of Education Reforms in Western Welfare States*. Cambridge, UK: Cambridge University Press.

Busemeyer, Marius, and Torben Iversen. 2014. "The Politics of Opting Out: Explaining Educational Financing and Popular Support for Public Spending." *Socio-Economic Review* 12 (2): 299–328.

Busemeyer, Marius, and Kathleen Thelen. 2008. "From Collectivism towards Segmentalism. Institutional Change in German Vocational Training." Max Planck Institute for the Study of Societies (MPIfG) Discussion Paper, 1–30.

Busemeyer, Marius R., and Christine Trampusch. 2012. *The Political Economy of Collective Skill Formation*. Oxford: Oxford University Press.

Busemeyer, Marius R., and Christine Trampusch. 2013. "Liberalization by Exhaustion: Transformative Change in the German Welfare State and Vocational Training System." *Zeitschrift für Sozialreform* 59 (3): 291–312.Bustikova, Lenka. 2014. "Revenge of the Radical Right." *Comparative Political Studies* 47: 1738–65.

Campbell, John L., and Ove K. Pedersen. 2007. "The Varieties of Capitalism and Hybrid Success: Denmark in the Global Economy." *Comparative Political Studies* 40 (3): 307–32.

Cantwell, John. 1989. *Technological Innovation and Multinational Corporations*. Oxford: Blackwell.

Cantwell, John, and Simona Iammarino. 2003. *Multinational Corporations and European Regional Systems of Innovation*. London: Routledge.

Cantwell, John, and Ram Mudambi. 2005. "MNE Competence-Creating Subsidiary Mandates." *Strategic Management Journal* 26 (12): 1109–28.

Caragliu, Andrea, Chiara Del Bo, and Peter Nijkamp. 2011. "Smart Cities in Europe." *Journal of Urban Technology* 18 (2): 65–82.

Card, David. 2001. "Estimating the Return to Schooling: Progress on Some Persistent Econometric Problems." *Econometrica* 69 (5): 1127–60.

Carlin, W., and David Soskice. 2014. *Macroeconomics: Institutions, Instability and the Financial System*. Oxford: Oxford University Press.

Casper, Steven. 2007. *Creating Silicon Valley in Europe: Public Policy Towards New Technology Industries*. New York: Oxford University Press.

Castilla, Emilio J., Hokyu Hwang, Ellen Granovetter, and Mark Granovetter. 2000. "Social Networks in Silicon Valley." In *The Silicon Valley Edge: A Habitat for Innovation and Entrepreneurship*, eds. Chong-Moon Lee, William Miller, Marguerite

Hancock, Henry Rowen, William F. Miller, Marguerite Gong Hancock, and Henry S. Rowen, 218–47. Stanford, CA: Stanford Business Books.

Castles, Francis, and Peter Mair. 1984. "Left-Right Political Scales: Some 'Expert' Judgments." *European Journal of Political Research* 12 (March): 73–88.

Cavaille, Charlotte, and Jeremy Ferwerda. "How Distributional Conflict over In-Kind Benefits Generates Support for Anti-Immigrant Parties." Paper presented at Annual Meetings of the Political Science Association, 2017.

Cavaille, Charlotte, and Kris-Stella Trump. 2015. "Support for the Welfare State In Western Democracies: The Two Dimensions of Redistributive Attitudes." *Journal of Politics* 77 (1): 146–60.

Chandler, Alfred D. 1967. *Strategy and Structure: Chapters in the History of the Industrial Enterprise.* Cambridge, MA: MIT Press.

Chandler, Alfred D. 1977. *The Invisible Hand: The Managerial Revolution in American Business.* Cambridge, MA: Belknap Press of Harvard University Press.

Chang, Ha-Joon. 2011. *23 Things They Don't Tell You about Capitalism.* New York: Bloomsbury.

Chinn, Menzie D. 2006. "What Matters for Financial Development? Capital Controls, Institutions, and Interactions." *Journal of Development Economics* 81 (1): 163–92.

Chinn, Menzie D., and Hiro Ito. 2008. "A New Measure of Financial Openness." *Journal of Comparative Policy Analysis* 10 (3): 309–22.

Cini, Michelle, and Lee McGowan. 1998. *Competition Policy in the European Union.* Basingstoke, UK: Macmillan.

Clark, Michael. 2009. "Valence and electoral outcomes in Western Europe, 1976–1998." *Electoral Studies* 28 (1): 111–22.

Coe, David T., Elhanan Helpman, and Alexander W. Hoffmaister. 2009. "International R&D Spillovers and Institutions." *European Economic Review* 53 (7): 723–41.

Collier, Ruth Berins. 1999. *Paths Towards Democracy: The Working Class and Elites in Western Europe and South America.* Cambridge, UK: Cambridge University Press.

Colomer, Joseph H. 2006. *Political Institutions: Democracy and Social Choice.* Oxford: Oxford University Press.

Cooke, Philip. 2001. "Regional Systems of Innovation, Clusters and the Knowledge Economy." *Industry and Corporate Change* 10 (4): 945–74.

Corak, Miles. 2013. "Income Inequality, Equality of Opportunity, and Intergenerational Mobility." *Journal of Economic Perspectives* 27: 79–102.

———. 2013b. "Inequality from Generation to Generation: The United States in Comparison." In *The Economics of Inequality, Poverty, and Discrimination in the Twenty-First Century,* ed. Robert S. Rycroft. Santa Barbara, CA: ABC-CLIO.

Costas Lapavitsas. 2014. *Profiting without Producing: How Finance Exploits Us All.* New York: Verso.

Cox, Gary. 1987. *The Efficient Secret.* Cambridge, UK: Cambridge University Press.

Crafts, Nicholas. 2018. *Forging Ahead, Falling Behind and Fighting Back: British Economic Growth from the Industrial Revolution to the Financial Crisis.* Cambridge, UK: Cambridge University Press.

Crepaz, Markus. 1998. "Inclusion versus Exclusion: Political Institutions and Welfare Expenditures." *Comparative Politics* 31 (1): 61–80.

Crouch, Colin. 1993. *Industrial Relations and European State Traditions*. Oxford: Oxford University Press.

Curtis, M. 2006. "Catalyzing the Collapse: The Computer and the Fall of the Soviet Union." AHS Capstone Projects, Paper 15.

Cusack, Thomas R., and Susanne Fuchs. 2002. "Documentation Notes for Parties, Governments, and Legislatures Data Set." Berlin, Germany: Wissenschaftszentrum Berlin für Sozialforschung. https://www.wzb.eu/system/files/docs/ende/meg/pgl_doc_notes_cf.pdf.

———. 2007. "Parties, Governments and Legislatures Data Set." Berlin, Germany: Wissenschaftszentrum Berlin für Sozialforschung. http://www.wzb.eu/en/persons/thomas-r-cusack?s=5662.

Cusack, Thomas, Torben Iversen, and David Soskice. 2007. "Economic Interests and the Origins of Electoral Systems." *American Political Science Review* 101 (3): 373–91.

———. 2010. "The Coevolution of Capitalism and Political Representation: Explaining the Choice of Electoral Systems." *American Political Science Review* 103 (May): 393–403.

Dahl, Robert A. 1971. *Polyarchy: Participation and Opposition*. New Haven: Yale University Press.

Dassonneville, Ruth, and Marc Hooghe. 2017. "Economic indicators and electoral volatility: economic effects on electoral volatility in Western Europe, 1950–2013." *Comparative European Politics* 15 (6): 919–43.

Davis, Gerald F. 2016. *The Vanishing American Corporation: Navigating the Hazards of a New Economy*. Oakland, CA: Berrett-Kochler.

De Waele, Jean-Michel. 2014. *European Social Democracy during the Global Economic Crisis: Renovation or Resignation?* Oxford: Oxford University Press.

Doner, Richard F. and Ben R. Schneider. 2016. "The Middle-Income Trap. More Politics than Economics." *World Politics* 68 (4): 608–44.

Dosi, Giovanni. 2000. *Innovation, Organization, and Economic Dynamics: Selected Essays*. Northampton, MA: Edward Elgar.

Downs, Anthony. 1957. *An Economic Theory of Democracy*. New York: Harper.

Due, Jesper, Jørgen Steen Madsen, Strøby Jensen, Carsten and Petersen, Lars K. 1994. *The Survival of the Danish Model: A Historical Sociological Analysis of the Danish System of Collective Agreement*. Copenhagen: DJØF.

Dunford, Michael, and Diane Perrons. 1994. "Regional inequality, regimes of accumulation and economic development in contemporary Europe." *Transactions of the Institute of British geographers*: 163–82.

Durlauf, Steven. 1996a. "A Theory of Persistent Income Inequality." *Journal of Economic Growth* 1: 75–93.

———. 1996b. "Neighborhood Feedbacks, Endogenous Stratification, and Income Inequality." In *Dynamic Disequilibrium Modelling*, eds. W. Barnett, G. Gandolfo, and C. Hillinger, 505–34. New York: Cambridge University Press.

Durlauf, Steven, and Ananth Seshadri. 2017. "Understanding the Great Gatsby Curve." *NBER Macroeconomics Annual* 32: 1–94.

Ebbinghaus, Bernhard. 1995. "The Siamese Twins: Citizenship Rights, Cleavage Formation, and Party-Union Relations in Western Europe." *International Review of Social History* 40 (3): 51–89.

Edgren, Gosta, Karl-Otto Faxen, and Carl-Erik Odhner. 1973. *Wage Formation and the Economy*. London: Allen and Unwin.

Ehrenhalt, Alan. 2012. *The Great Inversion and the Future of the American City*. New York: Vintage.

Eichengreen, Barry. 1997. "Institutions and Economic Growth: Europe after World War II." In *Economic Growth in Europe since 1945*, eds. Nicholas Crafts and Gianni Toniolo, 38–72. Cambridge, UK: Cambridge University Press.

Eichengreen, Barry, Donghyun Park, and Kwanho Shin. 2012. "When Fast-Growing Economies Slow Down: International Evidence and Implications for China." *Asian Economic Papers* 11 (1): 42–87.

Elkjær, Mads Andreas. 2017. "Unequal Representation in High Equality Contexts? A Study of Differential Responsiveness in Denmark." Typescript, Department of Government, Harvard University.

Elkjær, Mads Andreas, and Torben Iversen. 2018. "The Political Representation of Economic Interests: Subversion of Democracy or Middle-Class Supremacy?" Typescript, Department of Government, Harvard University.

Emmenegger, Patrick, Silja Häusermann, Bruno Palier, and Martin Seeleib-Kaiser, eds. 2012. *The Age of Dualization: The Changing Face of Inequality in Deindustrializing Societies*. New York: Oxford University Press.

Engerman, Stanley L., and Kenneth L. Sokoloff. 2005. "The Evolution of Suffrage Institutions in the New World." *Journal of Economic History* 65 (4): 891–921.

Esping-Andersen, Gösta. 1985. *Politics Against Markets: The Social Democratic Road to Power*. Princeton, NJ: Princeton University Press.

———. 1990. *The Three Worlds of Welfare Capitalism*. Princeton, NJ: Princeton University Press.

Estevez-Abe, Margarita, Torben Iversen, and David Soskice. 2001. "Social Protection and the Formation of Skills: A Reinterpretation of the Welfare State." In *Varieties of Capitalism: The Institutional Foundations of Comparative Advantage*, eds. Peter A. Hall and David Soskice, 145–83. Oxford: Oxford University Press.

Eurofound. 2015. "Workplace Practices—Patterns, Performance, and Well-being." Third European Company Survey, Overview Report. Luxembourg: Publications Office of the European Union.

Feldmann, Maryann P. 2000. "Location and Innovation: The New Economic Geography of Innovation, Spillovers, and Agglomeration." In *The Oxford Handbook of Economic Geography*, eds. Gordon Clark, Mayann P. Feldmann, Meric Gertler, and Kate Williams, 373–94. Oxford: Oxford University Press.

Fioretos, Orfeo. 2011. *Creative Reconstructions: Multilateralism and European Varieties of Capitalism after 1950*. Ithaca, NY: Cornell University Press.

Flanagan, Robert J., David Soskice, and Lloyd Ulman. 1983. *Unionism, Economic Stabilization, and Incomes Policies: European Experience*. Washington, DC: Brookings Institution.

Ford, Martin. 2015. *The Rise of the Robots: Technology and the Threat of a Jobless Future*. New York: Basic Books.

Frank, Mark G., and Paul Ekman, 2004. "Nonverbal Detection of Deception in Forensic Contexts." In *Handbook of Forensic Psychology: Resource for Mental Health and*

Legal Professionals, eds. William T. O'Donohue and Eric R. Levensky, 645–53. New York: Elsevier Science.

Freeman, Christopher. 2008. *Systems of Innovation: Selected Essays in Evolutionary Economics*. Cheltenham, UK: Edward Elgar.

Freeman, Christopher, and Francisco Louçã. 2001. *As Time Goes By. From the Industrial Revolutions to the Information Revolution*. New York: Oxford University Press.

Freeman, Gary P. 1986. "Migration and the political economy of the welfare state." *The Annals of the American Academy of Political and Social Science* 485 (1): 51–63.

Freeman, Richard B. 1980. "Unionization and the Dispersion of Wages." *Industrial and Labor Relations Review* 34 (1): 3–24.

———. 1988. "Labor Market Institutions and Economic Performance." *Economic Policy* 6: 62–80.

Freitag, Markus. 1999. "Politik und Währung. Ein internationaler Vergleich." PhD dissertation, University of Bern.

Frey, Carl Benedikt, and Michael A. Obsborne. 2017. "The Future of Employment: How Susceptible Are Jobs to Computerisation?" *Technological Forecasting and Social Change* 114: 254–80.

Friedman, T. L. 2005. *The World is Flat: A Brief History of the Twenty-First Century*. New York: Picador.

Galenson, Walter. 1952. *The Danish System of Industrial Relations: A Study in Industrial Peace*. Cambridge, MA: Harvard University Press.

Gamoran, Adam. 2010. "Tracking and Inequality: New Directions for Research and Practice." In *The Routledge International Handbook of the Sociology of Education*, eds. Michael W. Apple, Stephen J. Ball, and Luis A. Gandin, 213–28. New York: Routledge.

Garfinkel, Simson, and Beth Rosenberg. 2006. *RFID: Applications, Security, and Privacy*. Boston: Addison-Wesley.

Garrett, Geoffrey. 1998. "Global Markets and National Politics: Collision Course or Virtuous Circle?" *International Organization* 52 (4): 787–824.

Gawthrop, Richard, and Gerald Strauss. 1984. "Protestantism and Literacy in Early Modern Germany." *Past and Present* 104 (1): 31–55.

Georgiadis, Andreas, and Alan Manning. 2012. "Spend It Like Beckham? Inequality and Redistribution in the UK, 1983–2004." *Public Choice* 151 (3/4): 537–63.

Gerschenkron, Alexander. 1966. *Economic Backwardness in Historical Perspective: A Book of Essays*. Cambridge, MA: Harvard University Press.

Gidron, Noam, and Peter A. Hall. 2017. "The politics of social status: Economic and cultural roots of the populist right." *The British Journal of Sociology* 68: S57–S84.

Gilens, Martin. 2005. "Inequality and Democratic Responsiveness: Who Gets What They Want from Government?" *Public Opinion Quarterly* 69: 778–96.

———. 2012. *Affluence and Influence: Economic Inequality and Political Power in America*. Princeton, NJ: Princeton University Press.

Gingrich, Jane, and Ben Ansell. 2014. "Sorting for Schools: Housing, Education, and Inequality." *Socio-Economic Review* 12 (2): 329–51.

Gjerløff, Anne Katrine. 2014. "Skolens udvikling i 1960erne-70erne." In *Skole i 200 År*. Undervisningsministeriet, Copenhagen, Denmark.

Glaeser, Edward L., ed. 2010. *Agglomeration Economics*. National Bureau of Economic Research (NBER) conference volume, ed. E. L. Glaeser. Chicago: University of Chicago Press.

Glaeser, Edward L. 2011. *The Triumph of the City*. New York: MacMillan https://skole200 .dk/wp-.content/uploads/2014/08/Artikel_Skolens_Udvikling_1960_70.pdf

Glaeser, Edward. L., Hedi D. Kallal, José A. Scheinkman, and Andrei Shleifer. 1992. "Growth in Cities." *Journal of Political Economy* 100 (6): 1126–52.

Glaeser, Edward L., and Matthew G. Resseger. 2010. "The Complementarity between Cities and Skills." *Journal of Regional Science* 50 (1): 221–44.

Glyn, Andrew. 2007. *Capitalism Unleashed: Finance Globalization and Welfare*. Oxford: Oxford University Press.

Go, Sun, and Peter H. Lindert. 2010. "The Uneven Rise of American Public Schools to 1850." *Journal of Economic History* 70 (1): 1–26.

Goldin, Claudia, and Larry Katz. 1998. "The Origins of Technology-Skill Complementarity." *The Quarterly Journal of Economics* 103 (3): 693–732.

———. 2007. "Long-run Changes in the Wage Structure: Narrowing, Widening, Polarizing." *Brookings Papers on Economic Activity* 2: 135–67.

———. 2008. *The Race between Education and Technology*. Cambridge, MA: Belknap Press of Harvard University Press.

Goldthorpe, John. 1984. *Order and Conflict in Contemporary Capitalism*. Oxford: Oxford University Press.

Goodhart, D. 2013. *The British Dream: Successes and Failures of Postwar Immigration*. London: Atlantic Books.

Goos, Maarten, and Alan Manning. 2007. "Lousy and Lovely Jobs: The Rising Polarization of Work in Britain." *The Review of Economics and Statistics* 89 (1): 118–33.

Gordon, Robert. 2016. *The Rise and Fall of American Growth: The U.S. Standard of Living since the Civil War*. Princeton, NJ: Princeton University Press.

Granovetter, M. S. 1973. "The Strength of Weak Ties." *American Journal of Sociology* 78 (6): 1360–80.

Greenaway, David, and Richard Kneller. 2007. "Heterogeneity, Exporting, and Foreign Direct Investment." *Economic Journal* 117 (517): 134–61.

Hacker, J. S., P. Rehm, and M. Schlesinger. 2013. "The Insecure American: Economic Experiences, Financial Worries, and Policy Attitudes." *Perspectives on Politics* 11 (1): 23–49.

Hacker, Jacob, and Paul Pierson. 2011. *Winner-Take-All Politics: How Washington Made the Rich Richer—and Turned Its Back on the Middle Class*. New York: Simon & Schuster.

Haine, W. Scott. 2000. *The History of France*. Westport, CT: Greenwood Press.

Hall, Peter A. 1993. "Policy Paradigms, Social Learning, and the State: The Case of Economic Policymaking in Britain." *Comparative Politics* 25 (3): 275–96.

Hall, Peter A., and David Soskice, eds. 2001. *Varieties of Capitalism: The Institutional Foundations of Comparative Advantage*. Oxford: Oxford University Press.

Hallerberg, Mark. 2004. *Domestic Budgets in a United Europe: Fiscal Governance from the End of Bretton Woods to EMU*. Ithaca, NY: Cornell University Press.

Hallerberg, Mark, and Jürgen von Hagen. 1999. "Electoral Institutions, Cabinet Negotiations, and Budget Deficits in the European Union." In *Fiscal Institutions and Fiscal Performance*, eds. James M. Poterba and Jürgen von Hagen, 209–32. Chicago: University of Chicago Press.

Hancke, Robert. 2002. *Large Firms and Institutional Change: Industrial Renewal and Economic Restructuring*. Oxford: Oxford University Press.

Hanushek, Eric A., and Ludger Woessmann. 2006. "Does Educational Tracking Affect Performance and Inequality? Differences-in-Differences Evidence across Countries." National Bureau of Economic Research Working Paper, No. 11124: C63–C76.

Hayek, Friedrich A. 1944. *The Road to Serfdom*. London: Routledge.

———. 1966. "The Principles of a Liberal Social Order." *Il Politico* 31 (4): 601–18.

Hassel, Anke. 2010. "Twenty Years after German Unification: The Restructuring of the German Welfare and Employment Regime." *German Politics and Society* 28 (2): 102–115.

Häusermann, Silja. 2010. *The Politics of Welfare State Reform in Continental Europe: Modernization in Hard Times*. Cambridge, UK: Cambridge University Press.

Häusermann, Silja, and Hanspeter Kriesi. 2015. "What Do Voters Want? Dimensions and Configurations in Individual-Level Preferences and Party Choice." In *The Politics of Advanced Capitalism*, eds. Pablo Beramendi, Silja Häusermann, Herbert Kitschelt, and Hanspeter Kriesi, 202–30. Cambridge, UK: Cambridge University Press.

Hechter, Michael, and William Brustein. 1980. "Regional Modes of Production and Patterns of State Formation in Western Europe." *American Journal of Sociology* 85 (5): 1061–94.

Heckman, J. 2011. "The Economics of Inequality: The Value of Early Childhood Education." *American Educator* 35 (1): 31–35.

Heckman, J., and S. Mosso. 2014. "The Economics of Human Development and Social Mobility." *Annual Review of Economics* 6: 689–733.

Helpman, Elhanan, Marc J. Melitz, and Stephen R. Yeaple. 2004. "Export versus FDI." *American Economic Review* 94: 300–16.

Hellwig, T. 2001. "Interdependence, Government Constraints, and Economic Voting." *The Journal of Politics* 63 (4): 1141–62.

Herrigel, Gary. 1995. *Industrial Constructions: The Sources of German Industrial Power*. Cambridge, UK: Cambridge University Press.

Hochschild, Arlie R. 2016. *Strangers in Their Own Land: Anger and Mourning on the American Right*. New York: New Press.

Hofmann, Claudia, Alberto Osnago, and Michele Ruta. 2017. "Horizontal Depth: A New Database on the Content of Preferential Trade Agreements." World Bank, Trade, and Competitiveness Global Practice Group, February 2017.

Holzer, Harry J. 1987. "Informal Job Search and Black Youth Unemployment." *The American Economic Review* 77 (3): 446–52.

Hovenkamp, Herbert. 2015. *Federal Antitrust Policy, The Law of Competition, and Its Practice*. St. Paul, MN: West Academic.

Huber, Evelyne, and John D. Stephens. 2001. *Development and Crisis of the Welfare State: Parties and Policies in Global Markets*. Chicago: University of Chicago Press.

Huo, Jingjing. 2009. *Third Way Reforms: Social Democracy after the Golden Age*. Cambridge, UK: Cambridge University Press.

Iacoboni, Marco, Istvan Molnar-Szakacs, Vittorio Gallese, Giovanni Buccino, John C. Mazziotta, Giacomo Rizzolatti. 2005. "Grasping the Intentions of Others with One's Own Mirror Neuron System." *PLOS Biology* 3 (3): 529–35.

Iammarino, Simona, and Philip McCann. 2013. *Multinationals and Economic Geography: Location, Technology, and Innovation*. Cheltenham, UK: Edward Elgar.

Ibsen, Christian Lyhne, and Kathleen Thelen. Forthcoming. "Diverging Solidarity Labor Strategies in the New Knowledge Economy." *World Politics* 69 (3): 409–47.

Ignazi, Piero. 2003. *Extreme Right Parties in Western Europe*. New York: Oxford University Press.

———. 1992. "The Silent Counter-Revolution: Hypotheses on the Emergence of Extreme Right-Wing Parties in Europe." *European Journal of Political Research* 22: 3–34.

Inglehart, Ronald. 1971. "The Silent Revolution in Europe: Intergenerational Change in Postindustrial Societies." *American Political Science Review* 65 (4): 991–1017.

———. 1990. *Culture Shift in Advanced Industrial Society*. Princeton, NJ: Princeton University Press.

Inglehart, Roland, and Pippa Norris. 2017. "Trump and the Populist Authoritarian Parties: The Silent Revolution in Reverse." *Perspectives on Politics* 15 (2): 443–54.

Iversen, Torben. 1996. "Power, Flexibility, and the Breakdown of Centralized Wage Bargaining: Denmark and Sweden in Comparative Perspective." *Comparative Politics* 28 (4): 399–436.

———. 1998. "The Choices for Scandinavian Social Democracy in Comparative Perspective." *Oxford Review of Economic Policy* 14 (1): 59–75.

———. 1999. *Contested Economic Institutions: The Politics of Macroeconomics and Wage Bargaining in Advanced Democracies*. Cambridge, UK: Cambridge University Press.

Iversen, Torben, and Thomas R. Cusack. 2000. "The Causes of Welfare State Expansion: Deindustrialization or Globalization?" *World Politics* 52 (3): 313–49.

Iversen, Torben, and Frances Rosenbluth. 2010. *Women, Work, and Politics: The Political Economy of Gender Inequality*. New Haven: Yale University Press.

Iversen, Torben, and David Soskice. 2001. "An Asset Theory of Social Policy Preferences." *American Political Science Review* 95 (4): 875–93.

———. 2006. "Electoral Institutions and the Politics of Coalitions: Why Some Democracies Redistribute More Than Others." *American Political Science Review* 100 (2): 165–81.

———. 2010. "Real Exchange Rates and Competitiveness: The Political Economy of Skill Formation, Wage Compression, and Electoral Systems." *American Political Science Review* 104 (3): 601–23.

———. 2012. "Modern Capitalism and the Advanced Nation State: Understanding the Causes of the Crisis." In *Coping with Crisis: Government Reactions to the Great Recession*, eds. Nancy Bermeo and Jonas Pontusson, 35–64. New York: Russell Sage.

———. 2014. *Dualism and Political Coalitions: Inclusionary versus Exclusionary Reforms in an Age of Rising Inequality*. Cambridge, MA: Harvard University Press.

————. 2015. "Information, Inequality, and Mass Polarization: Ideology in Advanced Democracies." *Comparative Political Studies* 48 (13): 1781–1813.

Iversen, Torben, and John Stephens. 2008. "Partisan Politics, the Welfare State, and Three Worlds of Human Capital Formation." *Comparative Political Studies* 41 (4/5): 600–37.

Jensen, Carsten. 2011. "Capitalist Systems, Deindustrialization, and the Politics of Public Education." *Comparative Political Studies* 41 (4): 412–35.

Jessop, Bob. 1982. *The Capitalist State*. New York: New York University Press.

Johansson, Egil. 1988. "Literacy Campaigns in Sweden." *Interchange* 19 (3/4): 135–62.

Johnson, Chalmers. 1982. *MITI and The Japanese Miracle: The Growth of Industrial Policy, 1925–1975*. Stanford, CA: Stanford University Press.

Jordana, J., and D. Levi-Faur. 2004. *The Politics of Regulation: Institutions and Regulatory Reforms for the Age of Governance*. Cheltenham, UK: Edward Elgar.

Kaletsky, Anatole. 2010a. "Capitalism 4.0." *The OECD Observer* (279): 23.

————. 2010b. *Capitalism 4.0: The Birth of a New Economy in the Aftermath of Crisis*. Philadelphia: PublicAffairs.

Kalleberg, A. 2003. "Flexible Firms and Labor Market Segmentation Effects of Workplace Restructuring on Jobs and Workers." *Work and Occupations* 30 (2): 154–75.

Kalyvas, Stathis N. 1996. *The Rise of Christian Democracy in Europe*. Ithaca, NY: Cornell University Press.

Katzenstein, Peter. 1985. *Small States in World Markets*. Ithaca, NY: Cornell University Press.

Katznelson, Ira. 1981. *City Trenches: Urban Politics and the Patterning of Class in the United States*. Chicago: University of Chicago Press.

Katznelson, Ira, and Aristide Zolberg, eds. 1986. *Working-Class Formation: Nineteenth-Century Patterns in Western Europe and North America*. Princeton, NJ: Princeton University Press.

Keech, William. 2009. "A Scientifically Superior Definition of Democracy." Midwest Political Science Association Meeting, Chicago.

Kees Koedijk, Jeroen Kremers, Paul David, and Lars-Hendrik Röller. 1996. "Market Opening, Regulation and Growth in Europe." *Economic Policy* 11 (October): 443–67.

Kharas, Homi, and Harinder Kohli. 2011. "What is the Middle-Income Trap, Why Do Countries Fall into It, and How Can It Be Avoided?" *Global Journal of Emerging Market Economies* 3 (3): 281–89.

Kitschelt, Herbert. 1994. *The Transformation of European Social Democracy*. Cambridge, UK: Cambridge University Press.

————. 1995. "Formation of Party Cleavages in Post-Communist Democracies." *Party Politics* 1 (4): 447–72.

Kitschelt, Herbert, and Anthony J. McGann. 1995. *The Radical Right in Western Europe: A Comparative Analysis*. Ann Arbor: University of Michigan Press.

Kitschelt, Herbert, and Philipp Rehm. 2014. "Occupations as a Site of Political Preference Formation." *Comparative Political Studies* 47 (12): 1670–1706.

———. 2015. "Party Alignments: Change and Continuity." In *The Politics of Advanced Capitalism*, eds. Pablo Beramendi, Silja Häusermann, Herbert Kitschelt, and Hanspeter Kriesi, 179–201. Cambridge, UK: Cambridge University Press.

Kjær, Peter and Ove K. Pedersen. 2001. "Translating Liberalization: Neoliberalism in the Danish Negotiated Economy." In *The Rise of Neoliberalism and Institutional Analysis*, eds. John L. Campbell and Ove K. Pedersen, 219–48. Princeton, NJ: Princeton University Press pp. 219–248.

Kocka, Jürgen. 1986. "Problems of Working-Class Formation in Germany: The Early Years, 1800–1875." In *Working-Class Formation: Nineteenth-Century Patterns in Western Europe and the United States*, eds. Ira Katznelson and Aristide R. Zolberg, 279–351. Princeton, NJ: Princeton University Press.

Korpi, Walter. 1983. *The Democratic Class Struggle.* London: Routledge and Kegan Paul.

———. 1989. "Power, Politics, and State Autonomy in the Development of Social Citizenship: Social Rights during Sickness in 18 OECD Countries since 1930." *American Sociological Review* 54 (3): 309–28.

———. 2006. "Power Resources and Employer-Centered Approaches in Explanations of Welfare States and Varieties of Capitalism: Protagonists, Consenters, and Antagonists." *World Politics* 58 (2): 167–206.

Koske, I., I.Wanner, R. Bitetti, and O. Barbiero. 2015. "The 2013 Update of the OECD's Database on Product Market Regulation: Policy Insights for OECD and Non-OECD Countries." OECD Economics Department Working Papers, No. 1200. Paris: OECD Publishing.

Kriesi, Hanspeter, Edgar Grande, Romain Lachat, Martin Dolezal, Simon Bornschier, and Timotheos Frey. 2008. *West European Politics in the Age of Globalization.* Cambridge, UK: Cambridge University Press.

Kriesi, Hanspeter, and Takis S. Pappas, eds. 2015. *European Populism in the Shadow of the Great Recession.* Colchester, UK: EPCR Press.

Kristal, Tali, and Yinon Cohen, 2013. "The Causes of Rising Wage Inequality: What Do Computerization and Fading Pay-Setting Institutions Do?" Paper prepared for the Society for the Advancement of Socio-Economics Mini-Conference ("The Political Economy of Skills and Inequality"), Milan, June 27–29.

Kristensen, P. H. 2006. "The Danish Business System Transforming towards the New Economy." In *National Identity and the Varieties of Capitalism: The Danish Experience*, eds. J. L. Campbell, J. A. Hall, and O. K. Pedersen, 295–30. Montreal, Canada: McGill-Queen's University Press.

Krueger, Alan. 2012. "The Rise and Consequences of Inequality in the United States." Unpublished speech.

Krueger, Anne. 1974. "The Political Economy of the Rent-Seeking Society." *The American Economic Review* 64 (3): 291–303.

———. 1990. "Government Failures in Development." *Journal of Economic Perspectives* 4 (3): 9–25.

Krugman, Paul. 1991a. "Increasing Returns and Economic Geography." *Journal of Political Economy* 99 (3): 483–99.

———. 1991b. *Geography and Trade.* Cambridge, MA: MIT Press.

Kuemmerle, W. 1997. "Building Effective R&D Capabilities Abroad." *Harvard Business Review* 75: 61–72.

———. 1999. "Foreign Direct Investment in Industrial Research in the Pharmaceutical and Electronics Industries: Results from a Survey of Multinational Firms." *Research Policy* 28 (2): 179–93.

Kurzweil, Raymond. 2005. *The Singularity is Near*. London: Viking.

Lange, Peter, and Geoffrey Garrett. 1985. "The Politics of Growth: Strategic Interaction and Economic Performance in the Advanced Industrial Democracies." *Journal of Politics* 47 (3): 792–827.

Lehmbruch, Gerhard. 1967. *Proporzdemokratie. Politisches System Und Politische Kultur in Der Schweiz Und in Österreich*. Tübingen, Germany: Mohr/Siebeck.

———. 1993. "Consociational Democracy and Corporatism in Switzerland." *Publius: The Journal of Federalism* 23 (2): 43–60.

Lepsius, M. Rainer. 1966. "Parteiensystem und Sozialstruktur: zum Problem der Demokratisierung der deutschen Gesellschaft." In *Wirtschaft, Geschichte, und Wirtschaftsgeschichte. Festschrift zum 65. Geburtstag von Friedrich Lütge*, eds. Wilhelm Abel, Knut Borchardt, Hermann Kellenbenz, Wolfgang Zorn, 371–93. Stuttgart: Tübingen/ Göttingen: Fischer.

Levi-Faur, D. 2005. "The Global Diffusion of Regulatory Capitalism." *The Annals of the American Academy of Political and Social Science* 598 (1): 12–32.

Lewis-Beck, Michael S., and Mary Stegmaier. 2013. "The VP-Function Revisited: A Survey of the Literature on Vote and Popularity Functions after over 40 Years." *Public Choice* 157 (3/4): 367–85.

Lieberman, David. 2008. "Bentham's Democracy." *Oxford Journal of Legal Studies* 28 (3): 605–26.

Lijphart, Arend. 1968. "Typologies of Democratic Systems." *Comparative Political Studies*, 1968 (1): 3–44.

———. 1977. *Democracy in Plural Societies: A Comparative Exploration*. New Haven: Yale University Press.

———. 1984. *Democracies: Patterns of Majoritarian and Consensus Government in Twenty-One Countries*. New Haven: Yale University Press.

———. 1997. "Unequal Participation: Democracy's Unresolved Dilemma." *American Political Science Review* 91 (1): 1–14.

Lindblom, Charles. 1977. *Politics and Markets: The World's Political-Economic Systems*. New York: Basic Books.

Lindert, Peter H. 2004. *Growing Public: Social Spending and Economic Growth since the Eighteenth Century*. Cambridge, UK: Cambridge University Press.

Lipset, Seymour Martin. 1959. "Some Social Requisites of Democracy: Economic Development and Political Legitimacy." *The American Political Science Review* 53 (1): 69–105.

———. 1960. *Political Man: The Social Bases of Politics*. Garden City, NY: Doubleday.

Lipset, Seymour M., and Stein Rokkan. 1967. "Cleavage Structures, Party Systems, and Voter Alignments: An Introduction." In *Party Systems and Voter Alignments: Cross-National Perspectives*, eds. S. M. Lipset and S. Rokkan, 1–64. New York: Free Press.

Lizzeri, A., and N. Persico. 2004. "Why Did the Elites Extend the Suffrage? Democracy and the Scope Of Government, with an Application to Britain's 'Age Of Reform.'" *Quarterly Journal of Economics* 119 (2): 707–65.

Ljungberg, J. 2006. "Secular Movements of Earnings Differentials: Sweden 1870–2000." Paper presented at the Fourteenth International Economic History Congress, Helsinki.

Lubbers, Marcel, Mérove Gijsberts, and Peer Scheepers. 2002. "Extreme Right-Wing Voting in Western Europe." *European Journal of Political Research* 41 (3): 345–78.

Luebbert, Gregory. 1991. *Liberalism, Fascism, or Social Democracy: Social Classes and the Political Origins of Regimes in the Interwar Period*. Oxford: Oxford University Press.

Lundgreen, Peter. 1975. "Industrialization and the Educational Formation of Manpower in Germany." *Journal of Social History* 9 (1): 64–80.

Lundvall, Bengt-Åke. 1992. *National Systems of Innovation: Toward a Theory of Innovation and Interactive Learning*. New York: Pinter.

———. 2016. *The Learning Economy and the Economics of Hope*. London: Anthem Press.

MacDonagh, Oliver. 1977. *Early Victorian Government, 1830–1870*. London: Weidenfeld and Nicholson.

Magee, Stephen P., William A. Brock, and Leslie Young. 1989. *Black Hole Tariffs and Endogenous Policy Theory: Political Economy in General Equilibrium*. Cambridge, UK: Cambridge University Press.

Magnusson, Lars. 2000. *Economic History of Sweden*. New York: Routledge.

Magraw, Roger. 1986. *France, 1815 to 1915: The Bourgeois Century*. Oxford: Oxford University Press.

Malerba, Franco. 2004. *Sectoral Systems of Innovation: Concepts, Issues, and Analyses of Six Major Sectors in Europe*. Cambridge, UK: Cambridge University Press.

Manow, Philip. 2009. "Electoral Rules, Class Coalitions, and Welfare State Regimes, or How to Explain Esping-Andersen with Stein Rokkan." *Socio-Economic Review* 7: 101–21.

Manow, Philip, and Kees Van Kersbergen, eds. 2009. *Religion, Class Coalitions, and Welfare State Regimes*. Cambridge, UK: Cambridge University Press.

Mares, Isabela. 2003. *The Politics of Social Risk: Business and Welfare State Development*. Cambridge, UK: Cambridge University Press.

Margalit, Yotam. 2013. "Explaining Social Policy Preferences: Evidence from the Great Recession." *American Political Science Review* 107 (1): 80–103.

Marks, Gary. 1989. *Unions in Politics: Britain, Germany, and the United States in the Nineteenth and Twentieth Centuries*. Princeton, NJ: Princeton University Press.

Martin, Cathie Jo. 2000. *Stuck in Neutral: Business and the Politics of Human Capital Investment Policy*. Princeton, NJ: Princeton University Press.

———. 2006. "Sectional Parties, Divided Business." *Studies in American Development* 20 (2): 160–84.

———. 2012. "Political Institutions and the Origins of Collective Skill Formation Systems." In *The Political Economy of Collective Skill Formation*, eds. Marius R. Busemeyer and Christine Trampusch, 41–67. New York: Oxford University Press.

Martin, Cathie Jo, and Duane Swank. 2008. "The Political Origins of Coordinated Capitalism: Business Organization, Party Systems, and the State in the Age of Innocence." *American Political Science Review* 102 (2): 181–98.

———. 2011. "Gonna Party Like It's 1899: Electoral Systems and the Origins of Varieties of Coordination." *World Politics* 63 (1): 78–114.

———. Forthcoming. *The Political Construction of Corporate Interests.* Cambridge, UK: Cambridge University Press.

Martin, Cathie Jo, and Kathleen Thelen. 2007. "The State and Coordinated Capitalism: Contributions of the Public Sector to Social Solidarity in Postindustrial Societies." *World Politics* 60 (1): 1–36.

Maynes, Mary Jo. 1979. "The Virtues of Archaism: The Political Economy of Schooling in Europe, 1750–1850." *Comparative Studies in Society and History* 21 (4): 611–25.

McGowan, Lee. 2005. "Europeanization Unleashed and Rebounding: Assessing the Modernization of EU Cartel Policy." *Journal of European Public Policy* 12 (6): 986–1004.

———. 2010. *The Antitrust Revolution in Europe: Exploring the European Commission's Cartel Policy.* Cheltenham, UK: Edward Elgar.

McLean, Iain. 2001. *Rational Choice and British Politics: An Analysis of Rhetoric and Manipulation from Peel to Blair.* Oxford: Oxford University Press.

Miliband, Ralph. 1969. *The State in Capitalist Society.* New York: Basic Books.

Moene, Karl Ove, and Michael Wallerstein. 1997. "Pay Inequality." *Journal of Labor Economics* 15 (3): 403–30.

———. 2001. "Inequality, Social Insurance, and Redistribution." *American Political Science Review* 95 (4): 859–74.

Montgomery, James D. 1991. "Social Networks and Labor-Market Outcomes: Toward an Economic Analysis." *The American Economic Review* 81 (5): 1408–18.

Moretti, E., and P. Thulin. 2013. "Local Multipliers and Human Capital in the United States and Sweden." *Industrial and Corporate Change* 22 (1): 339–62.

Morrison, Bruce. 2011. "Channeling the 'Restless Spirit of Innovation': Elite Concessions and Institutional Change in the British Reform Act of 1832." *World Politics* 63 (4): 678–710.

Nahapiet, Janine, and Sumantra Ghoshal. 1998. "Social Capital, Intellectual Capital, and the Organizational Advantage." *The Academy of Management Review* 23 (2): 242–66.

Nannestad, Peter, and Martin Paldam. 1994. "The VP-Function: A Survey of the Literature on Vote and Popularity Functions After Twenty-Five Years." *Public Choice* 79 (3/4): 213–45.

———. 1997. "From the Pocketbook of the Welfare Man: A Pooled Cross-section Study of Economic Voting in Denmark, 1986–92." *British Journal of Political Science* 27: 119–36.

Nelson, Richard R. 1993. *National Innovation Systems: A Comparative Analysis.* New York: Oxford University Press.

Nickell, Stephen. 2004. "Poverty and Worklessness in Britain." *Economic Journal* 114 (494): C1–C25.

Nilsson, Anders, and Birgitta Svard. 1994. "Writing Ability and Agrarian Change in Early Nineteenth-century Rural Scania." *Journal of Swedish History* 19 (3): 251–74.

Nolan, Mary. 1986. "Economic Crisis, State Policy, and Working Class Formation in Germany, 1870 to 1900." In *Working-Class Formation: Nineteenth-Century Patterns in Western Europe and the United States*, eds. I. Katznelson and A. K. Zolberg, 352–93. Princeton, NJ: Princeton University Press.

Nord, Philip. 1996. *The Republican Moment: Struggles for Democracy in Nineteenth Century France*. Cambridge, MA: Harvard University Press.

North, Douglas. 1990. *Institutions, Institutional Change, and Economic Performance*. Cambridge, UK: Cambridge University Press.

OECD (Organisation for Economic Co-operation and Development). Social Expenditure Statistics. Online database edition. Accessed on 1/15, 2015.

———. 2000. *Literacy in the Information Age: Final Report of the International Adult Literacy Survey*. Paris: OECD.

———. 2010. Education at a Glance 2010: OECD Indicators. Paris: OECD.

———. 2012. Equity and Quality in Education: Supporting Disadvantaged Students and Schools. Paris: OECD.

———. 2013. *PISA 2012 Results: Excellence Through Equity: Giving Every Student the Chance to Succeed (Volume II)*. PISA, OECD. https://www.oecd.org/pisa/keyfindings/pisa-2012-results-volume-II.pdf.

———. 2016. *Skills Matter: Further Results from the Survey of Adult Skills*. Paris: OECD.

———. 2017. Education at a Glance 2017: OECD Indicators. Paris: OECD.

———. Distribution of Gross Earnings of Full-time Employees, OECD.stat. http://stats.oecd.org/Index.aspx?DatasetCode=DEC_I.

Oesch, Daniel. 2012. "The Class Basis of the Cleavage between the New Left and the Radical Right: An Analysis for Austria, Denmark, Norway and Switzerland." In *Class Politics and the Radical Right*, ed. Jens Rydren, 49–69. London: Routledge.

Okun, A. 1975. *Equality and Efficiency: The Big Trade-off*. Washington, DC: Brookings Institution.

Olson, Mancur. 1982. *The Rise and Decline of Nations*. New Haven: Yale University Press.

Orloff, Ann Shola. 1993. "Gender and the social rights of citizenship: The comparative analysis of gender relations and welfare states." *American sociological review*: 303–28.

Ottaviano, Gianmarco I. P., and Giovanni Peri. 2012. "Rethinking the Effect of Immigration on Wages." *Journal of the European Economic Association* 10 (1): 152–97.

Overman, Henry, and Diego Puga. 2010. "Labor Pooling as a Source of Agglomeration." In *Agglomeration Economics*, NBER conference volume, ed E. L. Glaeser. Chicago: Chicago University Press.

Pellizzari, Michele. 2004. "Do Friends and Relatives Really Help in Getting a Good Job?" CEP/LSE Discussion Paper, No. 623.

Peltzman, Sam. 1976. "Toward a More General Theory of Regulation." *Journal of Law and Economics* 19: 211–40.

Peters, Yvette, and Sander J. Ensink. 2015. "Differential Responsiveness in Europe: The Effects of Preference Difference and Electoral Participation." *West European Politics* 38 (3): 577–600.

Piketty, Thomas. 2005. "Top Income Shares in the Long Run: An Overview." *Journal of the European Economic Association* 3 (2–3): 382–92.

———. 2014. *Capital in the Twenty-First Century.* Cambridge, MA: Belknap Press of Harvard University Press.

Piketty, Thomas, and Emmanuel Saez, E. 2006. "The Evolution of Top Incomes: A Historical and International Perspective." American Economic Review 96 (2): 200–205.

Pincus, Steve C. A., and James Robinson. 2014. "What Really Happened during the Glorious Revolution?" In *Institutions, Property Rights, and Economic Growth: The Legacy of Douglass North*, eds. Sebastian Galiani and Itai Sened, 192–222. New York: Cambridge University Press.

Pontusson, Jonas. 2005. *Inequality and Prosperity: Social Europe vs. Liberal America.* Ithaca, NY: Cornell University Press.

Pontusson, Jonas, and Sarosh Kuruvilla. 1992. "Swedish Wage-earner Funds: An Experiment in Economic Democracy." *Industrial and Labor Relations Review* 45 (4): 779–91.

Pontusson, Jonas, and Peter Swenson. 1996. "Labor Markets, Production Strategies, and Wage Bargaining Institutions: The Swedish Employer Offensive in Comparative Perspective." *Comparative Political Studies* 29 (April): 223–50.

Popa, Mircea. 2015. "Elites and Corruption: A Theory of Endogenous Reform and a Test Using British Data." *World Politics* 67 (2): 313–52.

———. 2016. "The Politics of Housing Bubbles: Explaining Cross-National Variation in the 2000s." Manuscript.

Porter, Michael E. 1990. *The Comparative Advantage of Nations.* Glencoe, IL: Free Press.

———. 2000. "Location, Clusters and Company Strategy." In *The Oxford Handbook of Economic Geography*, eds. Gordon Clark, Maryann P. Feldmann, Meric Gertler, and Kate Williams. Oxford: Oxford University Press.

Poulantzas, Nicos. 1973. *Political Power and Social Classes.* New York: New Left Books.

———. 1978. *State, Power, Socialism.* New Left Books.

Powell, G. Bingham. 2000. *Elections as Instruments of Democracy: Majoritarian and Proportional Visions.* New Haven: Yale University Press.

Przeworski, Adam, Michael Alvarez, José Antonio Cheibub, and Fernando Limongi. 2000. *Democracy and Development: Political Institutions and Well-Being in the World, 1950–1990.* Cambridge, UK: Cambridge University Press.

Przeworski, Adam, and Fernando Limongi. 1997. "Modernization: Theories and Facts." *World Politics* 49 (January): 155–83.

Przeworski, Adam, and John Sprague. 1988. *Paper Stones: A History of Electoral Socialism.* Chicago: Chicago University Press.

Przeworski, Adam, and Michael Wallerstein. 1982. "The Structure of Class Conflict in Democratic Capitalist Societies." *American Political Science Review* 76 (June): 215–38.

Rehm, Philipp. 2009. "Risks and Redistribution: An Individual-Level Analysis." *Comparative Political Studies* 42 (7): 855–81.

———. 2011. "Social Policy by Popular Demand." *World Politics* 63 (2): 271–99.

———. 2016. *Risk Inequality and Welfare States: Social Policy Preferences, Development, and Dynamics.* Cambridge, UK: Cambridge University Press.

Rehm, Philipp, Jacob S. Hacker, and Mark Schlesinger. 2012. "Insecure Alliances: Risk, Inequality, and Support for the Welfare State." *American Political Science Review* 106 (2): 386–406.

Restuccia, D., and C. Urratia. 2004. "Intergenerational Persistence of Earnings: The Role of Early and College Education." *American Economic Review* 94 (5): 1354–78.

Riker, William. 1962. *The Theory of Political Coalitions.* New Haven: Yale University Press.

Rodrik, Dani. 1997. *Has Globalization Gone Too Far?* Washington, DC: Institute for International Economics.

———. 2018. "Populism and The Economics of Globalization." *Journal of International Business Policy* 1 (June).

Rogowski, Ronald. 1987. "Trade and the Variety of Democratic Institutions." *International Organization* 41 (2): 203–23.

Roine, Jesper, and Daniel Waldenstrom. 2008. "The Evolution of Top Incomes in an Egalitarian Society: Sweden, 1903–2004." *Journal of Public Economics* 92 (1/2): 366–87.

Rokkan, Stein. 1970. *Citizens, Elections, Parties: Approaches to the Comparative Study of the Processes of Development.* Oslo: Universitetsforlaget.

Rothstein, Bo. 1992. "Labor-market Institutions and Working-class Strength." In *Structuring Politics*, eds. Sven Steinmo, Kathleen Thelen, and Frank Longstreth, 33–56. New York: Cambridge University Press.

Rueda, D. 2005. "Insider-Outsider Politics in Industrialized Democracies: The Challenge to Social Democratic Parties." *American Political Science Review* 99 (1): 61–74.

———. 2008. *Social Democracy Inside Out: Partisanship and Labor Market Policy in Advanced Industrialized Democracies.* Oxford: Oxford University Press.

Rueda, David, and Jonas Pontusson. 2000. "Wage Inequality and Varieties of Capitalism." *World Politics* 52 (3): 350–83.

Rueschmeyer, Dieter, Evelyne Huber Stephens, and John D Stephens. 1992. *Capitalist Development and Democracy.* Chicago: University of Chicago Press.

Ruggie, John G. 1982. "International Regimes, Transactions and Change. Embedded Liberalism in the Post War Economic Order." *International Organization* 36 (2): 379–415.

———. 1983. "International Regimes, Transactions, and Change: Embedded Liberalism in the Post War Economic Order." In *International Regimes*, ed. Stephen D. Krasner, 195–232. Ithaca, NY: Cornell University Press.

Rugman, Alan. 2005. *The Regional Multinationals: MNEs and "Global" Strategic Management.* Cambridge, UK: Cambridge University Press.

———. 2012. *The End of Globalization.* New York: Random House.

Rustow, Dankwart A. 1955. *The Politics of Compromise: A Study of Parties and Cabinet Governments in Sweden.* Princeton, NJ: Princeton University Press.

Savage, M., et al. 2013. "A New Model of Social Class? Findings from the BBC's Great British Class Survey Experiment." *Sociology* 47 (2): 219–50.

Saxenian, Anna Lee. 1994. *Regional Advantage: Culture and Competition in Silicon Valley and Route 128*. Cambridge, MA: Harvard University Press.

———. 2006. *The New Argonauts: Regional Advantage in a Global Economy*. Cambridge, MA: Harvard University Press.

Scheve, Kenneth, and David Stasavage. 2007. "Political Institutions, Partisanship, and Inequality in the Long Run." Manuscript, Yale University.

———. 2016. *Taxing the Rich: A History of Fiscal Fairness in the United States and Europe*. Princeton, NJ: Princeton University Press.

Schmitter, Philippe. 1979. "Still the Century of Corporatism?" In *Trends toward Corporatist Intermediation*, eds. Philippe Schmitter and Gerhard Lehmbruch, 7–48. Beverly Hills, CA: Sage.

Schmitter, Philippe C., and Gerhard Lehmbruch, eds. 1979. *Trends toward Corporatist Intermediation*. Beverly Hills, CA: Sage.

Schneider, Ben Ross. 2009. *Hierarchical Market Economies and Varieties of Capitalism in Latin America*. Cambridge: Cambridge University Press.

———. 2013. *Hierarchical Capitalism in Latin America: Business, Labor, and the Challenge of Equitable Development*. New York: Cambridge University Press.

Schonfield, Andrew. 1965. *Modern Capitalism*. Oxford: Oxford Uiversity Press.

Schuetz, Gabriela, Heinrich W. Ursprung, and Ludger Woessmann. 2008. "Education Policy and Equality of Ppportunity." *Kyklos* 61 (2): 279–308.

Schumpeter, Joseph A. 1942. *Capitalism, Socialism, and Democracy*. London: Harper.

Scruggs, Lyle. 2004. Welfare State Entitlements Data Set: A Comparative Institutional Analysis of Eighteen Welfare States. http://sp.uconn.edu/~scruggs/#links. Accessed on 1/15, 2015.

Searle, G. 1993. *Entrepreneurial Politics in Mid-Victorian Britain*. Oxford: Oxford University Press.

Simmons, Beth and Zachary Elkins. 2004. "The Globalization of Liberalization: Policy Diffusion in the International Political Economy." *American Political Science Review* 98 (February): 171–89.

Singer, Natasha. 2017. "How Big Tech is Going After your Health Care." *New York Times*, December 26, 2017. https://www.nytimes.com/2017/12/26/technology/big-tech-health-care.html.

Slomp, Hans. 1990. *Labor Relations in Europe: A History of Issues and Developments*. Westport, CT: Greenwood.

Solt, Frederick. 2016. "The Standardized World Income Inequality Database." *Social Science Quarterly* 97 (5): 1267–81.

Soskice, David. 1990. "Wage Determination: The Changing Role of Institutions in Advanced Industrialized Countries." *Oxford Review of Economic Policy* 6 (4): 36–61.

Soskice, David, Robert Bates, and David Epstein. 1992. "Ambition and Constraint: The Stabilizing Role of Institutions." *Journal of Law, Economics, and Organization* 8 (3): 547–60.

Soskice, David, and Torben Iversen. 2000. "The Non-neutrality of Monetary Policy with Large Wage and Price Setters." *Quarterly Journal of Economics* (February): 265–84.

Standing, Guy. 2011. *The Precariat: The New Dangerous Class*. Edinburgh: A&C Black.

Stephens, John D. 1979. *The Transition from Capitalism to Socialism*. London: Macmillan.

Stewart, Gordon. 1986. *The Origins of Canadian Politics: A Comparative Approach*. Vancouver: University of British Columbia Press.

Stigler, George J. 1971. "The Theory of Economic Regulation." *Bell Journal of Economics and Management Science* 2; reprinted in Stigler, *The Citizen and the State: Essays on Regulation*. Chicago: University of Chicago Press, 1975.

Storper, Michael, 2013. *Keys to the City*. Princeton, NJ: Princeton University Press.

Streeck, Wolfgang. 1987. "The Uncertainties of Management in the Management of Uncertainty: Employers, Labor Relations, and Industrial Adjustment in the 1980s." *Work, Employment, and Society* 1 (3): 281–308.

———. 2009. *Re-Forming Capitalism: Institutional Change in the German Political Economy*. Oxford: Oxford University Press.

———2011a. "Taking Capitalism Seriously: Towards an Institutionalist Approach to Contemporary Political Economy." *Socio-Economic Review* 9 (1): 137–67.

———. 2011b. "The Crisis of Democratic Capitalism." *New Left Review* 71: 5–29.

———. 2016. *How Will Capitalism End? Essays on a Failing System*. New York: Verso.

Susskind, Richard, and Daniel Susskind. 2016. *The Future of the Professions: How Technology Will Transform the Work of Human Experts*. Oxford: Oxford University Press.

Svirydzenka, Katsiaryna. 2016. "Introducing a New Broad-based Index of Financial Development." IMF Working Papers.

Svolik, Milan. 2008. "Authoritarian Reversals and Democratic Consolidation." *American Political Science Review* 102 (2): 153–68.

Swank, Duane. 2002. *Global Capital, Political Institutions, and Policy Change in Developed Welfare States*. Cambridge, UK: Cambridge University Press.

Swank, Duane, and Sven Steinmo. 2002. "The New Political Economy of Taxation in Advanced Capitalist Democracies." *American Journal of Political Science* 46 (3): 642–55.

Swenson, Peter. 1991. "Bringing Capital Back in, or Social Democracy Reconsidered: Employer Power, Cross-class Alliances, and Centralization of Industrial Relations in Denmark and Sweden." *World Politics* 43 (4): 513–44.

———. 2002a. *Capitalists against Markets: The Making of Labor Markets and Welfare States in the United States and Sweden*. Oxford: Oxford University Press.

———. 2002b. *Labor Markets and Welfare States*. New York: Oxford University Press.

Teece, David J. 1986. "Profiting from Technological Innovation: Implications for Integration, Collaboration, Licensing, and Public Policy." *Research Policy* 15 (6): 285–305.

Thelen, Kathleen. 2004. *How Institutions Evolve: The Political Economy of Skills in Germany, Britain, the United States, and Japan*. New York: Cambridge University Press.

———. 2009. "Skill Formation and Training." In *The Oxford Handbook of Business History*, eds. G. Jones and J. Zeitlin. Oxford: Oxford University Press.

———. 2014. *Varieties of Liberalization and the New Politics of Social Solidarity*. Cambridge, UK: Cambridge University Press.

Thelen, Kathleen, and Marius Busemeyer. 2012. "Institutional Change in German Vocational Training: From Collectivism towards Segmentalism." In *The Political*

Economy of Collective Skill Formation, eds. Marius R. Busemeyer and Christine Trampusch, 68–100. Oxford: Oxford University Press.

Tiebout, Charles M. 1956. "A Pure Theory of Local Expenditures." *Journal of Political Economy* 64 (5): 416–24.

Tilton, Timothy A. 1974. "The Social Origins of Liberal Democracy: The Swedish Case." *American Political Science Review* 68 (02): 561–71.

Trampusch, Christine. 2010: "Employers, the State, and the Politics of Institutional Change: Training Regimes in Austria, Germany, and Switzerland." *Journal of Political Research* 49: 545–73.

Uterwedde, Henrik. 1998. "Mitterrand's Economic and Social Policy in Perspective." In *The Mitterrand Years: Legacy and Evaluation*, ed. Mairi Maclean, 133–50. New York: Macmillan.

Van Parijs, Philippe, and Yannick Vanderborght. 2017. *Basic Income: A Radical Proposal for a Free Society and a Sane Economy*. Cambridge, MA: Harvard University Press.

Vernon, Raymond. 1966. "International Investment and International Trade in the Product Cycle." *The Quarterly Journal of Economics* 80 (2): 190–207.

Verny, Douglas V. *Parliamentary Reform in Sweden, 1866-1921*. Oxford: Clarendon Press.

Visser, Jelle. 2015. ICTWSS: Database on Institutional Characteristics of Trade Unions, Wage Setting, State Intervention and Social Pacts in 34 Countries between 1960 and 2014, Version 5. Amsterdam: Amsterdam Institute for Advanced Labour Studies (AIAS).

Vliet, Olaf van, and Koen Caminada. 2012. "Unemployment Replacement Rates Dataset among 34 Welfare States 1971–2009: An Update, Extension, and Modification of the Scruggs's Welfare State Entitlements Data Set." NEUJOBS Special Report no. 2. Leiden, Netherlands: Leiden University.

Vogel, Steven. 2018. *Marketcraft: How States Make Markets Work*. Oxford: Oxford University Press.

Wade, Robert. 1990. *Governing the Market: Economic Theory and the Role of Government in East Asian Industrialization*. Princeton, NJ: Princeton University Press.

Wajcman, Judy. 2017. "Automation: Is It Really Different This Time?" *British Journal of Sociology* 68 (1): 119–27.

Wallerstein, Michael. 1990. "Centralized Bargaining and Wage Restraint." *American Journal of Political Science* 34 (4): 982–1004.

———. 1999. "Wage-Setting Institutions and Pay Inequality in Advanced Industrial Societies." *American Journal of Political Science* 43 (3): 649–88.

Whitley, Richard. 1999. *Divergent Capitalisms: The Social Structuring and Change of Business Systems*. Oxford: Oxford University Press.

———. 2007. *Business Systems and Organizational Capabilities: The Institutional Structuring of Competitive Competences*. Oxford: Oxford University Press.

———. 2010. "Changing Competition Models in Market Economies: The Effects of Internationalization, Technological Innovations, and Academic Expansion on the Conditions Supporting Dominant Economic Logics." In *The Oxford Handbook of Comparative Institutional Analysis*, eds. Glenn Morgan, John L. Campbell, Colin

Crouch, Ove Kaj Pedersen, and Richard Whitley, 363–98. Oxford: Oxford University Press.

Whitley, Richard, and Jochen Gläser. 2014. *Organizational Transformation and Scientific Change: The Impact of Institutional Restructuring on Universities and Intellectual Innovation.* Bingley, UK: Emerald Group.

Wucherpfennig, Julian and Franziska Deutsch. 2009. "Modernization and Democracy. Theories and Evidence Revisited." *Living Reviews in Democracy* 1. https://www.ethz.ch/content/dam/ethz/special-interest/gess/cis/cis-dam/CIS_DAM_2015/WorkingPapers/Living_Reviews_Democracy/Wucherpfennig%20Deutsch.pdf.

Winters, J. V. 2011. "Why Are Smart Cities Growing? Who Moves and Who Stays?" *Journal of Regional Science* 51 (2): 253–70.

Wintle, Michael. 2000. *An Economic and Social History of the Netherlands, 1800–1920.* Cambridge, UK: Cambridge University Press.

Wren, Anne, ed. 2013. *The Political Economy of the Service Transition.* Oxford: Oxford University Press.

Wright, Erik Olin. 1979. *Class Crisis and the State.* New York: New Left Books.

Zeldin, Theodore. 1973. *France 1848–1945: Ambition, Love, and Politics.* Vol. 1. Oxford: Oxford University Press.

Ziblatt, Daniel. 2006. "Review Article: How Did Europe Democratize?" *World Politics* 58 (January): 311–38.

Zysman, John. 1983. *Governments, Markets, and Growth: Financial Systems and the Politics of Industrial Change.* Ithaca, NY: Cornell University Press.

INDEX

Italic pages refer to figures and tables

A NOTE ON THE TYPE

This book has been composed in Adobe Text and Gotham.
Adobe Text, designed by Robert Slimbach for Adobe,
bridges the gap between fifteenth- and sixteenth-century
calligraphic and eighteenth-century Modern styles.
Gotham, inspired by New York street signs, was designed
by Tobias Frere-Jones for Hoefler & Co.